CNN GLENTS

オンラインテスト

CNN GLENTS
公式ガイド

笹尾洋介 **監修** 京都大学 国際高等教育院附属国際学術言語教育センター 准教授　　**朝日出版社**

音声・動画の視聴方法

本書の音声・動画データは、下記の方法でご利用いただけます。

音声のダウンロード

① パソコンの場合

MP3形式の音声ファイルを下記のURLよりダウンロードし、iTunesやWindows Media Playerなどの
MP3再生が可能なソフトに取り込んで聴くことができます。
ダウンロードしたファイルをパソコン上でiTunesやWindows Media Playerなどに取り込んだ上で、
ポータブルオーディオ機器やスマートフォンなどに同期してご利用いただくこともできます。
※「CNN音声版」に加えて、「ナレーター音声版」もダウンロード音声に含まれていますので、ご利用ください。

https://ee.asahipress.com/glents/guide/mp3.zip
(ブラウザの検索窓ではなく「URL入力窓」に入力してください)

② スマートフォンの場合

音声再生アプリ「**リスニング・トレーナー(リストレ)**」で、音声をダウンロードして聴くことができます。

STEP 1　App StoreまたはGoogle Playで「リストレ」をダウンロード

2　アプリを開き、「コンテンツを追加」をタップ

3　カメラへのアクセス許可を「OK」する

4　下記コードをカメラで読み込む

5　読み込めない場合は画面上部に **91334** を入力し「Done」をタップ

6　My Audioの中に本書が加わるので、それを選ぶ

7　目次画面上の「Play All」の右の ▶ をタップすると、最初から通しで再生される。

8　特定の音声を再生したい場合には、聴きたいものをタップする。

Listening Section Part 5の動画の視聴

動画を視聴するには、スマートフォンの場合、Part 5のDirections、
または設問の右上にあるQRコードを読み込んで再生ボタンをタップしてください。
PCの場合は、QRコードの横にあるURLにアクセスして再生ボタンをクリックしてください。

Contents オンラインテスト CNN GLENTS 公式ガイド

Practice Test 模擬試験

あなたのグローバル英語力を測定 | 新時代のオンラインテスト

GLENTS

詳しくは**CNN GLENTS特設ページへ**
https://www.asahipress.com/special/glents/

CNN GLENTSとは

GLENTSとは、**GL**obal **EN**glish **T**esting **S**ystemという名の通り、世界標準の英語力を測るシステムです。リアルな英語を聞き取る**リスニングセクション**、海外の話題を読み取る**リーディングセクション**、CNN GLENTS独自のセクションとして設けた、最新の世界情勢を理解するのに必要な知識を問う**国際教養セクション**から構成される、世界に通じる「ホンモノ」の英語力を測定するためのテストです。

※画像はイメージです。

1 作られた英語ではなく 生の英語ニュースが素材

リスニング問題、リーディング問題ともに、CNNの多彩なニュースから出題。ニュース映像を使った「動画視聴問題」もあります。

2 場所を選ばず受験できる オンライン方式

コンピューターやスマートフォン、タブレットなどの端末とインターネット接続環境があれば、どこでも好きな場所で受けられます。※パソコンのブラウザ、iOSアプリ、Androidアプリで受験できます。

※画像はイメージです。

3 自動採点で結果をすぐに表示 CEFR準拠のCEFR-Jにも対応

テスト終了後、自動採点によって即座に結果がわかります。国際指標CEFR準拠のCEFR-Jとの対照レベルや、TOEIC® Listening & Reading Testの予測スコアも表示されます。

4 コミュニケーションに必要な 社会・文化知識にも配慮

円滑なコミュニケーションには、英語力に加え、社会的・文化的知識が必須です。国際教養セクションでは、世の中の情勢や今日的なテーマに関する様々な問題が出題されます。

CNN GLENTSの問題構成

リスニングセクション

［30問（空所補充4問・3肢択一26問）／
配点60点／約30分（CNN音声版）・
約35分（ナレーター音声版）］

※リスニングセクションの所要時間は目安です。試験によって変わります。

書き取り、ショートニュース、ロングニュース、インタビューに加え、CNNの実際のニュース映像を使用した動画視聴問題からなります。

テストの音声は、CNNで実際に放送された音声を使う「CNN音声版」と、同じ内容をネイティブのナレーターが吹き込み直した「ナレーター音声版」の2種類から選択できます。

リーディングセクション

［20問（3肢択一）／配点40点／25分］

語彙、ショートニュース（約200ワード）、ロングニュース（約500ワード）からなります。

国際教養セクション

［10問（4肢択一）／配点20点／15分］

ニュースの理解に必要な背景知識を問います。10問すべて英語で出題されます。

各セクションの構成

セクション	パート別構成	設問数
リスニングセクション 配点60点	1. 書き取り	4
	2. ショートニュース	6
	3. ロングニュース	8
	4. インタビュー	8
	5. ビューイング（動画視聴）	4
リーディングセクション 配点40点	1. 語彙	4
	2. ショートニュース	6
	3. ロングニュース	10
国際教養セクション 配点20点	ニュースの理解に必要な 背景知識を問う問題	10

CNNとは CNN（Cable News Network）は、最新ニュースを24時間配信し、世界200以上の国と地域で20億人が視聴可能な世界最大のニュース専門メディア。ピュリツァー賞などを受賞した一流の記者が、世界が注目する政治・経済・社会の情報を届けている。

テスト画面

リスニング問題 PART 1 書き取り

リスニング問題 PART 2 ショートニュース

リスニング問題 PART 5 動画視聴

リーディング問題 PART 1 語彙

解答・解説

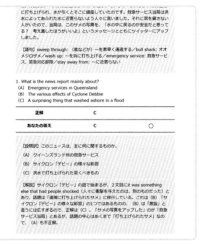

テストの受験可能期間が終了した翌日から1カ月間、マイページの「受験履歴」から詳細な「解答・解説」を閲覧することができ、英文トランスクリプト、訳、語注、解説などが確認できます。

テスト結果

スコアレポートの見方

テスト終了後、すぐにマイページから「スコアレポート」を閲覧することができます。「スコアレポート」には、「リスニングセクション」「リーディングセクション」「国際教養セクション」の得点と、CEFR-Jとの対照レベル、および項目別のレーダーチャートなどが表示されます。

※CEFRとは、Common European Framework of Reference for Languages（外国語の学習・教授・評価のためのヨーロッパ言語共通参照枠）を指し、外国語運用能力を示す国際指標の1つです。CEFR-JはCEFRをベースに、日本の英語教育での利用を目的に構築された、新しい英語教育の到達度指標です。

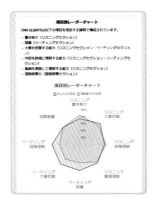

01. CEFR-Jに準拠したレベル診断

「CNN GLENTS」の得点を基に、相当するCEFR-Jのレベル、レベル別に「何ができるか」の達成度一覧、学習のヒントなどが表示されます。世界共通の指標と照らし合わせることで、現在の自分の実力を総合的に把握し、今後の学習に役立てることができます。

02. レーダーチャート

リスニングでは「書き取り」「大意把握」「詳細理解」「動画理解」、リーディングでは「語彙」「大意把握」「詳細理解」に関し、受験者の正解率に応じて項目別レーダーチャートが表示され、自分の弱点がひと目でわかります。

03. TOEIC® L & R Test 予測スコアとCEFR-Jレベル

CNN GLENTSのスコアを基に、TOEIC® L & R Testの予測スコア、および相当するCEFR-Jのレベルが表示されます。現在の自分の実力を総合的に把握し、今後の学習に役立てることができます。

公式認定証の発行

スコアレポートと同時に、公式認定証が発行されます。「ナレーター音声版」のテストを受験した場合には、「CNN音声版」に換算された点数も表示されます。

※テスト中に中断があった場合、その旨が公式認定証に記載されます。

受験料 3,960円（税込）

► CNN ENGLISH EXPRESS 誌の購読者などに受験料の割引があります。

テストスケジュール

► 年3回、3月、7月、11月に実施され、それぞれテストを受験できる期間は2週間です。

► 詳しいスケジュール、申し込み方法などについては、以下のURL、またはQRコードから、CNN GLENTS
ホームページにアクセスしてください。

https://www.asahipress.com/special/glents/

姉妹テスト 高校生・大学生向け団体受験テスト

CNN GLENTS Basic

詳しくはCNN GLENTS団体受験特設ページへ
https://www.asahipress.com/special/glents/organization/

CNN GLENTS Basicとは

テスト内容、試験時間、受験料等を学校で使いやすいよう構成した
高校生・大学生向け団体受験用テストです

► リスニングセクション［24問／配点60点／約20分］とリーディングセクション［16問／配点40点／20
分］で構成。リスニングは「CNN音声版」と「ナレーター音声版」の2種類。動画視聴問題も含みます。

► 語句の注釈があるなど、CNN GLENTSより取り組みやすい内容です。

► CEFR-Jに対応し、レベル別に「何ができるか」の達成度一覧、学習のヒントなどが表示されます。

► 高校生は1人880円（税込）、大学生は1人2,200円（税込）で受験可能。

► 受験可能期間は自由に設定でき、期間内であればいつでも受験ができます。

なぜ今、CNN GLENTSが
必要なのか?
――CNN GLENTSだけの特長

CNN GLENTS監修 **笹尾洋介** 京都大学 国際高等教育院
附属国際学術言語教育センター 准教授

CNN GLENTSは
現実世界とダイレクトにリンクしている

Q CNN GLENTSが、他のテストと違う点は何ですか?

CNN GLENTSは単なる英語能力を測るための試験ではありません。実際のコミュニケーションで不可欠な**背景知識も含めた総合的な英語運用能力**を測定します。テストに登場する人物や場所は実在し、テストが**現実世界とダイレクトにリンクしています**。

　CNN GLENTSでは時事知識が重要な役割を果たします。まず、国際教養セクションが全体の⅙（20点／120点満点）を占めます。さらに、国際教養セクションはリーディングセクションとリスニングセクションの合計点と正の相関（r = .336）が認められることから、リーディング・リスニング技能においても時事知識が一定の役割を果たすことがわかります※。参考までに、国際教養セクションのスコアとTOEIC® Listening & Reading Testのスコアとの間にはほとんど相関が認められませんでした（r = .151）※。

　さらに、様々な音声変化（同化や脱落など）が頻出する「**生の英語**」を素材としていること、映像情報と言語情報を統合した**Viewing（動画視聴）**の力が測れることが大きな特長です。

※2020年11月9日〜11月27日に実施したCNN英語検定第3回プレテスト通常スピード版受験データ（N＝249）をもとに算出

グローバル人材・
グローバルリーダーの育成につながる

Q CNN GLENTSを受けるメリットは何でしょう?

✓ **テスト対策がそのまま国際教養を高める**ことに直結します。

✓ 8つの項目（リスニングでは「書き取り」「大意把握」「詳細理解」「動画理解」、リーディングでは「語彙」「大意把握」「詳細理解」、および「国際教養」）ごとにレーダーチャートが表示されるので、自分の**弱点が一目でわかります**。

✓ 背景知識も含めた**実践的なコミュニケーション力**を測定することができます。

✓ CEFR-Jとの対照レベルやTOEIC® Listening & Reading Testの予測スコアも把握できるので、**英語習熟度の確認**にもなります。

✓ CNN GLENTSは、英語力の向上はもちろんのこと時事問題に関する見知を広げる効果も期待できるため、**グローバル人材・グローバルリーダーの育成**につながると思います。

世界の動向を客観的に理解し、英語でしっかり発信できる国際人を目指せ

小西克哉 国際ジャーナリスト
国際教養大学大学院客員教授

時事英語を用いたテストなら、時代に即した英語力が測れる

Q CNNのニュースを使った英語テストの意義は?

CNN GLENTSはCNNで放送されたニュースの理解力を試すテストとして、英語の初歩的なレベルから非常に高いレベルまで、幅広い設問が用意されていると思います。素材としての英語の新鮮さを生かした構成になっていますね。文化的背景が問われるというのも重要なポイントで、これまでは「英語試験で背景的な知識を設問に含めると、正確な英語力の測定が難しくなる」という意見がありましたが、知識と一体になったテストがあっていいはずです。背景知識も理解を助ける大切な情報ですから、

知っていることは大事な実力の1つだと思いますね。そういう意味でも、時事英語を用いたテストは、時代に即した英語力が測れる良いテストだと思います。

今後、海外の大学のコースをオンラインで受講することも盛んになっていくでしょう。その際のスクリーニングに英語の試験は必ず必要でしょうし、**本物の英語力を測れるCNN GLENTSのような試験の意味はどんどん大きくなる**と思います。

新たな視点を得ることこそ、英語を勉強する理由

Q 真の国際人を目指すにはどんな能力が必要ですか?

日本の主要メディアは横並びを意識し過ぎて、海外のことには選択的関心しか示さない。もっとバランスよく、様々なトピックを扱うべきでしょう。それに対し、CNNのニュースのようなコンテンツを通して学べば、世界の人々が何に関心を持っているかを理解できますし、その背景となる価値観や思考を理解するヒントを得ることもできます。そういう新たな視点を得ることこそが、英語を勉強す

る大きな理由であるべきだと思います。**世界の動向を客観的に理解できて、自分自身の好みや立場、大事なメッセージを英語でちゃんと言えるというのは国際人として非常に大切**です。

今の学生はとても恵まれていて、勉強する機会も多いし、ネットもあって勉強する道具もそろっている。意欲的に英語を学び続けてほしいと思います。

グローバル社会で求められる異文化コミュニケーションに欠かせない国際教養力

鈴木武生 （株）アジアユーロ言語研究所 代表取締役、言語学博士、企業研修コンサルタント

Q 国際ビジネスで求められる英語力は以前とは変わってきているのですか?

2020年ぐらいまでは、TOEIC® スコアがいくつであるとか、英語ができることが1つのスキルになっていましたが、海外では国際ビジネスで求められる英語力がどんどん変化しています。異文化に対する知識やトピックを知り、英語でどのようにシェアして、違う文化を持つ人をどのようにまとめていけばよいか、それを仕事でどのように行うか、というのがこれからの課題になっていきます。

具体的には、異文化対応力と、異文化を持つ人に対するコミュニケーション力が重要になります。

例えばビジネスでの会話は、ただ単に機械や金融のような専門の話ができるだけではなくて、仕事の内容プラス、スモールトークです。スモールトークというのは、相手との距離を縮めるための会話のスキルです。

欧米人はスモールトークの中で相手の人柄や信頼度を見抜くので、同じレベルの教養を持っていることが判断材料となり、友好な関係性を築く重要な基盤になります。

異文化対応力と、異文化を持つ人に対するコミュニケーション力が重要

Q 異文化理解、異文化対応力をどう測るのですか?

自然な英語力や語彙は当然のことながら、後は何をどう話すかというスキル、同時に相手の価値観とか、こういうふうに相手は考えているんだというコミュニケーションのパターン、それに対する理解、異文化的なプラスアルファの知識が必要になってきます。

今までは、異文化理解や異文化対応力について体系的なプログラムがなく、あとは「習うより慣れろ」「本人の資質」「時の運まかせ」になりがちでしたが、英語力のみならず国際教養力も測ることができるCNN GLENTSなら、異文化理解や異文化対応力のある人材かどうかを判断する指標にすることができますね。

CNN GLENTSなら異文化理解、異文化対応力が測れる

CNN GLENTSを受験！
ビジネスの現場の反応は？

CNN GLENTS（CNN音声版）を受験したお二人からテストについてお聞きしました。

野村證券株式会社

野村グループは、グローバルに拠点を持つ金融サービス・グループ。
営業部門、ホールセール部門、インベストメント・マネジメント部門という3つの部門が、
30を超える国や地域のネットワークを通じて、国内外のお客様に付加価値の高いサービスを提供しています。

前田大輔 氏
本店法人コンサルティング一部
部長（当時）

受験後の感想 「リスニングセクション」「リーディングセクション」「国際教養セクション」のそれぞれが実践的であり、その内容も事実に基づくものであるため、ビジネスや日常における実際の会話をイメージし、英語を学ぶ目的を想定しながら受験することができました。

今後に向けて 「国際教養セクション」は知らないと解けない問題であり、テストとしては解けないと悔しく残念ではありますが、現実世界では一般的な教養について知らないとビジネスチャンスを逃してしまうことや、信頼を勝ち取れないことが多く、示唆の多い受験の機会となりました。復習して知識を身につけたいと感じました。

渡邊 皓 氏
本店法人コンサルティング一部（当時）

受験後の感想 「リスニングセクション」「リーディングセクション」「国際教養セクション」の全セクションを通じて、内容が高度でありながら実用的なものだと感じました。さらに、他のテストに比べて試験時間が短く、受験料も手頃であり、パソコンやスマホなどの端末のみで受験ができる点も大変便利に感じました。

今後に向けて 特に「国際教養セクション」は、問題内容も含めて他のテストにないユニークさを感じましたが、実際のビジネス・日常生活の場面でコミュニケーションを取っていく際には知っておくべき内容ばかりでしたので、日々の学習姿勢を猛省いたしました。私自身は海外留学を志望しておりますが、今回のCNN GLENTS受験を通じて一層学習の意欲が湧き上がってきました。

CNN GLENTSの
企業向けセミナー導入例

**千葉銀行で「1日セミナー＋CNN GLENTS受験」からなる
英語リスニング力強化セミナーを実施しました。**

千葉銀行　ちばぎん

**国内181店舗、海外6拠点の店舗ネットワークを有する千葉銀行、
行員の英語力強化に力を入れています。**

写真は、千葉銀行市場営業部のお二人と、CNNのニュースを用いた研修で講師を務めた鈴木武生氏（中央）。

セミナーの目的
海外拠点や市場関連業務への従事を目指す職員を中心に、英語に対するモチベーションアップと効果的かつ継続的な学習法の習得を目的として、オンライン形式で35名による研修を実施、セミナー後にCNN GLENTSで効果測定を行いました。

セミナーの内容
❶ 事前のアンケートで参加者の英語学習の状況や課題、英語レベルを把握。

❷ リスニング力の強化を図るために、CNNのニュースを使って実際にシャドーイングや反訳トレーニングなど具体的な学習を実行。

❸ CNN GLENTSを使って効果を測定。

CNN GLENTS受験者の声
満足度について

- 生きた英語に触れられるだけでなく、習熟度を数値で把握することのできるテストなので実践的でよかった。
- 自分の英語力の把握に役立った。
- 英語の学習はサボりがちなので、たまにこういう機会があるといいと思った。

テスト活用の利点

- 続けて学習する上で、理解度が進んでいることを把握しやすくなると思う。
- 自分の本当の英語力がわかると思う。
- いつも受験しているTOEIC®とは異なり、実際のニュースなどが問題で出題されるので、英語を学ぶ上で非常に勉強になった。

CNN GLENTS
受験者の反応は?

会社員　30代　女性　神奈川県
英検®2級

『CNN English Express』を3年間定期購読しています。別冊付録にある「今月のEE問題集」を活用して力試ししていましたが、本格的に実力を測りたいと思っていたところ、「CNN GLENTS」があると知り、受験しました。今回はナレーター音声版を受けたので、これからも精進し、次回はCNN音声版の高得点を目指します!

学生　20代　男性　福岡県
英検®2級、TOEIC®605点

コロナで留学が中止になり、「ガクチカ(学生時代に力を入れたこと)」で履歴書に書く内容に困っていました。「CNN GLENTS」はオンラインテストなので自宅で受験でき、結果がすぐにわかるので、大学の授業で忙しい身にとって、大変助かりました。

教員　50代　男性　東京都
TOEIC®680点

今後、社会に出ていく学生たちには「異文化理解力」が必要だと思い、良い教材を探していました。「CNN GLENTS」はオンラインテストですが、受験後に解答と解説を見ることができると聞き、まずは自分で受験してみました。国際教養問題は手ごたえがあり、学生たちには日頃からニュースに触れることの大切さがわかる、よいきっかけになるのではと思います。

会社員　40代　女性　大阪府
TOEIC®615点

オンライン英会話でネイティブと話していますが、話題に困り、CNNのニュースを見るようになりました。だいぶ語彙が増えたと思い、海外出張も決まったので、受験しました。日頃から聴いているCNNのアンカーたちの声を聴きながら問題に答えるのは新鮮でした。

実力がレーダーチャートで表示されるので、「自分の足りない部分を強化したい」というモチベーションアップにつながりました。

銀行員　20代　男性　千葉県
TOEIC®955点

苦手分野と得意分野がレーダーチャートで端的にわかる点が大変参考になりました。どこで間違えたのか、明確に振り返ることができるため、特に得点にバラつきがある部分を強化したいと思いました。

通常のリーディングとリスニングパートだけではなく、国際教養セクションの問題がある点が大変面白かったです。大学時代は国際政治学を専攻していたことから、知的好奇心をそそられる問題ばかりで、テストであることを忘れてしまうくらい楽しかったです。

塾講師　男性　神奈川県
英検®1級、TOEIC®990点

英検1級のリスニング・リーディングの練習として受験してみましたが、動画問題や語彙問題、国際教養セクションと盛りだくさんで楽しめました(動画問題で字幕にぼかしが入っていたのには最初びっくりしました)。国際教養セクションはほとんどわかりませんでしたが、背景知識を知るきっかけになって、いい刺激になりました。解説も充実しているので、復習するのにとても役立ちました。

岡山県立岡山朝日高等学校

村井容子 教諭

Q CNN GLENTS Basic を受験して生徒の反応はいかがでしたか？

高校1年の生徒を対象に、第1回はナレーター音声版で、第2回はCNN音声版で受験をしました。使用されている素材が、机の上や教室の中のものではなく、自分たちの身の回りや世界で起こっていること、そして、これから解決に向けて考えていくべきことであるため、生徒も興味を持って取り組んでいたようです。

Q オンラインテストの運用はいかがでしたか？

受験については、1人1台端末を用いて行いました。生徒一人一人にメールで受験案内を送っていただき、その指示に従えば受験も簡単です。すぐにスコアレポートを見ることができるので、強み・弱みを把握でき、復習につなげることができました。時間の負担も、費用の負担も少なく、継続的に使用するのに大変便利だと思います。

工学院大学附属中学校・高等学校

中川千穂 教諭

Q CNN GLENTS Basic を受験して生徒の反応はいかがでしたか？

試験の後の休み時間、生徒たちは試験で読んだ内容や、聴いた内容について話をしていました。現実社会で起きたことですので、興味・関心を持ったのだと思います。単語がわからなかったため、十分に理解できなかったものに関しては、自ら調べ、会得していました。それだけ内容が鮮明に記憶に残っていたためですし、調べて学んだ単語は内容と関連付けられているので、記憶に定着すると考えます。

Q オンラインテストの運用はいかがでしたか？

受験に際して、画面上の操作などに関する質問は1つも出ませんでした。手引を見なくても、次のステップや指示がわかるように作られていたおかげです。結果がスコアだけでなく、レベル表示されることで、現在の自分のレベルを認識することができるのも、大きな利点です。共通テストのリスニング対策として、全員でイヤホンをして教室で取り組むのは、本番に向けての練習となり、意欲向上につながったと思います。

立命館大学

山中 司 生命科学部生物工学科 教授

「多様な英語を
聞き取れるようになりたい」という
新たな動機づけを得た学生もいました

Q CNN GLENTS Basic を試してみようと思ったきっかけは何ですか?

1. テストの素材がCNNのニュース(=この世界でリアルに語られた英語)である点
2. 試験時間が40分程度の上、スマホを使ってオンラインで手軽に受験できる点
3. CEFR-Jとの対照レベルやTOEIC® L&R Testの予測スコアが確認できる点

以上の3点が一番大きな要因と言えると思います。

Q 学生の反応はいかがでしたか?

動画視聴問題は、初めての経験だったようで面白いと感じる学生が多かったと思います。ネイティブ話者のナチュラルスピードなので苦戦する学生もいましたが、「リアルな英語を体験できた」という感想を持った学生や、こういった様々な英語を聞き取れるようになりたいと、新たな動機づけを得た学生も見受けられました。

スコアが良くてもそうでなくても、グローバルな英語力に関して「自分の立ち位置」を確認すること(診断的価値)が英語アセスメントの本来の役割です。その意味で有意義な経験を提供できたと思いますし、今後も継続したいと思いました。

CNN GLENTSは、単なる言語能力だけではなく
総合的な英語力を評価する
非常に優れたテストだと思います

普段から世界の出来事にアンテナを張り、深い教養や幅広い知識に磨きをかけることは、大学生だけでなく、社会人になってからもとても重要なことです。こうした普段からの意識的な努力が、CNN GLENTSを受験する際には役に立ちます。

一般社会において、英語ができる人は、単に言語能力だけ独立して「できる」ことは稀で、仕事もできる人がほとんどです。そして往々にして、多少英語力が足りなくても、教養や知識で補って強引にでもコミュニケーションを成り立たせてしまう特徴があります。

CNN GLENTSはこうした総合的な英語力を評価してくれると考えており、とても優れたテストだと思っています。

CNN GLENTS:
出題形式と例題

リスニングセクション │ 出題形式と例題

リスニングセクションはPart 1〜Part 5からなり、試験時間はCNN音声版で約30分、ナレーター音声版で約35分です。

▶ 問題に関する指示文・指示音声はすべて英語です。

▶ 問題文の音声は、Part 1では2回、Part 2〜Part 4では1回、Part 5の動画は1回流れます。

▶ Part 1のディクテーション問題では、空所に該当する単語を文字入力します。他のPartは3肢択一式問題です。

▶ リスニングセクションで問われる設問は、以下の4種類です。

	設問構成	設問内容	設問数
1	書き取り	ディクテーション	4
2	大意把握	ニュースの主題を問う	7
3	詳細理解	ニュースの中で重要な細部を問う	15
4	動画理解	動画を視聴して内容を把握する	4

合計 30問／配点60点
※リスニングセクションの試験時間は、テストごとに多少変動があります。

▶ 配点の大きいリスニングセクション（60点）にうまく対応することがスコアを上げる大きなポイントになりますが、リスニングの練習でスタジオ録音のクリアな音声ばかり聴いていた場合、CNNのナチュラルスピードの音声が聞き取れないことが多いかもしれません。

　これは、ネイティブスピーカーが話す場合、特に単語の語尾の音にしばしば変化が起こり、そのために聞き取りにくいことが1つの原因です。そこで生の英語に対応するためには、こうした音声変化に慣れておくことが大切です。

Part 1　ディクテーション問題

▶ 問題は2題出題されます。

▶ 20〜30秒程度のニュース（またはニュースの一部）を聴き、英文の空所に聞き取った単語を入力します。音声は2度流れ、2度目の音声の後に30秒間、入力する時間があります。空所は1題につき2カ所あります。

▶ 入力する単語は1語のみです。

例題1

例題の音声は「CNN音声版」のみです。 01↓

The UK is on track for its worst __①_____ in more than 300 years. The Bank of England says the country's GDP could shrink by 14 percent this year, a dip that has not been seen —get this—since 1706. That's several years before the __②_____ *prime minister* even existed in England. But, for all the gloom, the bank is hoping for a swift recovery in 2021.

訳 イギリスは300余年ぶりに最悪の急落を経験しそうです。イングランド銀行は英国のGDPが今年（2020年）14%縮小する可能性があると述べています。それほどの下落は、なんと1706年以来のことです。その年は「首相」という言葉自体がイングランドに生まれる数年前にあたります。しかし、そんな暗い見通しにもかかわらず、同銀行は2021年には迅速に回復することを期待しています。

正解 ①crash　②term

例題2

02↓

This plain-looking rock has propped open a door in Michigan for the past 30 years—that's a nice doorstop—but it is __①_____ out of this world. A geology professor at Central Michigan University was asked to check it out and found that the oddly shaped, 22-pound rock was actually a meteorite __②_____ $100,000.

訳 この何の変哲もない石は過去30年間、ミシガン州でドアを開けたまま支えておく役割を果たしてきました——良いドアストッパーですね——でもそれは文字通り、この世界の外から来たのです。セントラルミシガン大学の地質学の教授が調査を依頼され、その奇妙な形の22パウンド（約10キロ）の石は実のところ10万ドルの価値がある隕石だと突き止めました。

正解 ①literally　②worth

Part 2　ショートニュース問題

▶ 問題は3題出題されます。

▶ 30〜40秒程度の短めのニュースを聴き、1題につき2問の設問に答えます。

▶ 選択肢3つの中から答えを選ぶ3肢択一式問題です。

▶ ニュースの音声が1回流れた後に設問の音声も流れ、そのあと解答時間が15秒あります。

例題3

03↓

1. What is the news report mainly about?

(**A**) Emergency services in Queensland

(**B**) The various effects of Cyclone Debbie

(**C**) A surprising thing that washed ashore in a flood

2. What did some people tweet?

(**A**) A photo of a shark

(**B**) Warnings to stay away from floodwaters

(**C**) Messages saying that it was safe to go back in the water

問題文

Well, after Cyclone Debbie swept through parts of Australia, severe flooding followed. But it was something else that had people shocked: a dead, 1.5-meter-long bull shark washed up on the side of the road in Queensland, just sittin' there when the water went away. Emergency services did tell people to stay away from floodwaters. When some didn't listen, they did tweet this photo of the shark with a message saying, "Think it's safe to go back in the water? Think again."

訳

さて、サイクロン「デビー」がオーストラリアの一部を通過した後、続いて大洪水が起こりました。しかし、人々に衝撃を与えたのは、別のものでした。それは、体長1.5メートルの息絶えたオオメジロザメで、クイーンズランド州の道端に打ち上げられ、水が引くとそこに鎮座していたのです。救急サービス当局は洪水によってあふれた水に近寄らないよう人々に言いました。それに耳を貸さない人がいたので、当局は、このサメの写真を、「水の中に戻るのが安全だと思ってる？　考え直したほうがいいよ」というメッセージとともにツイッターにアップしました。

正解 1. C　2. A

► 設問の内容は「大意把握」が1問、「詳細理解」が1問になります。

設問例

[**大意把握**]

● **What is the main point of the news report?**

訳 このニュースの要点は何か。

● **What is the news report mainly about?**

訳 このニュースは主に何について述べているか。

● **What problem in the US is the main topic of the news report?**

訳 米国のどのような問題がこのニュースの主なトピックか。

[**詳細理解**]

● **What happened at the restaurant in Georgia?**

訳 ジョージア州のレストランで起こったことは何か。

● **What was San Francisco the first US city to do?**

訳 サンフランシスコが米国の市として初めて行ったことは何か。

- **What does the news report say about most of the rescued animals?**

  訳　このニュースでは、救助された動物たちの多くについて何と述べているか。

Part 3　ロングニュース問題

▶ 問題は2題出題されます。

▶ 2分前後の長めのニュースを聴き、1題につき4問の設問に答えます。

▶ 選択肢3つの中から答えを選ぶ3肢択一式問題です。

▶ ニュースの音声が1回流れた後に設問の音声も流れ、そのあと解答時間が15秒あります。

▶ 設問の内容は「大意把握」が1問、「詳細理解」が3問になります。

　「大意把握」と「詳細理解」の設問例は「ショートニュース問題」の解説を参照してください。

例題4　

1. What is the news report mainly about?

　(**A**) Cyberbullying among teens

　(**B**) Teenage smartphone addiction in South Korea

　(**C**) Medical problems resulting from smartphone use

2.　What is the main purpose of the activities at the camp?

　(**A**) To help the teens overcome an obsession

　(**B**) To educate the parents of smartphone addicts

　(**C**) To give the teens better reasons to use their smartphones

3. How do the camp participants usually feel about being at the camp?

　(**A**) They feel lonely for the whole 12 days.

　(**B**) They hate it at first but only for a couple of days.

　(**C**) They like it at first but get bored after a few days.

4. What does one doctor say can result from too much smartphone use?

　(**A**) Muscle weakness

　(**B**) Decreased brain usage

　(**C**) Depression and anxiety

正解　**1. B　2. A　3. B　4. C**

トランスクリプト・訳・解説は、スマートフォンの場合はQRコードから、PCの場合はURLから見ることができます。
https://ee.asahipress.com/glents/guide/p21.pdf

Part 4 インタビュー問題

► 問題は2題出題されます。

► 3分～3分30秒程度のインタビューを聴き、1題につき4問の設問に答えます。

► 選択肢3つの中から答えを選ぶ3肢択一式問題です。

► インタビューの音声が1回流れた後に設問の音声も流れ、そのあと解答時間が15秒あります。

► 設問の内容は「大意把握」が1問、「詳細理解」が3問になります。

　「大意把握」と「詳細理解」の設問例はpp.20-21の「ショートニュース問題」の解説を参照してください。

例題5

1. What are the speakers mainly discussing?

(**A**) Slavery in the US

(**B**) The treatment of black people in the US

(**C**) The way American police officers are trained

2. What does Bryan Stevenson say the great evil of slavery in the US was?

(**A**) The myth of white supremacy

(**B**) The fact that slaves could not vote

(**C**) The fact that slaves could not own land

3. What does the interviewer say about reforms in the justice system?

(**A**) Sentencing reforms have not been made.

(**B**) No one at the top has tried to do the right thing.

(**C**) The reforms have had no effect on black people's real experience.

4. What does Stevenson say police officers should be trained to do?

(**A**) Shoot

(**B**) Wrestle

(**C**) Manage conflict

`正解` **1. B　2. A　3. C　4. C**

トランスクリプト・訳・解説は、スマートフォンの場合はQRコードから、PCの場合はURLから見ることができます。
https://ee.asahipress.com/glents/guide/p22.pdf

Part 5　動画視聴問題

スマートフォンの場合はQRコードから、PCの場合はURLから動画をご視聴ください。
https://eqm.page.link/Po4N

▶ 問題は2題出題されます。

▶ 30〜40秒程度の短めのニュース動画を見て、1題につき2問の設問に答えます。

▶ 選択肢3つの中から答えを選ぶ3肢択一式問題です。

▶ ニュース動画が1回流れた後に設問の音声も流れ、そのあと解答時間が15秒あります。

▶ 設問の内容は「大意把握」が1問、「詳細理解」が1問になります。

▶ 「大意把握」と「詳細理解」の設問例はpp.20-21の「ショートニュース問題」の解説を参照してください。

例題6

1. What is the main point of the news report?

(**A**) Humans have altered the land to make it more suitable for animals.

(**B**) Humans are to blame for a number of environmental problems.

(**C**) Humans are responsible for the recent decrease in ocean pollution.

2. What does the news report say has happened since 1980?

(**A**) Ocean plastic pollution has increased 10 times.

(**B**) Around 1 million species of animals have become extinct.

(**C**) Around 75 percent of all land has been altered.

正解　**1. B　2. A**

トランスクリプト・訳・解説は、スマートフォンの場合はQRコードから、PCの場合はURLから見ることができます。
https://ee.asahipress.com/glents/guide/p23.pdf

リーディングセクション｜出題形式と例題

リスニングセクションの解答制限時間がきたら、「This is the end of the Listening Section. It is now time for the Reading Section.」とアナウンスが流れ、**自動でリーディングセクションに進みます**。

▶ リーディングセクションは Part 1〜Part 3 からなり、試験時間は25分です。

▶ 画面上部にセクション全体の残り時間が表示されます。テスト画面の「Next」で次に進み、「Back」で前に戻ります。時間内であれば、前の問題に戻って解答し直すことができます。

▶ リーディングセクションでは、マークした設問をあとで見直すことができる「レビュー機能」がついています。設問下の「Mark for review」を選択しておけば、画面右上の「Review」を押すと、解答状況が一覧で表示されます。見直したい設問に色がついているので、そこを押せば設問に戻ることができます。試験時間内であれば、解答内容の見直し・訂正が何度でもできます。

▶ リーディングセクションで問われる設問は、以下の3種類です。

	設問構成	設問内容	設問数
1	**語彙**	ニュースの理解に必要な語彙力を問う	4
2	**大意把握**	ニュースの主題を問う	5
3	**詳細理解**	ニュースの中で重要な細部を問う	11

合計 20問／配点40点／試験時間25分

Part 1　語彙問題

▶ 問題は4題出題されます。

▶ ニュースから抜粋した英文に空所が設けられており、そこに入る最も適切な単語を3つの選択肢の中から選びます。

例題1

When the world comes back online after the coronavirus, demand is likely to surge, causing further (　　　　).

(**A**) facility　　　(**B**) laxity　　　(**C**) volatility

［訳］ 新型コロナウイルス終息後に世界が（社会・経済活動を）再開したとき、需要は急増し、さらなる不安定をもたらすものとみられます。

例題2

In Venice, the city is bracing for another day of flooding, its fourth（　　　　）day.

(**A**) consecutive　　　　(**B**) progressive　　　　(**C**) recurrent

---

訳　ベネチアでは今日もまた浸水の備えをしている。4日連続だ。

正解　**A**

Part 2　短文読解問題

▶ 問題は3題出題されます。

▶ 200語程度の短めのニュースを読み、1題につき2問の設問に答えます。

▶ 選択肢3つの中から答えを選ぶ3肢択一式問題です。

▶ 設問の内容は「大意把握」が1問、「詳細理解」が1問になります。

問題文は、スマートフォンの場合はQRコードから、PCの場合はURLから見ることができます。
https://ee.asahipress.com/glents/guide/p25A.pdf

例題3

1. What is the news report mainly about?

(**A**) Hunting in Uganda

(**B**) The killing of a rare gorilla

(**C**) A popular gorilla group

2. Who has been jailed?

(**A**) Rafiki

(**B**) Sam

(**C**) Byamukama

正解　1. B　　2. C

訳・解説は、スマートフォンの場合はQRコードから、PCの場合はURLから見ることができます。
https://ee.asahipress.com/glents/guide/p25B.pdf

Part 3　長文読解問題

▶ 問題は2題出題されます。

▶ 500〜550語程度の長めのニュースを読み、1題につき5問の設問に答えます。

▶ 選択肢3つの中から答えを選ぶ3肢択一式問題です。

▶ 設問の内容は「大意把握」が1問、「詳細理解」が4問になります。

問題文は、スマートフォンの場合はQRコードから、PCの場合はURLから見ることができます。
https://ee.asahipress.com/glents/guide/p26A.pdf

1. What is the research described in the news report mainly about?

(**A**) Volcanic eruptions in India

(**B**) The potential impact of a future asteroid strike

(**C**) Why the dinosaurs became extinct

2. What is implied about the volcanic-eruptions theory?

(**A**) It is the most likely to be correct.

(**B**) It no longer seems to be correct.

(**C**) It describes only one cause of the ultimate bad day.

3. What did the researchers want to find out about dinosaurs?

(**A**) What geological markers they left behind

(**B**) How long it would have taken for them to die

(**C**) Where they could have lived after each of the two disasters

4. What was concluded about the impact of the asteroid strike?

(**A**) The gases sent into the atmosphere made the Earth very hot.

(**B**) The Earth's climate became too cold for dinosaurs to survive.

(**C**) Vegetation at the bottom of the food chain increased.

5. What did the research team conclude about the Deccan Traps eruptions?

(**A**) They may have helped recovery after the asteroid strike.

(**B**) They didn't begin until after the dinosaurs became extinct.

(**C**) They released too much carbon dioxide for any animals to have survived.

正解   1. C   2. B   3. C   4. B   5. A

訳・解説は、スマートフォンの場合はQRコードから、PCの場合はURLから見ることができます。
https://ee.asahipress.com/glents/guide/p26B.pdf

国際教養セクション｜出題形式と例題

リーディングセクションの解答制限時間がきたら、自動で国際教養セクションに進みます。

▶ 国際教養セクションの試験時間は15分です。

▶ 設問は10題出題され、**選択肢4つの中からその内容が誤っているものを選ぶ4肢択一式**です。

▶ 画面上部にセクション全体の残り時間が表示されます。

▶ 国際教養セクションでは、リーディングセクションと同様に、マークした設問をあとで見直すことができる「レビュー機能」がついています。設問下の「Mark for review」を選択しておけば、画面右上の「Review」を押すと、解答状況が一覧で表示されます。見直したい設問に色がついているので、そこを押せば設問に戻ることができます。試験時間内であれば、解答内容の見直し・訂正が何度でもできます。

▶ **試験時間が過ぎると、自動でテストが終了します。早く終了したい場合は、右下の「Click to end the test」をクリックすれば（アプリでは「Tap to end the test」をタップ）、試験時間が過ぎる前にテストを終了できます。**

例題

1. **Which of the following statements about Iran is NOT true?**

   (**A**) About 90% of Iranians practice Shiite Islam.

   (**B**) Iran borders the Persian Gulf.

   (**C**) Iran and Saudi Arabia, which had severed diplomatic ties since 2016, agreed to normalize diplomatic relations in March 2023.

   (**D**) The official language of Iran is Arabic.

   設問訳　イランに関する次の記述のうち、誤っているものはどれか。

   (**A**) イラン国民の約90%がイスラム教シーア派を信仰している。

   (**B**) イランはペルシャ湾に面している。

   (**C**) 2016年から断交していたイランとサウジアラビアは、2023年3月、外交関係を正常化することで合意した。

   (**D**) イランの公用語はアラビア語である。

   正解　**D**

2. **Which of the following statements about American presidential elections is NOT true?**

   (**A**) A person may run for president without being in either the Republican Party or the Democratic Party.

   (**B**) States that tend to back Republican candidates are called red states, and states that tend to back Democratic candidates are called blue states.

   (**C**) The Tuesday in February or early March when primary elections and caucuses are held in more states than on any other day is called Super Tuesday.

(**D**) The candidate who receives the most votes cast by the general voting public in November wins the election.

設問訳 アメリカの大統領選に関する次の記述のうち、誤っているものはどれか。

(**A**) 共和党、民主党に属していなくても大統領選に立候補できる。

(**B**) 共和党を支持する傾向がある州を赤い州、民主党を支持する傾向がある州を青い州と呼ぶ。

(**C**) 2月または3月上旬の火曜日で、予備選挙や党員集会が最も多くの州で開催される日を「スーパーチューズデー」と呼ぶ。

(**D**) 11月の一般投票で、最も得票数が多かった候補者が当選する。

正解 **D**

3. **Which of the following statements about abbreviations is NOT true?**

(**A**) UNICEF is an agency of the United Nations that works to protect the rights and lives of children.

(**B**) A company's CFO is the top person in charge of its financial operations and financial strategy.

(**C**) The CDC is a comprehensive research institute of the United Nations for controlling infectious diseases.

(**D**) The IAEA is an international organization that promotes the peaceful use of nuclear energy and seeks to prevent the development of nuclear weapons.

設問訳 ニュースで使われる略語に関する次の記述のうち、誤っているものはどれか。

(**A**) UNICEFとは、子どもの権利と命を守るために活動する国連機関のことである。

(**B**) 企業のCFOとは、企業の財務運営と財務戦略を担当する責任者である。

(**C**) CDCとは、国連に所属する感染症対策の総合研究所のことである。

(**D**) IAEAとは、原子力の平和的利用の促進と核兵器開発の防止を目的とする国際機関である。

正解 **C**

問題の傾向

1. 国際関係で近年話題になっているトピック・国・イベントに関する問題

例 （以下、誤っている選択肢を太字にしてあります）

■「ウクライナについて」 選択肢 ▶ **カスピ海に面する**／1991年までソ連の一部だった／2021年の小麦、トウモロコシ、大麦の生産量は世界で10位以内だった／2021年の名目GDPはロシアの約10分の1だった

■「難民の増加について」 選択肢 ▶ 2020年末時点で、最も多くの難民を出している国はシリアである／**同時点で、最も多くの難民を受け入れている国はドイツである**／同時点で、EU加盟国では反移民の傾向が拡大してい

る／同時点で、難民の約40％は18歳未満の子どもである

■「中国経済について」　選択肢▶2022年の自動車生産台数は中国が世界一だった／2022年の中国の名目GDPは日本の4倍以上だった／**2022年の中国のGDPに占める割合が最も高いのは、製造業や建設業などの第2次産業だった**／2021年末時点で純資産が5000万ドルを超える超富裕層の数では、中国は米国に次ぎ世界2位だった

2. アメリカ国内の政治・社会に関する問題

例

■「米国での薬物過剰摂取問題」　選択肢▶2020年、米国では約5万5000人が薬物過剰摂取で死亡した／同年、米国では薬物過剰摂取の死亡者数が自動車事故の死亡者数を1万人以上上回った／同年、米国では鎮痛剤と称されるオピオイドが薬物過剰摂取の死亡原因の第1位だった／**マイケル・ジャクソンは、2009年にオピオイドの過剰摂取で死亡した**

■「米国の州政府について」　選択肢▶州は独自の憲法を持つ／**州知事の任期は4年である**／州政府は州兵の指揮権を持つ／州政府は新型コロナウイルス感染の拡大抑制のために、州内で検疫・隔離を実施する権限を持つ

■「米国連邦最高裁判所の仕組み」　選択肢▶連邦最高裁は1人の長官と8人の判事の9人からなる／**最高裁判事は大統領が指名し、下院が承認する**／最高裁判事は死亡、引退、または上院による有罪判決が出るまで在職する／判決は最高裁判事の多数決で決まる

3. 科学・テクノロジー・環境・医学関連の知識を問う問題

例

■「ウイルスについて」　選択肢▶ウイルスは細菌よりはるかに小さい／ペストはウイルスによる感染症ではない／ウイルスは単独では増殖できない／**抗生物質はウイルス治療に有効である**

■「AIについて」　選択肢▶ディープラーニングはAIの急速な進歩に寄与している／**AIの軍事利用は禁止されている**／自動運転車にはAI技術が必須である／AI技術でがんを診断する機器が市場に出始めている

■「リチウムイオン電池について」　選択肢▶くりかえし充電と放電が可能である／過充電や過放電によって発熱することがある／**電池の残量がある状態で充電を始めるとフル充電できない**／急速充電が可能である

4. 略語（abbreviation）が何を意味するかを問う問題

例

■**PKO:** United Nations Peacekeeping Operations（国連平和維持活動）

■**ILO:** International Labour Organization（国際労働機関）

■**FTA:** Free Trade Agreement（自由貿易協定）

■**OECD:** Organization for Economic Co-operation and Development（経済協力開発機構）

■**JAXA:** Japan Aerospace Exploration Agency（宇宙航空研究開発機構）

対策

1. 国際ニュースを伝えるニュースサイトに日常的に目を通す。

  例

  ■ **CNN.com**（https://edition.cnn.com/）

2. 英語のみでは難しい場合、日本語でもニュースに触れる。

  例

  ■ **CNN.co.jp**（https://www.cnn.co.jp/）

このほか、新聞、書籍、テレビ、ニュース動画、ニュースサイトなど、自分に合った形で日本語でも日々のニュースに触れるよう心がける。

3. 英語ニュースのポッドキャストを聴く。

  ニュースを知るだけでなく、リスニングの練習にもなるので一石二鳥。

  例

  ■ **CNN Tonight**（https://edition.cnn.com/audio/podcasts/cnn-tonight）

  ■ **Anderson Cooper 360°**（https://edition.cnn.com/audio/podcasts/anderson-cooper-360）

  ■ **Amanpour**（https://www.cnn.com/audio/podcasts/amanpour）

  ■ **Fareed Zakaria GPS**（https://www.cnn.com/audio/podcasts/fareed-zakaria-gps）

※ Apple社のPodcast、Spotifyなどでも聴けます。

Practice Test 1

※Practice Test 1は2021年7月実施の第1回CNN GLENTSの問題を基に若干の変更を加えています。

Listening Section

Part 1

CNN音声版 06 ナレーター音声版 26

Directions

Here are the directions for **Part 1**. You will hear two short news reports. Enter the missing words in the spaces below the text. Enter only one word in each space. You will hear each report two times. For each report, after listening two times, you will have 30 seconds to enter the missing words.

No.1

CNN音声版 07 ナレーター音声版 27

European human-rights ambassadors say they are deeply concerned about a group of female activists ①(   ) in Saudi Arabia, and they are calling on the kingdom to release them. One of the women, who has already spent more than two years in ②(   ), will now be tried by a terrorism court. Her apparent crime? Demanding the right to drive.

Enter the word for ①

Enter the word for ②

No.2

CNN音声版 08 ナレーター音声版 28

Scientists thought the elephant shrew had been extinct for 50 years. Thankfully, they were wrong. Why thankfully? 'Cause it's cute. It's related to an elephant but ①(   ) like a mouse. The last time scientists saw one was in the 1970s, but in the African nation of Djibouti, where the elephant shrew was recently rediscovered, local ②(   ) had said they'd seen them. These little mammals can run at over 18 miles per hour—faster than some elephants.

Enter the word for ①

Enter the word for ②

Part 2

Directions

CNN音声版 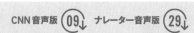 ナレーター音声版

Here are the directions for **Part 2**. You will hear three short news reports. Each report will be followed by two questions. You will hear each report and question only once. For each question, you will have 15 seconds to choose the best answer.

問題文 設問 問題文 設問
CNN音声版 10 11 ナレーター音声版 30 31

No.1

1. **What is the main topic of this news report?**

   (**A**) The attitudes of Americans toward wearing masks

   (**B**) The different benefits of various types of masks

   (**C**) The availability of masks in the United States

2. **What is reported as some men's reason for their decision about masks?**

   (**A**) They don't want to seem criminal.

   (**B**) They are worried about their health.

   (**C**) They want others to wear masks more often.

問題文 設問 問題文 設問
CNN音声版 12 13 ナレーター音声版 32 33

No.2

1. **What is the main topic of this news report?**

   (**A**) An accident that occurred during a boat race

   (**B**) The rescue of three sailors from an island

   (**C**) The search for survivors of a helicopter crash

2. **What does the news report say about a message written in sand?**

   (**A**) It got washed away a number of times.

   (**B**) It was first seen by sailors on a patrol ship.

   (**C**) It was seen from Australian and US aircraft.

Listening Section

No.3

1. What is this news report mainly about?

(**A**) The response to a theme park's increase in ticket prices

(**B**) Problems with Wi-Fi spots in Tokyo

(**C**) A place where people can do remote work

2. What does the news report suggest about Yomiuriland?

(**A**) It has suffered financially during the pandemic.

(**B**) Visitors think it needs to make more changes.

(**C**) Its employees appreciate the new safety measures.

Part 3

Directions   CNN音声版 (16↓) ナレーター音声版 (36↓)

Here are the directions for **Part 3**. You will hear all of or excerpts from two news reports. Each report will be followed by four questions. You will hear each report and question only once. For each question, you will have 15 seconds to choose the best answer.

問題文 設問   問題文 設問
CNN音声版 (17↓) (18↓) ナレーター音声版 (37↓) (38↓)

No.1

1. What is the main topic of this news report?

(**A**) A famous athlete's charity efforts

(**B**) A campaign to get young people involved in sports

(**C**) A failed UK-government policy

2. What childhood experience does Marcus Rashford mention?

(**A**) Being unable to play sports for health reasons

(**B**) His parents' efforts to help other families

(**C**) His mother's struggles to support her family

3. What does the interviewee say about poverty in the UK?

(**A**) It has been decreasing in recent years.

(**B**) People often fail to understand how severe it is.

(**C**) It is less widespread than it is in other developed nations.

4. What did Rashford help persuade the British government to do?

(**A**) Ask the UK's major supermarkets to join a task force

(**B**) Provide free meals during the coronavirus lockdown

(**C**) Allow children to go to school during the coronavirus lockdown

Listening Section

No.2

1. What is the main point of this news report?

　(**A**) China announced it will join another country's space mission.

　(**B**) An unexpected discovery was made on the moon.

　(**C**) A Chinese spacecraft completed a historic mission to the moon.

2. What is true with regard to the landing site on the moon?

　(**A**) It was not the one that had originally been planned.

　(**B**) This was the first time any probe had been there.

　(**C**) It had more dangers than expected.

3. According to the news report, what happened in the 1970s?

　(**A**) Material obtained by a Chinese spacecraft was lost.

　(**B**) Chinese scientists had difficulty building a moon-landing spacecraft.

　(**C**) Samples from the moon were brought to Earth.

4. What does the news report say scientists hope to learn more about?

　(**A**) The activity of past volcanoes on the moon

　(**B**) How to protect astronauts from radiation

　(**C**) The way Earth was formed

Part 4

Directions

CNN音声版 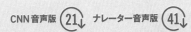 21↓ ナレーター音声版 41↓

Here are the directions for **Part 4**. You will hear excerpts from two interviews. Each interview will be followed by four questions. You will hear the interviews and each question only once. For each question, you will have 15 seconds to choose the best answer.

問題文 設問　　　　　　　　問題文 設問
CNN音声版  22↓ 23↓ ナレーター音声版 42↓ 43↓

No.1

1. What is the main point made by Al Gore?

(**A**) Climate change is becoming a harder problem to solve.

(**B**) The pandemic has taken attention away from climate change.

(**C**) We are developing more ways to deal with the climate crisis.

2. According to Al Gore, what lesson can the COVID-19 crisis teach us?

(**A**) It is important to listen to scientists' warnings.

(**B**) Virus outbreaks can become uncontrollable within months.

(**C**) Pandemics have a larger effect on racial minorities.

3. What does Al Gore say about alternative energy sources such as solar and wind?

(**A**) People mistakenly think they are unreliable.

(**B**) They are becoming cheaper to use.

(**C**) More efforts should be focused on battery storage.

4. What point does Al Gore emphasize with regard to climate change?

(**A**) The atmosphere is already very polluted.

(**B**) Sewage systems contribute to the problem.

(**C**) Fossil fuels can be burned in different ways.

Listening Section

No.2

1. What are the speakers mainly discussing?

(**A**) Why some leaders are more effective than others

(**B**) Characteristics that are important for leadership

(**C**) The differences between leadership and success

2. What does David Rubenstein say about learning to lead?

(**A**) It happens early in life.

(**B**) It is not necessary for some leaders.

(**C**) It can have an unintended effect.

3. Why does Rubenstein mention Bill Gates?

(**A**) To support his point about the importance of luck

(**B**) To stress the importance of the Internet

(**C**) To explain how meeting certain people has helped him

4. What does Rubenstein say about leaders?

(**A**) They tend to enjoy studying.

(**B**) Most begin to have success at a young age.

(**C**) Most are not raised in wealthy families.

► リスニング・トレーナーの「Play All」機能やiTunes、Windows Media Playerなどの音声再生ソフトでPart 1から連続で再生している場合は、"It is now time for Part 5."の音声が流れたら、音声を止めてください。

► Part 5の動画視聴問題は、スマートフォンの場合はQRコードから、PCの場合はURLから動画をご視聴ください。

Part 5

Directions

https://eqm.page.link/BZ95

Here are the directions for **Part 5**. You will watch two short news reports. Each report will be followed by two questions. You will watch each report and hear each question only once. For each question, you will have 15 seconds to choose the best answer.

※ Directionsと設問の音声も動画に含まれています。

No.1

1. What is the main topic of this news report?

(**A**) A ban on the use of pigeons for racing

(**B**) A new way for racing pigeons to be sold internationally

(**C**) A racing pigeon that was sold for a record amount of money

2. According to the news report, what is happening in China?

(**A**) More people are becoming interested in pigeon racing.

(**B**) Pigeons are being raised for buyers in Belgium.

(**C**) Raising pigeons is becoming more difficult.

No.2

https://eqm.page.link/Ex7F

1. What is this news report mainly about?

(**A**) The effects of airplane design on public safety

(**B**) An airplane with a new type of design

(**C**) An airline's effort to attract more customers

2. According to the news report, what do experts hope will happen?

(**A**) An airline will agree to collaborate with researchers.

(**B**) Airlines will design cabins with more space.

(**C**) Airplane fuel costs will become lower.

Reading Section

Part 1

> **Directions**
>
> **Part 1** contains four short excerpts from news reports. Each excerpt has one blank space and is followed by three answer options. Choose the best word from the answer options to fill each blank space.

No.1

While Hollywood movies have stumbled in China lately, some films produced by Chinese studios and production companies have (   ).

(**A**) accomplished   (**B**) distinguished   (**C**) flourished

No.2

The concept of (   ) passports remains deeply contentious, and anyone banking on it for a 2021 summer vacation could be disappointed.

(**A**) efficacy   (**B**) immunity   (**C**) vitality

No.3

Vincent van Gogh was (   ) undervalued throughout his career.

(**A**) progressively   (**B**) serially   (**C**) severally

No.4

US car sales have (   ) again, and Americans are back to buying vehicles at their pre-pandemic pace.

(**A**) picked up   (**B**) pulled up   (**C**) rounded up

Part 2

No.1

The pandemic has not only upended millions of lives around the world, it's now threatening the world's oceans. Discarded disposable masks, gloves and wipes are floating into waterways and oceans. The proof is in the waste that's already washed ashore on beaches.

As many as 62,210 PPE items, including single-use masks and gloves, were collected during the annual International Coastal Cleanup event in September 2020, according to preliminary data. It's the world's largest volunteer effort, held every September, involving participants from dozens of countries who remove and log a sample volume of plastics and marine waste from the ocean and waterways.

In 2020, 76 countries participated in the cleanup and collected at least 1.6 million pounds of trash, including tens of thousands of PPE products. It was the first time in the 35-year history of the event that PPE was added as a data category, along with cigarette butts, food wrappers, plastic straws and bottles, said Dr. George Leonard, chief scientist with Ocean Conservancy, a nonprofit working to protect oceans and advance marine conservation. "We absolutely believe that PPE waste is a significant threat to oceans and marine life," said Leonard.

Reading Section

1. **What is the main point of the news report?**

   (**A**) Waste resulting from the pandemic is polluting the oceans.

   (**B**) More equipment is needed to fight the pandemic.

   (**C**) A new swimming event had to be canceled.

2. **What is reported about the September 2020 event?**

   (**A**) Some types of waste harmed volunteers.

   (**B**) The volunteers used new methods to do their work.

   (**C**) Volunteers from various countries participated.

No.2

Two notebooks that once belonged to Charles Darwin, believed to be worth millions of pounds, have "likely been stolen" after being missing for two decades, Cambridge University Library said.

The notebooks—one of which contains Darwin's 1837 "Tree of Life" sketch—had been removed from the university's special collections strong rooms, where rare and valuable items are kept, to be photographed in September 2000, the library said in a statement.

The items were logged as photographed in November of the same year, but a routine check in January 2001 found that the small box containing the books had not been returned to its correct place.

Darwin sketched his ideas around an evolutionary tree in the summer of 1837 after returning from his round-the-world trip aboard HMS *Beagle*—decades before he published more developed ideas around the tree of life in *On the Origin of Species*.

For years, librarians at the university had assumed the books were simply lost in the vast library, which is home to more than 210 kilometers of shelving and some 10 million books, maps, and manuscripts.

"I am heartbroken that the location of these Darwin notebooks, including Darwin's iconic 'Tree of Life' drawing, is currently unknown, but we're determined to do everything possible to discover what happened," Jessica Gardner, university librarian and director of library services since 2017, said in a statement.

Reading Section

1. **What is the main point of the news report?**

   (**A**) An important library had to close down.

   (**B**) A university lost much of its digital security.

   (**C**) Valuable historical items have probably been stolen.

2. **When did Darwin do the drawing mentioned in this report?**

   (**A**) During his time aboard the *Beagle*

   (**B**) A long time before *On the Origin of Species* was published

   (**C**) Just before his round-the-world trip

No.3

Diamonds might be forever, but that doesn't mean they have to take eons to form. The gemstones are usually created after carbon is crushed and heated far beneath the Earth's surface over billions of years—which is what makes them so coveted.

Now, scientists in Australia say they have sped up the process into just a matter of minutes—and at room temperature. An international team of researchers led by the Australian National University (ANU) and RMIT University in Melbourne, Australia said they have created two types of diamonds at room temperature by using high pressure equivalent to 640 African elephants balancing on the tip of a ballet shoe.

The researchers said they were able to create two types of structurally distinct diamonds—one similar to those typically worn in jewelry, and another type called Lonsdaleite, which is found naturally at the sites of meteorite impacts and is harder than most diamonds.

Synthetic diamonds are not themselves new, and have already been created in labs since the 1940s in a bid to find cheaper, ethical and environmentally friendly stones. But researchers were excited to create such diamonds at room temperature, especially the harder Lonsdaleite diamond, which has the potential to be used to cut through "ultra-solid" materials on mining sites, they said.

Reading Section

1. **What is the main topic of the news report?**

   (**A**) The use of animals at a diamond-mining site

   (**B**) A new method for making diamonds

   (**C**) The discovery of a new type of diamond

2. **What does the news report say about Lonsdaleite?**

   (**A**) It might be useful in mining.

   (**B**) It was first discovered in the 1940s.

   (**C**) It is not found in nature.

Part 3

Directions

Part 3 contains all of or excerpts from two news reports, each followed by five questions. For each question, choose the best answer from the answer options.

No.1

As China grows richer, the waistlines of adults in the country are also expanding. More than half of Chinese adults are now considered overweight, a study conducted by the country's National Health Commission revealed on December 23, 2020. Obesity rates among Chinese adults have also more than doubled in less than two decades, from 7.1% in 2002 to 16.4% in 2020.

According to the report, 50.7% of Chinese adults are overweight, including those who are obese. In a country of 1.4 billion, that amounts to more than half a billion people—more than the entire US population.

That's a sharp increase over the past two decades. In 2002, 29.9% of Chinese adults were overweight, including obese. In 2012, that figure rose to 42%, according to previous reports released by Chinese health authorities.

"Our country's residents face a severe problem of overweight and obesity. The overweight and obesity rates among residents in both urban and rural areas and across all age groups are steadily rising," Li Bin, deputy director of the National Health Commission, said at a news conference.

It's partly due to huge changes in diet and eating habits brought on by the country's rapid economic growth. During the 1950s and 60s, famine saw an estimated 45 million Chinese people starve to death. And until 1993, people had to use government-distributed food vouchers to get staples such as rice, oil, eggs and meat.

The days of food shortages are long over. Now, Chinese people are free to eat largely as they choose, and the country's new wealth has brought ever more nutritious and calorie-rich food to the dining table.

The increase in spending power has also given rise to the problem of food waste, which Chinese President Xi Jinping has called "shocking and distressing." On December 22, 2020, a draft law on preventing food waste was submitted to the country's national legislature.

Rising overweight and obesity rates pose an additional burden to public health. Excessive weight increases the risk for serious disease and health conditions, including high blood pressure, diabetes, coronary heart disease and stroke, the US Centers for Disease Control and Prevention says.

"The overweight and obesity rates in China have been climbing fast, with a high prevalence and affecting all groups in the population. This brings enormous challenges," said Zhao Wenhua, chief nutritionist at the Chinese Center for Disease Control and Prevention.

According to the World Health Organization, at least 4 million people die each year as a result of being overweight or obese. Worldwide, obesity has been on the rise too, having nearly tripled since 1975, according to WHO. In 2016, 39% of adults globally—or more than 1.9 billion people—were overweight, including over 650 million who were obese.

In the United States, 71.6% of adults were classified as overweight, including obese, between 2015 and 2016, according to the CDC.

But China has a tougher measurement than global standards. WHO considers a body mass index (BMI)—a ratio of weight to height—over 25 to be overweight, and more than 30 obese. In China, a BMI greater than 24 is considered overweight, and over 28 is obese.

---

1. **What is the main topic of this news report?**

   (**A**) Changing attitudes about obesity among Chinese adults

   (**B**) The failure of the Chinese government to reduce food waste

   (**C**) Rising overweight and obesity rates in China

2. **What point is made by describing China in previous decades?**

   (**A**) The country's economic situation has improved.

   (**B**) Food shortages today are dealt with more effectively.

   (**C**) Some problems caused by poverty in the past still remain.

3. **What does the news report say about food waste in China?**

   (**A**) Its overall economic effects are not yet known.

   (**B**) The availability of more-nutritious foods would help reduce it.

   (**C**) The government is addressing the issue.

4. **According to the WHO, what has happened since 1975?**

   (**A**) Deaths resulting from obesity have tripled in the United States.

   (**B**) Obesity has become a bigger problem globally.

   (**C**) Some obesity-related health problems have decreased.

5. **What is true about China's standards for determining obesity?**

   (**A**) They are often changed by the government.

   (**B**) They are stricter than those used by the WHO.

   (**C**) They have been criticized by the WHO.

Reading Section

In an unusual collision, an airplane hit and killed a brown bear while landing at the Yakutat Airport in Alaska on November 14, 2020. Alaska Airlines Flight 66 was arriving from Cordova into Yakutat when the flight crew saw two bears crossing the runway, according to a statement by Alaska Airlines.

"The nose gear missed the bears, but the captain felt an impact on the left side after the bears passed under the plane," the airline's statement said. Pilots then spotted a bear lying several feet off the center of the runway while taxiing the Boeing 737-700 aircraft for parking.

The left engine cowl of the plane was damaged in the collision and maintenance technicians are currently working to repair the aircraft. Six passengers were on the flight at the time, but no injuries were reported.

After being informed of the incident, airport maintenance and operations crews removed the bear's carcass and brought it to a storage warehouse, according to Sam Dapcevich, a public information officer for the Alaska Department of Transportation and Public Facilities. The Alaska Department of Fish and Game was contacted to arrange for proper disposal of the bear.

"It's a rare occurrence for something like this to happen," Dapcevich told CNN. "I've been in Alaska my whole life and we've had aircraft strike birds and other animals —but this is the first instance of a bear that I've ever heard of."

The airport is partially fenced. The airport's operations crews are trained by the US Department of Agriculture to use pyrotechnics and vehicles to deter animals from coming near the runway and interfering with aircraft operations, Dapcevich said.

Crews had previously seen two bears in the area and believed them to be a female bear and a cub. On the day of the incident, crews had not seen any wildlife during snow removal operations, according to Dapcevich.

Local photographer and biologist Robert Johnson said he was surprised by the incident. He went out to capture the scene after speaking with his neighbors who were passengers on the flight. "It was an unusual occurrence, actually a first in Alaska at least," Johnson told CNN. "I've worked with bears most of my adult life up here."

In 1987, another unlikely collision occurred between wildlife and an Alaska Airlines airplane—but that aircraft hit a fish. An Alaska Airlines flight was departing from Juneau when a large fish hit the Boeing 737-200 aircraft just behind the cockpit window. An eagle that had crossed paths with the flight had been gripping the fish in its talons.

"In the process, the eagle either voluntarily released its meal or the rapid turn ripped it out of its claws," Anchorage-based Alaska Airlines pilot Captain Mac af Uhr wrote in a 2005 story about the incident, according to an Alaska Airlines blog post.

Dapcevich said it was too soon to say what steps would be taken to prevent a rare incident like the bear collision from happening in the future.

Reading Section

1. **What is the main topic of this news report?**

   (**A**) One airline's wildlife-conservation efforts

   (**B**) The closure of an airport

   (**C**) An accident at an airport

2. **Which of the following statements about the Flight 66 airplane is true?**

   (**A**) It was not carrying any passengers.

   (**B**) It suffered some damage.

   (**C**) Its design was criticized for being dangerous to animals.

3. **What does Sam Dapcevich say about what happened?**

   (**A**) The fence around the airport helped.

   (**B**) The bear is lucky to have survived.

   (**C**) Such an event is uncommon.

4. **What are the airport's operations crews trained to do?**

   (**A**) Contact the US Department of Agriculture if they see any bears

   (**B**) Keep wildlife from getting in the way of airplanes

   (**C**) Remove snow from the area without harming wildlife

5. **What happened when an eagle flew near an Alaska Airlines plane in 1987?**

   (**A**) The bird dropped its meal on the plane.

   (**B**) The bird suffered serious injuries.

   (**C**) The plane had to land in the water.

General-Knowledge Section

試験時間15分

Directions

This section contains 10 questions testing your understanding of English for communicating about world affairs. For each question, choose the best answer from the answer options. You will have a total of 15 minutes to answer all of the questions.

1. **Which of the following statements about US President Biden is NOT true?**

   (**A**) He previously served as governor of Delaware.

   (**B**) He was elected president on his third attempt.

   (**C**) He is the oldest US president in history.

   (**D**) He served two terms as vice president.

2. **Which of the following statements about US Vice President Harris is NOT true?**

   (**A**) She is the first female US vice president.

   (**B**) Her father is from Jamaica and her mother was from India.

   (**C**) She is qualified as a lawyer in the state of California.

   (**D**) Before becoming vice president, she was a US House of Representatives member representing California.

3. **Which of the following statements about the United Nations Security Council (UNSC) is NOT true?**

   (**A**) The UNSC consists of a total of 15 permanent and nonpermanent members.

   (**B**) The term for UNSC nonpermanent members is four years, and nonpermanent members can serve on the Council for consecutive terms.

   (**C**) All United Nations members must comply with UNSC resolutions.

   (**D**) If even one UNSC permanent member opposes a UNSC draft resolution, the resolution does not pass.

General-Knowledge Section

4. **Which of the following statements about the European Union (EU) is NOT true?**

   (**A**) The United Kingdom is the first state to have left the EU.

   (**B**) Norway is not a member of the EU.

   (**C**) All EU member states use the euro as their currency.

   (**D**) Germany has the largest GDP of all EU member states.

5. **Which of the following statements about Hong Kong is NOT true?**

   (**A**) It was a British colony for more than 150 years.

   (**B**) In 2019, Hong Kong's average life expectancies for males and females were longer than Japan's, according to Japan's Ministry of Health, Labour and Welfare.

   (**C**) The 2014 demonstrations against the Hong Kong government were called the Yellow Vests Movement.

   (**D**) In June, 2020, the Chinese government passed a new security law to crack down on antigovernment activities in Hong Kong.

6. **Which of the following statements about Jerusalem is NOT true?**

   (**A**) It is a sacred place in Judaism, Christianity and Islam.

   (**B**) It has the second-largest population in Israel, after Tel Aviv.

   (**C**) Israel has designated Jerusalem as its capital, but the United Nations does not recognize it as the capital.

   (**D**) In 2017, President Trump officially recognized Jerusalem as the capital of Israel.

7. **Which of the following statements about abbreviations used in the news is NOT true?**

   (**A**) The WHO is a specialized agency of the United Nations that was established to achieve health for people all over the world.

   (**B**) The WTO is an international organization that sets various international rules regarding communications.

   (**C**) ASEAN is a regional organization comprised of Southeast Asian countries for the purpose of cooperation in economic, political and other affairs.

   (**D**) An ICBM is a ballistic missile with a very long effective range, able to fly from one continent to another.

8. **Which of the following statements about COVID-19 vaccines is NOT true?**

   (**A**) The first COVID-19 vaccine to be approved in the United States was of the new, mRNA type.

   (**B**) No mRNA vaccines had been approved for use in humans until the COVID-19 vaccines were.

   (**C**) The mRNA vaccines use inactivated pathogens.

   (**D**) It is necessary to keep mRNA vaccines at extremely low temperatures to transport and store them.

General-Knowledge Section

9. **Which of the following statements about the 5G mobile-communications system is NOT true?**

    (**A**) The "G" in "5G" stands for gigahertz.

    (**B**) Mobile-communication systems have developed from 1G to 2G, 3G, 4G and 5G.

    (**C**) The introduction of 5G will mean higher transmission speeds than with 4G.

    (**D**) The introduction of 5G will enable more devices to be connected at the same time than with 4G.

10. **Which of the following is NOT mentioned in a World Bank report in 2020 on global poverty?**

    (**A**) North Africa is the poorest region in the world.

    (**B**) Half of the world's poorest people are children younger than age 15.

    (**C**) Some 3.3 billion people live on less than $5.50 a day.

    (**D**) It is estimated that climate change may drive 100 million people into poverty by 2030.

Practice Test 2

※Practice Test 2は2021年11月実施の第2回CNN GLENTSの問題を基に若干の変更を加えています。

Listening Section

Part 1

Directions CNN音声版 (46↓) ナレーター音声版 (66↓)

Here are the directions for **Part 1**. You will hear two short news reports. Enter the missing words in the spaces below the text. Enter only one word in each space. You will hear each report two times. For each report, after listening two times, you will have 30 seconds to enter the missing words.

CNN音声版 (47↓) ナレーター音声版 (67↓)

No.1

Living on the edge in central Mexico—the edge being a ①(   ) sinkhole which suddenly appeared in a family's backyard on Saturday. At first, it was 5 meters wide, but six days later, it's now at least 60 meters across and 20 meters deep. The family has been ②(   ). Officials say farming and the extraction of groundwater may be to blame.

Enter the word for ①

[   ]

Enter the word for ②

[   ]

CNN音声版 (48↓) ナレーター音声版 (68↓)

No.2

Dire warnings about the hunger ①(   ) in Ethiopia, and signs it's going to get worse: The United Nations and other aid groups have a new report saying more than 350,000 people in the country's Tigray Region are experiencing catastrophic levels of hunger, the most ②(   ) rating. The UN aid chief calls it a famine, and some compare the situation to Somalia's famine a decade ago.

Enter the word for ①

[   ]

Enter the word for ②

[   ]

Part 2

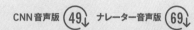

Directions 　　　　　　　CNN音声版 (49) ナレーター音声版 (69)

Here are the directions for **Part 2**. You will hear three short news reports. Each report will be followed by two questions. You will hear each report and question only once. For each question, you will have 15 seconds to choose the best answer.

問題文　設問　　　　　　　問題文　設問
—— CNN音声版 (50) (51) ナレーター音声版 (70) (71)

No.1

1. **What is the main point of this news report?**

   (**A**) An elephant injured a woman in a national park.

   (**B**) An elephant attempted to get food from a person's kitchen.

   (**C**) An elephant damaged a home as it fought with another animal.

2. **What does the news report say about Asia?**

   (**A**) Wild animals are losing their natural habitats.

   (**B**) Funding for national parks has been decreasing.

   (**C**) Illegal hunting of elephants is becoming a bigger problem.

問題文　設問　　　　　　　問題文　設問
—— CNN音声版 (52) (53) ナレーター音声版 (72) (73)

No.2

1. **What is this news report mainly about?**

   (**A**) A recent change in Spain's immigration policies

   (**B**) The increasing danger faced by migrants who leave Morocco by sea

   (**C**) Large numbers of migrants trying to enter a part of Spain from Morocco

2. **What is true about the boy mentioned in the news report?**

   (**A**) He was caught by authorities.

   (**B**) He is a legal resident of Spain.

   (**C**) He helped other people survive in the water.

Listening Section

No.3

1. What is this news report mainly about?

(**A**) The reason that the northern lights appear

(**B**) The decreasing strength of the northern lights

(**C**) The effect that the northern lights have on space weather

2. According to the news report, what have scientists been able to do in a lab?

(**A**) Use plasma to block electromagnetic waves

(**B**) Disprove a long-held theory about space weather

(**C**) Reproduce the northern lights

Part 3

Directions   CNN音声版 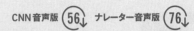 (56) ナレーター音声版 (76)

Here are the directions for **Part 3**. You will hear all of or excerpts from two news reports. Each report will be followed by four questions. You will hear each report and question only once. For each question, you will have 15 seconds to choose the best answer.

問題文 設問   問題文 設問
CNN音声版 (57) (58) ナレーター音声版 (77) (78)

No.1

1. **What is the main point of this news report?**

   (**A**) Businesses in Taiwan are being criticized for certain practices.

   (**B**) A water shortage in Taiwan is affecting an important industry.

   (**C**) Flooding in Taiwan is damaging facilities that produce electronics.

2. **According to the news report, what is one thing that climate-change models show?**

   (**A**) Rain will occur more frequently throughout Taiwan.

   (**B**) Rising sea levels will cause economic problems for Taiwan.

   (**C**) Taiwan will experience stronger storms.

3. **What is one solution that semiconductor manufacturers are exploring?**

   (**A**) Changing the location of their factories

   (**B**) Making seawater usable for chip production

   (**C**) Producing new types of chips that require less energy

4. **What does the news report suggest about Taiwan's semiconductor industry?**

   (**A**) Green energy is one of its priorities.

   (**B**) It no longer requires large amounts of water.

   (**C**) The Taiwanese people do not approve of its activities.

Listening Section

No.2

1. What is this news report mainly about?

(**A**) A new tax agreement that has received international support

(**B**) A trade agreement proposed by a number of multinational companies

(**C**) The global reaction to a proposed tax agreement between China and India

2. According to the news report, what is true of big international companies?

(**A**) They have been dishonest about their profits.

(**B**) They have been moving their headquarters abroad.

(**C**) They have refused to sell products in certain countries.

3. What is one problem that the deal described in the news report addresses?

(**A**) The recent decrease in the profits of certain US companies

(**B**) The failure of the world's biggest companies to release their tax records

(**C**) The fact that countries have been reducing rates of tax on corporations

4. What does the news report say about the Biden administration?

(**A**) A shift in its policy was a crucial step toward realizing the deal.

(**B**) Some of its recent decisions have been challenged by big tech companies.

(**C**) It has lowered its corporate-tax rate as part of a deal with certain companies.

Part 4

 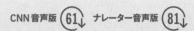
問題文　設問　　　　　問題文　設問
 CNN音声版 62↓ 63↓　ナレーター音声版 82↓ 83↓

No.1

1. What is the main issue that is discussed in this interview?

(**A**) China could soon get ahead of the United States in the field of AI.

(**B**) The US government believes China has used AI to damage US industries.

(**C**) US companies that develop AI are increasingly relying on Chinese technology.

2. What does the interviewer say about the future of AI?

(**A**) The importance of AI will vary greatly depending on the industry.

(**B**) Use in military applications will remain the primary purpose of AI.

(**C**) The further development of AI will result in major changes in society.

3. What is one thing Eric Schmidt suggests about China?

(**A**) US tech companies might move there if US spending on AI is not increased.

(**B**) Some of its officials do not believe AI is worth investing more money in.

(**C**) Its central-planning structure has resulted in billions of dollars being wasted.

4. What does Schmidt say the United States needs to do?

(**A**) Encourage foreign start-ups to move to the United States

(**B**) Significantly increase the amount of money it spends on AI development

(**C**) Open new universities where US and Chinese researchers can work together

Listening Section

No.2

1. What is the main topic of this interview?

(**A**) Factors behind the increase in people's life spans

(**B**) Mistaken ideas about modern diets and lifestyles

(**C**) The effect of pandemics on scientists' view of human health

2. What is one thing Steven Johnson says about the middle of the 19th century?

(**A**) Water often had to be added to milk.

(**B**) The drinking water in cities was a danger to people's health.

(**C**) A significant number of people had no access to water.

3. What does Johnson say about New York City in 1850?

(**A**) More children than adults died.

(**B**) Lack of access to doctors contributed to poor human health.

(**C**) The work of transporting milk was done mostly by children.

4. What is one thing that is shown by the example of pasteurization?

(**A**) Scientists do not always think their studies can be put to practical use.

(**B**) Activists who support science sometimes do more harm than good.

(**C**) Scientific advances are not always quickly accepted in society.

> ► リスニング・トレーナーやiTunes、Windows Media Playerなどの音声再生ソフトで
> 「Play All」で再生している場合は、設問の音声が終了後、止めてください。
> ► Part 5の動画問題は、スマートフォンの場合はリスニング・トレーナー、またはQRコード
> から、パソコンの場合はURLから動画をご視聴ください。

Part 5

No.1

1. What was the main purpose of the event described in this news report?

(**A**) To raise money for pandemic relief efforts

(**B**) To recognize certain groups of workers for their contribution

(**C**) To celebrate the joining of two organizations in New York City

2. What is one thing that the news report suggests about New York City?

(**A**) Its situation with regard to COVID has improved greatly.

(**B**) It was the first US city to track its COVID infection routes..

(**C**) Its COVID-infection rate is the lowest among all major US cities.

No.2

https://eqm.page.link/hzPF

1. What is the main point of this news report?

(**A**) The Ecuadoran government will pass new laws to protect tortoises.

(**B**) Conservation practices in the Galapagos Islands have harmed tortoises.

(**C**) Someone in the Galapagos Islands cruelly tried to transport tortoises.

2. What does the news report say about the tortoises?

(**A**) Plastic was found inside their stomachs.

(**B**) Some of them have not yet been located.

(**C**) They were not in good physical condition.

Reading Section

Part 1

Directions

Part 1 contains four short excerpts from news reports. Each excerpt has one blank space and is followed by three answer options. Choose the best word from the answer options to fill each blank space.

No.1

Louisiana public schools are allowed to let parents choose whether they want to (　　　) children after exposure to Covid-19.

(**A**) forbid   (**B**) quarantine   (**C**) disperse

No.2

Tokyo is considered one of the world's top food cities, drawing travelers from around the world who spend their days sampling (　　　) Japanese dishes, from sushi to ramen.

(**A**) auspicious   (**B**) reverent   (**C**) renowned

No.3

A growing power-supply (　　　) in China is triggering blackouts for households and forcing factories to cut production.

(**A**) crush   (**B**) cramp   (**C**) crunch

No.4

The Notre Dame cathedral is (　　　) reopen to the public in 2024.

(**A**) on track to   (**B**) committed to   (**C**) sitting tight to

Part 2

Directions

Part 2 contains excerpts from three short news reports, each followed by two questions. For each question, choose the best answer from the answer options.

No.1

As the climate crisis escalates, the world is banking on carbon-free energy to achieve a future with zero greenhouse gas emissions, or a net-zero future, where we remove just as much greenhouse gas from the atmosphere as we emit.

One potential form of clean energy is green hydrogen—which can be derived from sources like water, rather than fossil fuels, and is produced with renewable energy. It can be used to power heavy industry and fuel large vehicles, like planes and ships.

Facilities to produce this cleaner form of the gas have popped up across the globe—in the United States, Western Europe, China, Australia, Chile and South Africa, among other countries. The burgeoning global green hydrogen market is projected to be worth $11 trillion by 2050, by Goldman Sachs' estimates.

But critics of green hydrogen say using solar or wind energy to produce another fuel right now is a waste of precious renewables, as the world struggles to transition away from fossil fuels.

Reading Section

1. **What is the main topic of this news report?**

    (**A**) Key facts about one type of clean energy

    (**B**) The high cost of producing clean energy

    (**C**) A major shift to solar and wind energy

2. **What do critics of green hydrogen believe?**

    (**A**) It will not be widely used as a fuel.

    (**B**) Making it with renewable energy is currently not a good idea.

    (**C**) The facilities that produce it use a lot of fossil fuels.

No.2

Decades-long research into Leonardo da Vinci's purported remains has revealed how many people currently alive can claim to be descendants of the family of the Renaissance genius and *Mona Lisa* painter. It's 14.

The conclusion, published in the journal *Human Evolution*, comes from a new genealogical tree going through 21 generations and four branches. It's part of the Leonardo da Vinci DNA Project, which aims to confirm remains thought to be his and to "better understand his extraordinary talents and visual acuity through genetic associations."

The researchers wrote these results are "eagerly awaited from an historical viewpoint" as they will help researchers "scientifically explore the roots of his genius, to find information on his physical prowess and on his possibly precocious ageing, on his being left-handed and his health and possible hereditary sicknesses, and to explain certain peculiar sensory perceptions, like his extraordinary visual quality and synesthesia."

Researchers gathered data from historical documents in public and private archives and direct accounts by da Vinci descendants. The study did not provide much information on the living descendants, to protect their privacy.

Reading Section

1. **What is the main topic of this news report?**

   (**A**) A disagreement among Leonardo da Vinci's descendants

   (**B**) Effort to gain a better understanding of Leonardo da Vinci

   (**C**) Mistakes in historical documents about Leonardo da Vinci

2. **What does the news report say about the research?**

   (**A**) The researchers discovered new works by Leonardo da Vinci.

   (**B**) The researchers were surprised by the findings of their study.

   (**C**) Some of the data was provided by Leonardo da Vinci's relatives.

No.3

Hong Kong has reclaimed its status as the host of a marquee Asian tech conference it lost last year, as organizers cite the city's success in battling the coronavirus pandemic.

Rise, an annual tech conference whose recent speakers have included executives from Uber, Alibaba and Stripe, said that it would return to the city next year, with plans to stay for the next five years.

Organizers had announced in late 2020 that they would move the event to the Malaysian city of Kuala Lumpur, saying they wanted to seek opportunities in Southeast Asia's fast-growing tech scene.

At the time, the move raised questions about Hong Kong's ability to hold on to its image as Asia's premier global business hub as it was still grappling with the aftermath of mass protests in 2019.

Now, "Hong Kong has once again won as the host city of Rise for the coming five years," the event's organizers said in a joint statement with the Hong Kong Tourism Board.

The event in 2022 will be staged in-person. Hong Kong Secretary for Commerce and Economic Development Edward Yau touted this as "a testimony of Hong Kong's success in containing the pandemic and keeping the infection rate among the lowest in the world, thereby giving international event organizers confidence that they can stage their events here safely."

Reading Section

1. **What is the main point of this news report?**

    (**A**) Hong Kong will once again host a major event that it hosted in the past.

    (**B**) Hong Kong companies will be celebrated at a global business conference.

    (**C**) Hong Kong tech leaders will give aid to countries during the pandemic.

2. **What point does Edward Yau highlight with regard to Hong Kong?**

    (**A**) Its history as a center of global business

    (**B**) Its ability to keep the pandemic under control

    (**C**) The fact that its political situation has changed since the 2019 protests

Part 3

Directions

Part 3 contains all of or excerpts from two news reports, each followed by five questions. For each question, choose the best answer from the answer options.

No.1

The tiny goldfish you can pick up at pet stores for a few cents might not look like an environmental threat, but they can grow into a huge problem if set free in lakes or ponds—mainly because they can grow to be surprisingly huge.

Burnsville, Minnesota, which is south of Minneapolis, drew viral attention to the global issue when it posted pictures on social media of some of the whoppers that were caught during an ongoing survey of fish in Keller Lake. The city urged residents not to release their unwanted pet fish. They caught 10 goldfish last week and another 18 this week—each was more than a foot long, with the largest being 15 inches long and weighing about four pounds.

Burnsville natural resources specialist Caleb Ashling told CNN that the city partnered with neighboring Apple Valley and the company Carp Solutions to find out how many goldfish are in the lake. "We had some reports from residents of some increasingly large groups of goldfish out on the lake," Ashling said.

Goldfish root around on the bottom of lakes and ponds looking for food, which stirs up sediment and can uproot plants. This can impact water quality and the diversity of native species when the goldfish become established, said Carp Solutions owner Przemek Bajer, who is a research assistant professor at the University of Minnesota.

"Often, they don't eat aquatic plants, but the plants simply cannot establish roots in those lakes; they're just uprooted physically," Bajer said. "So if you have a lot of goldfish and carp in the lake, usually the first thing that happens is all the aquatic plants disappear." The fish also kick up nutrients that had settled on the bottom, and their waste, which can promote algae blooms that "turn clear lakes into green lakes."

Goldfish are native to China and eastern Asia and have traveled the world, thanks to their popularity as pets and ornamental fish. The US Geological Survey says that they've been established or reported in every US state, except Alaska, which eradicated a population of illegally introduced goldfish in 2019 from a pond in Anchorage. "All goldfish are invasive, basically worldwide," Bajer said. "In the whole of North America, Australia, parts of Europe, they are really, really widespread." They are closely related to the common carp, which are another invasive, non-native species, Bajer said.

"It's most likely that somebody just released them, but they can reproduce in the wild, too," Bajer said. "We don't know if these particular ones were released by somebody or they were spawned out in the lake from parents that maybe were introduced by somebody."

Ashling said they've worked hard to improve the water quality at Keller Lake and the communities want to protect their investment. He said the cities will decide what to do next once Carp Solutions finishes its assessment of how many goldfish are in the lake. "We know it's not good to have goldfish in the lake, but in some situations, goldfish can be in a lake and not be causing a lot of severe problems, but in the right lake in the right conditions they can cause a lot of problems," Ashling said. "So we're still in the process of trying to figure out what our situation is at Keller Lake."

1. **What is the main point of this news report?**

   (**A**) Fishing is having a negative effect on lake ecosystems.

   (**B**) A population of invasive fish has been found in a lake.

   (**C**) Poor water quality is harming a lake's goldfish population.

2. **What is true with regard to the behavior of goldfish in lakes and ponds?**

   (**A**) They make it difficult for plants to grow.

   (**B**) They eat plants that native species need to survive.

   (**C**) They destroy important fish that keep lakes and ponds clean.

3. **What does the news report say about the popularity of goldfish?**

   (**A**) It has led to effects on common carp populations.

   (**B**) It is the reason why goldfish are found in many places around the world.

   (**C**) Goldfish are more popular in the United States than in other countries.

4. **What is one thing Przemek Bajer says about the goldfish in Keller Lake?**

   (**A**) Their size will likely continue to increase.

   (**B**) They probably cannot reproduce successfully in the lake.

   (**C**) Whether they were put into the lake or born in it is unknown.

5. **What does Caleb Ashling suggest about the goldfish?**

   (**A**) They may not have a significant negative effect on Keller Lake.

   (**B**) There are a lot more of them than Carp Solutions says there are.

   (**C**) They are hard to study, because conditions in Keller Lake change frequently.

Reading Section

No.2

Smartphone season is underway, and the headlines will almost certainly be the same as always: thinner, sleeker, faster models are coming to consumer pockets. But if a new push from the US government succeeds, future smartphones may also have to be designed for something extra—the ability to be repaired however a device owner chooses.

President Joe Biden last month urged the Federal Trade Commission to set rules preventing manufacturers from imposing restrictions on independent device repair shops and DIY repairs, a principle known as "right to repair." A week later, the FTC vowed to "root out" illegal repair restrictions on various products, including phones.

Companies such as Apple have been criticized for using tactics that make it harder for independent repair businesses to access devices, such as using non-removable memory or batteries, or sealing devices with special glue. (The companies argue that this is done to ensure the products are properly repaired.) New regulation would likely prohibit this practice and require smartphone manufacturers to make parts, tools, repair manuals, and diagnostics for out-of-warranty repairs more readily available to third-party businesses.

"In many cases, the price to fix a smartphone or computer is close to, if not more than, replacing it altogether—a strategy that encourages people to buy new devices rather than fixing them. This needs to change," Pedro Pacheco, a senior director at market research firm Gartner, told CNN Business. "Manufacturers will need to make design choices to keep the cost to repair devices down."

While smartphone makers aren't the only ones facing criticism for obstructing repairs, the order specifically calls them out for practices that make repairs "more costly and time-consuming." Regulatory pressure could change not only how consumers choose to fix their devices but how manufacturers build them in subtle ways.

"Current right-to-repair laws proposed in the US don't impact device design in any way, but a focus on repair opportunities could incentivize the manufacturers to swap screws for more standard ones or make the battery easier to remove," said Kyle Wiens, CEO and founder of iFixit, an online repair website for consumer electronics.

David McQueen, research director at market research firm ABI Research, agrees, noting even the smallest of changes could impact the construction of smartphones on some level. For example, adding new screws or more holes may impact a device's IP ratings—the degree of protection a device's components provide against dust and water. "Smartphone vendors have worked hard to get this to high levels, but if devices do have more screw holes and have to be easier to take apart, then would these ratings be compromised or have to be lowered?" said McQueen.

McQueen also pointed to a possible dilemma that some smartphone manufacturers might face in a right-to-repair world: "Would some companies still use high-end components across all their models if they know it will be easy to have them repaired or replaced?" On the one hand, companies may find more of their customers could replace these parts with cheaper components. On the other hand, he argues, "It could damage a vendor's brand value if they're selling products with noticeably inferior components to combat this possibility."

Reading Section

1. **What is the main topic of this news report?**

   (**A**) A new feature of smartphones that would limit their life span

   (**B**) Rules that would allow device users more freedom in repairing their devices

   (**C**) An increase in illegal practices in the repair of devices like smartphones

2. **What is one thing that companies like Apple have faced criticism for?**

   (**A**) Making parts of their devices difficult to access

   (**B**) Failing to use caution when repairing their devices

   (**C**) Providing unclear information about the warranties they offer

3. **What does Pedro Pacheco say about device manufacturers?**

   (**A**) The deals they make with other businesses are not good for consumers.

   (**B**) The design choices they make lead to frequent problems with their devices.

   (**C**) They make repairs costly to discourage users from having devices repaired.

4. **According to David McQueen, what could result from changes in smartphone design?**

   (**A**) The devices could become more difficult to take apart.

   (**B**) People might think the devices pose a danger to their safety.

   (**C**) The devices could be more easily damaged by dust and water.

5. **What difficult choice does McQueen suggest smartphone manufacturers might have to make?**

   (**A**) Whether to stop selling cheaper models or try to improve their quality

   (**B**) Whether to keep using high-end parts or switch to using cheaper parts

   (**C**) Whether to change their marketing strategy or focus more on product quality

General-Knowledge Section

Directions

This section contains 10 questions testing your understanding of English for communicating about world affairs. For each question, choose the best answer from the answer options. You will have a total of 15 minutes to answer all of the questions.

1. **Which of the following statements about NATO (the North Atlantic Treaty Organization) is NOT true?**

   (**A**) It was formed in 1949, after World War II.

   (**B**) As of September 2023, the NATO alliance consists of 31 European and North American countries.

   (**C**) Turkey is a member of NATO.

   (**D**) The NATO headquarters is located in Geneva, Switzerland.

2. **Which of the following statements about China's political system is NOT true?**

   (**A**) The only officially recognized political party in China is the Communist Party of China.

   (**B**) The Chinese Communist Party celebrated its 100th anniversary in 2021.

   (**C**) The National People's Congress is a legislative body equivalent to Japan's Diet, and it convenes every March.

   (**D**) There is currently no term limit for the office of president of the People's Republic of China.

3. **Which of the following statements about Russia is NOT true?**

   (**A**) According to IMF statistics, Russia's nominal GDP in 2022 was the fifth largest in the world, after Germany.

   (**B**) As of September 2023, the president of Russia was Vladimir Putin.

   (**C**) Russia annexed the Crimean Peninsula in Ukraine in 2014.

   (**D**) As of September 2023, Russia was under economic sanctions from countries such as the United States and EU members.

General-Knowledge Section

4. Which of the following statements about Myanmar is NOT true?

(**A**) According to the Myanmar Statistical Yearbook 2019, Buddhists make up nearly 90 percent of Myanmar's population.

(**B**) As of September 2023, most of the Rohingya refugees who had fled to Bangladesh have returned to Myanmar.

(**C**) In February 2021, the national armed forces of Myanmar staged a coup d'état and seized control of the government.

(**D**) As of September 2023, an armed resistance movement against the military forces that staged the coup.

5. Which of the following statements about abbreviations used in the news is NOT true?

(**A**) The IMF is a specialized agency of the United Nations whose purpose is to ensure the stability of the international financial system.

(**B**) The FDA is a government agency that sets rules for the safety of food, drugs and medical devices in the United States.

(**C**) OPEC is an organization that regulates oil production and oil prices on behalf of oil-importing countries.

(**D**) UNESCO is a specialized agency of the United Nations that aims to promote international cooperation in education, science and culture.

6. According to the US Census Bureau's 2020 statistics, which of the following statements about population size and household income by race in the US is NOT true?

(**A**) The white population, not including Hispanics, makes up less than 60 percent of the overall US population.

(**B**) The black population in the US is larger than the Hispanic population.

(**C**) The estimated average household income of black people in the US is about 60 percent that of whites, not including Hispanics.

(**D**) The estimated average household income of Asians in the US is higher than that of whites, not including Hispanics.

7. **Which of the following statements about guns and gun control in the United States is NOT true?**

   (**A**) The Second Amendment to the US Constitution stipulates the "right of the people to keep and bear arms."

   (**B**) According to the CDC, there were nearly 40,000 firearm-related deaths in the United States in 2019.

   (**C**) The NRA is a pressure group that campaigns for gun abolition.

   (**D**) Regulations regarding firearm ownership are not the same in every state in the US.

8. **Which of the following statements about booster vaccinations for COVID-19 is NOT true?**

   (**A**) A COVID-19 booster vaccination is an additional vaccine dose given after the protection provided by the original shot(s) has begun to decrease.

   (**B**) As of October 2021, the FDA had authorized booster doses of three COVID-19 vaccines already approved in the US.

   (**C**) As of October 2021, some European countries had started providing booster vaccinations for COVID-19.

   (**D**) According to the FDA, the COVID-19 vaccine used for a booster vaccination must be the same type as was used for the recipient's original vaccination.

9. **Which of the following statements about cyberattacks is NOT true?**

   (**A**) A ransomware attack is one that makes a computer inoperable until a fee is paid.

   (**B**) IoT devices connected to the Internet may become targets of cyberattacks.

   (**C**) Malware is any type of malicious software designed to interfere with, damage or destroy a programmable device, service, system or network.

   (**D**) To prevent infection by malware, it is better not to update the OS.

General-Knowledge Section

10. **Which of the following statements about space development is NOT true?**

    (**A**) According to China's state media, in 2019, a Chinese spacecraft became the first ever to land on the far side of the moon.

    (**B**) The ISS is a space station operated exclusively by the United States and Russia.

    (**C**) NASA has outsourced the development of manned spacecraft to the private sector since the Space Shuttle program ended in 2011.

    (**D**) Three billionaires—Jeff Bezos, Elon Musk and Richard Branson—are competing in the space business.

Practice Test 1
解答・解説

Practice Test 1 | 解答一覧

解答欄にご自身の解答を書き写しておくと、スコアを出しやすくなります。

Listening Section リスニングセクション

Part	No.	Question	解答欄	正解	測定する力
1	1	1		detained	書き取り
		2		jail	書き取り
	2	1		tiny	書き取り
		2		residents	書き取り
2	1	1		A	大意把握
		2		A	詳細理解
	2	1		B	大意把握
		2		C	詳細理解
	3	1		C	大意把握
		2		A	詳細理解
3	1	1		A	大意把握
		2		C	詳細理解
		3		B	詳細理解
		4		B	詳細理解
	2	1		C	大意把握
		2		B	詳細理解
		3		C	詳細理解
		4		A	詳細理解
4	1	1		C	大意把握
		2		A	詳細理解
		3		B	詳細理解
		4		A	詳細理解
	2	1		B	大意把握
		2		A	詳細理解
		3		A	詳細理解
		4		C	詳細理解
5	1	1		C	動画理解
		2		A	動画理解
	2	1		B	動画理解
		2		C	動画理解

Reading Section リーディングセクション

Part	No.	Question	解答欄	正解	測定する力
1	1	——		**C**	語彙
	2	——		**B**	語彙
	3	——		**B**	語彙
	4	——		**A**	語彙
2	1	1		**A**	大意把握
		2		**C**	詳細理解
	2	1		**C**	大意把握
		2		**B**	詳細理解
	3	1		**B**	大意把握
		2		**A**	詳細理解
3	1	1		**C**	大意把握
		2		**A**	詳細理解
		3		**C**	詳細理解
		4		**B**	詳細理解
		5		**B**	詳細理解
	2	1		**C**	大意把握
		2		**B**	詳細理解
		3		**C**	詳細理解
		4		**B**	詳細理解
		5		**A**	詳細理解

General-Knowledge Section 国際教養セクション

Question	解答欄	正解	Question	解答欄	正解
1		**A**	6		**B**
2		**D**	7		**B**
3		**B**	8		**C**
4		**C**	9		**A**
5		**C**	10		**A**

試験結果

Total Score	/120
L&R Score	/100

セクション	スコア
	あなたの得点／満点
Listening Section	/60
Reading Section	/40
General-Knowledge Section	/20

※ナレーター音声版の場合、実際のテストではCNN音声版に得点調整したスコアも算出されます。

pp.84-85の表から、リスニングセクションとリーディングセクションの「測定する力」の正解数を数え、
下の欄に記入しましょう。あなたの強みと弱点がわかります。

リスニング	書き取り /4	大意把握 /7	詳細理解 /15	動画理解 /4

リーディング	語彙 /4	大意把握 /5	詳細理解 /11

Practice Test 1 | 解答・解説

Listening Section リスニングセクション

Part 1 ディクテーション問題

<table>
<tr><td>No.1</td><td>CNN音声版 07</td><td>ナレーター音声版 27</td></tr>
<tr><td></td><td colspan="2">オーストラリア英語</td></tr>
</table>

問題文・解答

European human-rights ambassadors say they are deeply concerned about a group of female activists ①detained in Saudi Arabia, and they are calling on the kingdom to release them. One of the women, who has already spent more than two years in ②jail, will now be tried by a terrorism court. Her apparent crime? Demanding the right to drive.

訳

欧州の人権大使たちは、サウジアラビアで拘束されている女性活動家の一団について深く憂慮していると述べ、同王国に彼女たちを釈放するよう要請しています。その女性たちの1人はすでに2年以上拘置所におり、今度テロ法廷で裁判にかけられることになっています。彼女が犯したとみられる罪とは? 車を運転する権利を求めたことです。

語句

human-rights: 人権の／ambassador: 大使／be concerned about: 〜について懸念している、憂慮している／deeply: 深く、非常に／activist: 活動家／detain: 〜を拘束する／call on...to do: …に〜するよう求める、要請する／kingdom: 王国／release: 〜を解放する、釈放する／jail: 刑務所、拘置所／try: 〜を裁判にかける／terrorism court: テロ法廷 ▶テロ容疑者を裁く特別法廷のこと。／apparent: (実際には違うかもしれないが)〜とみられる／crime: 犯罪／demand: 〜を求める、要求する

※リスニングセクションの各問題文の「アメリカ英語」などの記載は、CNN音声版の話者についてです。ナレーター音声版の話者の英語は、CNN音声版と異なる場合があります。
※ナレーター音声版の問題文は、スクリプトと多少異なる箇所があります。ご了承ください。

<table>
<tr><td>No.2</td><td>CNN音声版 08</td><td>ナレーター音声版 28</td></tr>
<tr><td></td><td colspan="2">アメリカ英語</td></tr>
</table>

問題文・解答

Scientists thought the elephant shrew had been extinct for 50 years. Thankfully, they were wrong. Why thankfully? 'Cause it's cute. It's related to an elephant but ①tiny like a mouse. The last time scientists saw one was in the 1970s, but in the African nation of Djibouti, where the elephant shrew was recently rediscovered, local ②residents had said they'd seen them. These little mammals can run at over 18 miles per hour—faster than some elephants.

訳

科学者たちは、ハネジネズミは50年前に絶滅したものだと思っていました。幸い、彼らは間違っていました。なぜ幸いかって? かわいいからです。ハネジネズミはゾウと関係がありますが、ネズミのようにとても小さな生き物です。科学者たちが最後にそれを目にしたのは1970年代のことでしたが、アフリカの国ジブチで、このほどハネジネズミが再び見つかりました。地元住民たちがそれを見たと言ったのです。この小さな哺乳類は時速18マイル(約29キロメートル)以上で走ることができます。これは一部のゾウを上回る速さです。

語句

elephant shrew: ハネジネズミ ▶ゾウやツチブタなどが含まれるアフリカ獣上目に分類される。／extinct: 絶滅した／thankfully: ありがたいことに、幸いなことに／be related to: 〜と関係している／tiny: とても小さな／Djibouti: ジブチ ▶アフリカ北東部に位置する共和制国家。／rediscover: 〜を再発見する／local resident: 地元住民／mammal: 哺乳類

Part 2 ショートニュース問題

No.1

CNN音声版
問題文 ⑩↓ 設問 ⑪↓

ナレーター音声版
問題文 ㉚↓ 設問 ㉛↓

オーストラリア英語

問題文

New research from the Brookings Institute has attempted to answer why so many Americans still refuse to wear masks. Now, according to the study, the number one reason Americans gave is that it is simply their right to not have to wear one. With that, researchers concluded that, quote, "American individualism could be causing significant health consequences across the country." Other people also say they don't use masks because they don't want to be mistaken for criminal. In fact, that's the answer most men of color who don't wear masks provided.

訳

ブルッキングス研究所による新たな調査は、なぜこれほど多くのアメリカ人がいまだにマスクの着用を拒否するのかについて答えを出そうとするものです。さて、その調査によれば、アメリカ人が挙げた理由で最も多かったのは、マスクを着用する義務を負わないことは単純に自分たちの権利だから、というものです。この回答を受けて、研究者らはこう結論付けました、いわく「アメリカ人の個人主義が、重大な健康被害を全国で引き起こしている可能性がある」と。また、マスクを着用しないのは犯罪者と間違えられたくないからだ、と言う人もいます。実は、これが、マスクを着用しない有色人種の男性の大半が理由として挙げたものでした。

語句

Brookings Institute: ブルッキングス研究所 ➤ワシントンDCにあるシンクタンク。Brookings Institutionの言い間違いと思われる。/ attempt to do: 〜しようと試みる / refuse to do: 〜することを拒む / right to not do: 〜しない権利 ➤ right not to doとも言う。/ conclude that: 〜であると結論付ける / quote: 引用始め / individualism: 個人主義 / significant: 重大な、深刻な / health consequences: 健康上の影響 / mistake A for B: AをBと間違える / criminal: 罪を犯している ➤

criminalを名詞として使って「mistaken for a criminal」とする方が一般的だが、ここでは形容詞として用いている。

1. 正解 **A**

What is the main topic of this news report?
(**A**) The attitudes of Americans toward wearing masks
(**B**) The different benefits of various types of masks
(**C**) The availability of masks in the United States

> **設問訳** このニュースの主なトピックは何か。
> (**A**) マスク着用に対するアメリカ人の考え方
> (**B**) マスクの種類別の利点
> (**C**) アメリカにおけるマスクの入手可能性

> **解説** ブルッキングス研究所が why so many Americans still refuse to wear masks（なぜこれほど多くのアメリカ人がいまだにマスクの着用を拒否するのか）について調査したことと、それに対してアメリカ人が挙げた理由が述べられているので、正解は（**A**）。（**B**）の「マスクの種類別の利点」や（**C**）の「マスクの入手可能性」には触れられていない。

2. 正解 **A**

What is reported as some men's reason for their decision about masks?
(**A**) They don't want to seem criminal.
(**B**) They are worried about their health.
(**C**) They want others to wear masks more often.

> **設問訳** 一部の男性のマスクについての判断理由として報じられていることは何か。
> (**A**) 罪を犯していると思われたくない。
> (**B**) 健康を気にしている。
> (**C**) 他人にもっと頻繁にマスクを着用してほしいと思っている。

> **解説** アメリカ人がマスクを着用しない理由は、it is simply their right to not have to wear one（マスクを着用する義務を負わないことは単純に自分たちの権利だから）のほか、Other people also say they don't use masks because they don't want to be mistaken for

criminal.（マスクを着用しないのは犯罪者と間違えられたくないからだ、と言う人もいます）と、that's the answer most men of color who don't wear masks provided.（これがマスクを着用しない有色人種の男性の大半が理由として挙げたものでした）で述べられている。よって、正解は（**A**）。

No.2

CNN音声版 問題文 ⑫ 設問 ⑬

ナレーター音声版 問題文 ㉜ 設問 ㉝

オーストラリア英語

問題文

Three sailors from Micronesia are in good condition after being rescued from a remote island in the western Pacific. Australian and US aircraft spotted their giant SOS message in the sand and sent in a helicopter with food and water. A patrol ship from Micronesia picked up the men a short time later. The sailors started their 23-nautical-mile journey on Thursday but veered off course and ran out of fuel.

訳

ミクロネシアの3人の船乗りは、西太平洋に浮かぶ孤島から救出され、今は良好な健康状態にあります。オーストラリアと米国の航空機（の乗員）が、船乗りたちが砂浜に書いた巨大なSOSメッセージを見つけ、食料と水を積んだヘリコプターを送り込みました。ミクロネシアの巡視船が程なくして彼らを救出しました。船乗りたちは木曜日に23カイリ（約43キロメートル）の航海に出ましたが、航路を外れ、燃料切れになったのでした。

語句

sailor: 船員、船乗り／rescue A from B: AをBから救出する／remote island: 離島、孤島／aircraft: 航空機 ►単複同形。／spot: ～を見つける／patrol ship: 巡視船、監視船／pick up: ～を（乗り物に）乗せる／nautical mile: カイリ　►1カイリは1852メートル。／veer off course: 航路を外れる／run out of fuel: 燃料切れになる

1. 正解 B

What is the main topic of this news report?

（**A**）An accident that occurred during a boat race
（**B**）The rescue of three sailors from an island

（**C**）The search for survivors of a helicopter crash

設問訳 このニュースの主なトピックは何か。
（**A**）ボートレース中に起きた事故
（**B**）3人の船乗りの島からの救出
（**C**）ヘリコプター事故の生存者の捜索

解説 sailorは「船乗り」であり、boat racer（ボート選手）ではないので、（**A**）は無関係。冒頭のThree sailors from Micronesia are in good condition after being rescued from a remote island in the western Pacific.（ミクロネシアの3人の船乗りは、西太平洋に浮かぶ孤島から救出され、今は良好な健康状態にあります）から、「遭難した船乗りたちが救出された話」だとわかるので、正解は（**B**）となる。sent in a helicopter with food and water（食料と水を積んだヘリコプターを送り込みました）とヘリコプターに言及しているが、ヘリコプター事故の話ではないので、（**C**）も誤り。

2. 正解 C

What does the news report say about a message written in sand?

（**A**）It got washed away a number of times.
（**B**）It was first seen by sailors on a patrol ship.
（**C**）It was seen from Australian and US aircraft.

設問訳 このニュースは、砂に書かれたメッセージについて何と言っているか。
（**A**）何度も流された。
（**B**）初めに巡視船の船員に見つけられた。
（**C**）オーストラリアと米国の航空機から見つけられた。

解説 Australian and US aircraft spotted their giant SOS message in the sand...（オーストラリアと米国の航空機［の乗員］が、船乗りたちが砂浜に書いた巨大なSOSメッセージを見つけ……）を正しく聞き取れれば、正解は（**C**）だとわかる。「巡視船」は船乗りを救出したが、彼らのメッセージを見つけたわけではないので、（**B**）は不適。（**A**）のwash awayは「〈波などが〉～を流し去る」の意味。

問題文

A Tokyo theme park is offering remote workers a change of scene. Here at Yomiuriland, visitors can take a break from the confines of the home office. For about $18, they can pick up a mobile Wi-Fi hotspot and work in the fresh air. A ticket also includes a spin on the park's Ferris wheel. One remote worker says it is a very much welcome change. It's a way for the theme park to bring in some extra cash as it feels the pinch of the corona-virus pandemic.

訳

東京のあるテーマパークが、リモートワークをする人たちに気分転換を提供しています。ここ、よみうりランドでは、来園者は自宅の仕事場という狭い空間をしばらく離れることができます。18ドルほど（の入園料）で、モバイルWi-Fiを受け取ったり、新鮮な空気の中で仕事をしたりすることができるのです。チケット代には同パークの大観覧車の乗車料金も含まれています。あるリモートワーカーは、これはとてもうれしい気分転換になる、と話しています。このテーマパークにとっては、コロナ禍のあおりを受ける中、収益にちょっとした上乗せをするための策となっています。

語句

a change of scene: 眺めの変化、気分転換／ **Yomiuriland:** よみうりランド　▶東京都稲城市にあるテーマパーク。ニュースで述べられているサービスは2020年秋冬に行われたもの。／ **take a break from:** ～をしばらく離れている／ **the confines of:** ～の限られた範囲／ **pick up:** ～を受け取る、もらう／ **a spin on:** ～に一乗りすること／ **Ferris wheel:** 大観覧車／ **welcome:** 歓迎すべき、ありがたい／ **bring in:**（収益などを）もたらす／ **extra:** 余分の／ **feel the pinch of:** ～の厳しい影響を受ける

1.　正解 C

What is this news report mainly about?

(A) The response to a theme park's increase in ticket prices

(B) Problems with Wi-Fi spots in Tokyo

(C) A place where people can do remote work

設問訳 このニュースは、主に何に関するものか。

(A) あるテーマパークの入園料値上げに対する反応

(B) 東京のWi-Fiスポットに関する問題

(C) 人々がリモートワークできる場所

解説 冒頭のA Tokyo theme park is offering remote workers a change of scene.（東京のあるテーマパークが、リモートワークをする人たちに気分転換を提供しています）と、For about $18, they can pick up a mobile Wi-Fi hotspot and work in the fresh air.（18ドルほど［の入園料］で、モバイルWi-Fiを受け取ったり、新鮮な空気の中で仕事をしたりすることができるのです）から、正解は（C）と判断できる。（A）の「入園料値上げ」や（B）の「Wi-Fiスポットに関する問題」の話は出てこない。

2.　正解 A

What does the news report suggest about Yomiuri-land?

(A) It has suffered financially during the pandemic.

(B) Visitors think it needs to make more changes.

(C) Its employees appreciate the new safety mea-sures.

設問訳 このニュースがよみうりランドについて示唆していることは何か。

(A)（新型コロナウイルスの）感染が拡大している中、財政的に苦しんでいる。

(B) 利用者は、同パークがもっと改善を行う必要があると考えている。

(C) 同パークの従業員は新しい安全対策を評価している。

解説 It's a way for the theme park to bring in some extra cash as it feels the pinch of the coronavirus pandemic.（このテーマパークにとっては、コロナ禍のあおりを受ける中、収益にちょっとした上乗せをするための策となっています）から、「よみうりランドは（コロナ禍で）財政面で苦しんでいる」ことがうかがえるので、（A）が正解となる。「利用者の声」として挙げられているのはit is a very much welcome change（これはとてもうれしい気分転換になる）なので、（B）は誤り。

Part 3 ロングニュース問題

No.1　CNN音声版　問題文 17↓　設問 18↓　ナレーター音声版　問題文 37↓　設問 38↓　イギリス英語

問題文

He's a famous young footballer with Manchester United and England who scores goals on the pitch and, away from it, campaigns to feed children who are unable to get enough food.

Marcus Rashford has already influenced British government policy and is now asking for lawmakers to act again. In an open letter to members of the country's parliament, Rashford is urging them to back three recommendations from a new task force he has set up.

Mentioning his own experience of child food poverty, he writes, "I remember the sound of my mum crying herself to sleep to this day, having worked a 14-hour shift, unsure how she was going to make ends meet."

Because this cause is so personal to him, Rashford teamed up with FareShare, which uses surplus food to provide millions of meals to charities, feeding those who can't provide enough for themselves.

"Four point two million people live in poverty in the United Kingdom. That's shocking. And quite often, you come up against a sort of dogmatic position where people go, 'Well, I just don't believe these numbers.' And that's where having the authenticity of somebody like Marcus Rashford—who has been there in terms of being hungry as a young man himself, needing to rely on breakfast clubs and after-school clubs in order to get enough food—is absolutely fantastic." (Lindsay Boswell, CEO, FareShare)

Earlier this year, the sports star helped persuade the British government to extend the scheme to provide free school meals to vulnerable children during the coronavirus lockdown. And now, he's lobbying for a longer-term solution after persuading the UK's major supermarkets to join his task force.

The British government says it will carefully consider the task force's recommendations as it approaches the next spending review—an acknowledgment that the star footballer with number 10 on his jersey is being listened to at the number 10 where Britain's prime minister lives.

Alex Thomas, CNN.

訳

彼はマンチェスターユナイテッドとイングランド（代表）の有名若手サッカー選手で、ピッチではゴールを決め、ピッチの外では満足に食事を得られない子どもたちに食べ物を提供する活動を行っています。

マーカス・ラッシュフォード選手は、すでに英国政府の政策に影響を与えており、今、議員たちに再び行動するよう呼びかけています。同国議会の議員たちに向けた公開書簡で、ラッシュフォード選手は、自身が新たに立ち上げたタスクフォースによる3つの提言を支援するよう求めているのです。

彼は食べ物に困っていた自身の幼少期の経験に触れ、こう書いています。「今でも母が寝るときに漏らしていた嗚咽を覚えています。母は14時間のシフトで働いても、どう家計をやりくりしていけばいいかわからなかったのです」

その目的は彼にとって個人的な意義がとても大きいため、ラッシュフォード選手は「フェアシェア」と提携しました。フェアシェアは余った食料で用意した何百万食分もの食事を慈善団体に提供し、満足に食事ができない人に食事を与えています。

「英国では420万人が貧困状態にあります。衝撃的な数ですよ。そのうえかなり頻繁に、ある種独断的な見解にも出くわすんです。『うーん、そんなにたくさんいるとはちょっと信じられない』なんて言うね。だからマーカス・ラッシュフォード選手のような、信頼性のある人が（この活動に協力してくださって）いるというのは——（しかも）自身が子どもの頃にひもじい思いをし、十分な食事を得るために（無償で食事が提供される）朝食クラブや放課後クラブに頼らざるをえなかった人です——本当に素晴らしいことです」（リンジー・ボズウェル　フェアシェアCEO）

今年すでに、このスポーツ界のスター選手は、コロナ対策のロックダウンの間、弱い立場の子どもたちに学校給食を無償で提供するプログラムを延長するよう英国

政府を説得するのに一役買いました。そして現在は、彼のタスクフォースに参加してもらうよう英国の大手スーパーを説得後、より長期的な解決に向けたロビー活動を展開しています。

英国政府は、次の歳出見直しが控えるなか、そのタスクフォースの提言を慎重に検討するとしています——10番のユニフォームを着るこのサッカー界のスター選手の言葉が、英国首相の住む「10番地」にも届いていることの証しです。

CNNのアレックス・トーマスがお伝えしました。

語句

footballer: サッカー選手／score a goal: ゴールを決める、1点入れる／pitch:《英》サッカーフィールド／campaign to do: 〜するための活動を行う／feed: 〜に食べ物を与える／influence: 〜に影響を与える／lawmaker: 立法者、議員／open letter: 公開状、公開書簡／parliament: 議会／back: 〜を支援する／recommendation: 勧告、提言／task force: 特別専門委員会、対策本部／poverty: 貧困／cry oneself to sleep: 泣いているうちに寝入る／to this day: 今日に至るまで／(be) unsure: 自信がない、確信がない／make ends meet: 家計をやりくりする／cause: 大義、目的／surplus: 余分の、余った／charity: 慈善団体／come up against: (困難などに)出くわす、直面する／dogmatic: 独断的な、独りよがりな／go:《話》〜と言う／authenticity: 信頼できること、本物であること／in terms of: 〜の点で／rely on: 〜に頼る、依存する／breakfast club: 朝食クラブ　➤学校で授業開始前に無償で子どもに朝食を提供する場。直後の after-school club はその放課後版。／persuade...to do: …を説得して〜させる／extend: 〜を延長する／scheme to do: 〜するための計画、構想／vulnerable: 弱い立場にある、被害を受けやすい／lobby for: 〜を求めてロビー活動を行う、働きかける／approach: (〜の時期などを)迎える、(出来事などに)近づく／spending review: 歳出見直し／acknowledgment that: 〜ということを事実だと認めること／jersey: ジャージー、スポーツユニフォーム／at the number 10: ➤ここでは英国首相官邸の住所(ダウニング街10番地)を指す。／prime minister: 首相

1. 正解 A

What is the main topic of this news report?

(**A**) A famous athlete's charity efforts

(**B**) A campaign to get young people involved in sports

(**C**) A failed UK-government policy

設問訳 このニュースの主なトピックは何か。

(**A**) 有名なアスリートの慈善活動

(**B**) 若者にスポーツをさせるためのキャンペーン

(**C**) 失敗に終わった英国政府の政策

解説 He's a famous young footballer with Manchester United and England who scores goals on the pitch and, away from it, campaigns to feed children who are unable to get enough food.（彼はマンチェスターユナイテッドとイングランド［代表］の有名若手サッカー選手で、ピッチではゴールを決め、ピッチの外では満足に食事を得られない子どもたちに食べ物を提供する活動を行っています）や Rashford teamed up with FareShare, which uses surplus food to provide millions of meals to charities, feeding those who can't provide enough for themselves（ラッシュフォード選手は「フェアシェア」と提携しました。フェアシェアは余った食料で用意した何百万食分もの食事を慈善団体に提供し、満足に食事ができない人に食事を与えています）などの説明から、有名サッカー選手が貧困状態にある人々に食事を提供する活動を行っていることがわかる。これを端的に表した（**A**）が正解。

2. 正解 C

What childhood experience does Marcus Rashford mention?

(**A**) Being unable to play sports for health reasons

(**B**) His parents' efforts to help other families

(**C**) His mother's struggles to support her family

設問訳 マーカス・ラッシュフォード選手は子ども時代のどんな経験について言及しているか。

(**A**) 健康上の理由でスポーツができなかったこと

(**B**) 彼の両親が他の家族を助けようと努めていたこと

(**C**) 家族を養うために彼の母親が苦労していたこと

解説 ラッシュフォード選手が子ども時代の経験について言及したこととして、I remember the sound of my mum crying herself to sleep to this day, having worked a 14-hour shift, unsure how she was going to make ends meet.（今でも母が寝るときに漏らしていた嗚咽を覚えています。母は14時間のシフトで働いて

も、どう家計をやりくりしていけばいいかわからなかったのです）という記述が紹介されている。彼が自身の子ども時代や家族について述べた内容がわかるのはこの箇所だけなので、正解は（**C**）。

3. 正解 B

What does the interviewee say about poverty in the UK?

（**A**）It has been decreasing in recent years.

（**B**）People often fail to understand how severe it is.

（**C**）It is less widespread than it is in other developed nations.

設問訳 インタビューを受けた人は、英国の貧困について何と言っているか。

（**A**）近年減ってきている。

（**B**）その深刻さを理解していない人が多い。

（**C**）他の先進諸国と比べて、貧困の広がりは少ない。

解説 インタビューを受けた人が英国の貧困について述べているのは、Four point two million people live in poverty in the United Kingdom. That's shocking. And quite often, you come up against a sort of dogmatic position where people go, 'Well, I just don't believe these numbers.'（英国では420万人が貧困状態にあります。衝撃的な数ですよ。そのうえかなり頻繁に、ある種独断的な見解にも出くわすんです、『うーん、そんなにたくさんいるとはちょっと信じられない』なんて言うね）の箇所である。正解は（**B**）。（**A**）はこれと正反対の内容なので選べない。他国と比較して述べた発言もないので（**C**）も不適。

4. 正解 B

What did Rashford help persuade the British government to do?

（**A**）Ask the UK's major supermarkets to join a task force

（**B**）Provide free meals during the coronavirus lockdown

（**C**）Allow children to go to school during the coronavirus lockdown

設問訳 ラッシュフォード選手は、英国政府に何をしてもらうよう説得するのに一役買ったか。

（**A**）英国の大手スーパーにタスクフォースへの参加を頼むこと

（**B**）コロナ対策のロックダウンの間、無料の食事を提供すること

（**C**）コロナ対策のロックダウンの間、子どもたちに学校に行くのを許可すること

解説 Earlier this year, the sports star helped persuade the British government to extend the scheme to provide free school meals to vulnerable children during the coronavirus lockdown.（今年すでに、このスポーツ界のスター選手は、コロナ対策のロックダウンの間、弱い立場の子どもたちに学校給食を無償で提供するプログラムを延長するよう英国政府を説得するのに一役買いました）という箇所から、the sports star（＝ラッシュフォード選手）の働きかけのおかげもあり、このプログラムの延長が決まったことがわかるので、正解は（**B**）。そのすぐ後でも after persuading the UK's major supermarkets to join his task force（彼のタスクフォースに参加してもらうよう英国の大手スーパーを説得後）と persuading が使われているが、英国政府の話とは別なので、（**A**）は選べない。（**C**）の「通学」に関する話は出てこない。

No.2　CNN音声版　問題文 19　設問 20　ナレーター音声版　問題文 39　設問 40　カナダ英語

問題文

Touching down in Inner Mongolia during the early morning hours Thursday, a piece of China's history successfully returned to Earth. After a 23-day mission, the *Chang'e 5* brings home the first lunar samples collected in nearly half a century. China is now only the third country to deliver such precious cargo, its flag now proudly planted at the site of the lunar probe's touchdown.

Named after the mythical Chinese goddess of the moon, the *Chang'e 5* mission had a twofold objective, one part discovery, the other to advance China's ambition in space with one of the most complicated and challenging missions in the country's aerospace history.

The four-part *Chang'e 5* probe blasted off from an island on China's southern coast November 24th. It touched down seven days later on a part of the moon that's never been visited before.

There, a lander began collecting samples with a drill and robotic arm before loading it onto an ascent vehicle. Two kilograms of the material was sealed in a re-entry capsule, which left the moon Sunday and brought to Earth the first lunar samples since the 1970s.

Soon, scientists will be analyzing the structure, physical properties and material composition of the soil and rock samples. They hope to find informtion that helps explain the moon's origins, how long it was volcanically active and when its magnetic field, which protects life from the sun's radiation, disappeared.

Possibly, other clues can be found with answers to long-held mysteries about our nearest celestial body.

Kim Brunhuber, CNN.

訳

木曜日の早朝の時間帯に内モンゴル自治区に着陸し、中国の歴史の一部となるものが無事に地球に帰還しました。23日間のミッションを終えた「嫦娥5号」は、約半世紀ぶりに回収された月面サンプルを持ち帰ってきました。このような貴重な積み荷を運んだ国として中国はまだ3番目の国であり、その月面探査機の着陸地点に今、中国旗が誇らしげに立っています。

中国の神話に出てくる月の女神にちなんで名づけられた嫦娥5号のミッションの目的には2つの要素がありました。1つは発見であり、もう1つは、中国の宇宙航空史上有数の複雑で困難なミッションを行うことで同国の宇宙への野心を進めることでした。

4つの部分から成る嫦娥5号の探査機は、11月24日に中国南岸の島から打ち上げられました。7日後、同機は月面の中でこれまで宇宙船が送られたことのない場所に着陸しました。

そこで着陸機はドリルとロボットアームを使ってサンプルの収集を開始し、そのサンプルを離陸機に積み込みました。2キログラムの物質は大気圏再突入カプセルに密封され、カプセルは日曜日に月（周回軌道）から離れ、地球に1970年代以来となる月のサンプルを持ち帰りました。

まもなく科学者たちがその土壌や岩のサンプルの構造、物理的特性、物質組成を分析することになっていま

す。彼らは月の起源、火山活動をしていた期間、そして太陽放射線から生命を守る月の磁場がいつ消失したのかを解明する助けとなる情報が得られることを望んでいます。

もしかすると、別の手がかりが見つかることで、地球から最も近い天体の長年の謎に答えが出るかもしれません。

CNNのキム・ブルンフーバーがお伝えしました。

語句

touch down: 着陸する／**Inner Mongolia**: = Inner Mongolia Autonomous Region　内モンゴル自治区／**the *Chang'e 5***: 嫦娥5号　➤中国の月探査機。／**lunar**: 月の／**precious**: 貴重な／**cargo**: 積み荷／**proudly**: 誇らしげに、堂々と／**plant**: 〜をしっかりと据える、設置する／**lunar probe**: 月面探査機／**name A after B**: BにちなんでAと名づける／**mythical**: 神話の／**goddess**: 女神／**twofold**: 2つの、2つの部分から成る／**objective**: 目標、目的／**advance**: 〜を前進させる、進める／**ambition**: 野心、野望／**complicated**: 複雑な／**challenging**: 困難な／**aerospace**: 航空宇宙の／**blast off from**: 〜から飛び立つ、打ち上げられる／**lander**: （月面などへの）着陸機／**drill**: ドリル／**load A onto B**: A（荷）をBに積み込む　➤ loading it の it は、samples を受けるため them とするのが適切。／**ascent vehicle**: 離陸機、上昇機　➤人や貨物を乗せて月面などから宇宙空間にある軌道船などへ飛び立つための機体。／**material**: 物質／**seal A in B**: AをBの中に封じ込める、密封する／**re-entry capsule**: 大気圏再突入カプセル／**analyze**: 〜を分析する／**structure**: 構造／**physical property**: 物理的特性／**material composition**: 物質組成／**soil**: 土、土壌／**origin**: 起源、起こり／**volcanically active**: 火山活動中の／**magnetic field**: 磁場、磁界／**radiation**: 放射線／**clue**: 手がかり、ヒント／**long-held**: 長年抱いてきた、昔からの／**celestial body**: 天体

---

1. 正解 C

What is the main point of this news report?

(A) China announced it will join another country's space mission.

(B) An unexpected discovery was made on the moon.

(C) A Chinese spacecraft completed a historic mission to the moon.

設問訳 このニュースの要点は何か。

(A) 中国が他国の宇宙ミッションへの参加を表明した。

(**B**) 月面で思わぬ発見があった。

(**C**) 中国の宇宙船が月への歴史的ミッションを成し遂げた。

解説 a piece of China's history successfully returned to Earth. After a 23-day mission, the *Chang'e 5* brings home the first lunar samples collected in nearly half a century.（中国の歴史の一部となるものが無事に地球に帰還しました。23日間のミッションを終えた「嫦娥5号」は、約半世紀ぶりに回収された月面サンプルを持ち帰ってきました）と述べられていることから、（**C**）が正解だと判断できる。「これまで宇宙船が送られたことのない場所に着陸した」と言っている箇所はあるが、「思わぬ発見があった」とは述べられていないので、（**B**）は不適。

2. 正解 B

What is true with regard to the landing site on the moon?

(**A**) It was not the one that had originally been planned.

(**B**) This was the first time any probe had been there.

(**C**) It had more dangers than expected.

設問訳 月の着陸地点に関して正しいのはどれか。

(**A**) もともと計画されていた場所ではなかった。

(**B**) そこに探査機が着陸するのは初めてだった。

(**C**) 予想以上の危険があった。

解説 It touched down seven days later on a part of the moon that's never been visited before.（7日後、同機は月面の中でこれまで宇宙船が送られたことのない場所に着陸しました）とあるので、正解は（**B**）。「これまで宇宙船が送られたことのない場所に着陸した」ことが「計画外だった」とは述べられていない。また「危険が伴った」とも述べられていないので、（**A**）や（**C**）は選べない。

3. 正解 C

According to the news report, what happened in the 1970s?

(**A**) Material obtained by a Chinese spacecraft was lost.

(**B**) Chinese scientists had difficulty building a moon-landing spacecraft.

(**C**) Samples from the moon were brought to Earth.

設問訳 このニュースによれば、1970年代に何が起こったか。

(**A**) 中国の宇宙船が入手した物質が紛失した。

(**B**) 中国の科学者たちが月着陸船の製造に苦労した。

(**C**) 月のサンプルが地球にもたらされた。

解説 1970年代について述べられているのは、and brought to Earth the first lunar samples since the 1970s（地球に1970年代以来となる月のサンプルを持ち帰りました）という箇所。「1970年代に月のサンプルが持ち帰られて以来、初めて月のサンプルが持ち帰られた」ということなので、1970年代に月のサンプルが地球にもたらされたことがわかる。よって、（**C**）が正解。（**A**）と（**B**）については触れられていない。

4. 正解 A

What does the news report say scientists hope to learn more about?

(**A**) The activity of past volcanoes on the moon

(**B**) How to protect astronauts from radiation

(**C**) The way Earth was formed

設問訳 このニュースによれば、科学者たちは何についてもっと知りたがっているか。

(**A**) かつてあった月の火山活動

(**B**) 宇宙飛行士を放射線から守る方法

(**C**) 地球がどのように形成されたか

解説 They hope to find information that helps explain the moon's origins, how long it was volcanically active and when its magnetic field, which protects life from the sun's radiation, disappeared.（彼らは月の起源、火山活動をしていた期間、そして太陽放射線から生命を守る月の磁場がいつ消失したのかを解明する助けとなる情報が得られることを望んでいます）という部分に注目しよう。the moon's origin（月の起源）とはあるが、「地球の起源」には言及されていないので（**C**）は不可。また「放射線」について触れられているが、「宇宙飛行士を守る」という文脈ではないため（**B**）も選べない。how long it was volcanically active（火山活動をしていた期間）を言い換えた（**A**）が正解である。

Part 4 インタビュー問題

問題文

The following is an interview with former vice president of the United States Al Gore.

Fareed Zakaria　In 2006, 14 years ago, Al Gore released his magnum opus, *An Inconvenient Truth*. The documentary laid out the calamities that would befall the earth if humans didn't change their ways and quickly. Fourteen years later, it's obvious that though millions of people have seen the film, not enough heeded its warnings.

In my new book, one of the things I try to stress is that the pandemics, the fires, the droughts, the hurricanes—this is all part of a kind of problem, which is that we are continuing human development without thought to what it is doing to nature, and meanwhile, you are seeing these natural backlashes. Do you think COVID-19 could be the wake-up call that we need?

Al Gore　Well, it could be, because, first of all, it gives us obvious evidence that when the leading scientists—in this case, virologists and epidemiologists—start warning of an impending danger, we'd best listen to them and prepare. In the same way, the climate scientists have been warning in even more dire terms about the danger we're facing with the climate crisis—a danger whose consequences don't last months and years but centuries and, if we don't get a handle on it quickly, millennia.

So I do think that it is part of a broader awakening, which we've also seen in the recognition of these long-standing institutional-racism problems and injustices. So I do think that it is a wake-up call for many.

We are seeing an historic drop in the cost of solar electricity, wind electricity, battery technology, electric vehicles, and a lot of other, less well-known efficiency improvements, hyper-efficiency options that are really creating new options. Last year, worldwide, 80 percent of all of the new electricity generation installed was solar and wind. And we're seeing, now, the cost of new solar plus battery storage is significantly cheaper now than a new gas plant. It already beat coal-powered generation.

Five years ago, electricity from solar and wind was cheaper than fossil electricity in 1 percent of the world. Now, it's cheaper in 70 percent of the world. And within five years, it will be cheaper in 100 percent of the world.

The key fact is what is already accumulated in the earth's atmosphere. It stays there roughly 100 years on average, and the accumulation already traps as much extra heat as would be released by 600,000 Hiroshima-class atomic bombs exploding every single day.

We've got to stop using the thin shell of atmosphere around our planet as an open sewer. And that means moving as quickly as possible toward the elimination of burning all fossil fuels.

訳

元合衆国副大統領アル・ゴア氏へのインタビューです。

ファリード・ザカリア　2006年、14年前のことですが、アル・ゴア氏は代表作『不都合な真実』を発表しました。このドキュメンタリー映画は、人類がその行動を、それもただちに変えなければ地球に降りかかるであろう惨事について詳細に描いたものです。それから14年後の今、数え切れないほど多くの人々がその映画を見たにもかかわらず、その警告が十分に聞き入れられていないのは明らかです。

私が新著の中で強く言おうとしていることの1つは、パンデミック、山火事、干ばつ、ハリケーン——これらはすべてある種の問題の一部で、人類は自然に与える影響を考えずに発展を続けており、そうしている間に、こうして自然からの反発にあっているということです。新型コロナウイルスは私たちに必要な警鐘になりうると思いますか。

アル・ゴア　ええ、そうでしょうね。まず、今回のコロナ禍

は私たちに明白な証拠を示してくれましたから、優れた科学者たち——今回で言えばウイルス学者、疫学者ですが——彼らが迫り来る危険に警鐘を鳴らし始めたら、彼らの言うことに耳を傾け、それに備えるべきだという証拠をね。これと同じように、気候科学者たちは、私たちが気候危機のせいで直面している危険について、はるかに切迫した言葉で警告し続けています——その危険の影響が残るのは数カ月や数年ではなく数世紀に及び、早急に対処しなければ数千年単位になると。

ですから、新型コロナウイルスから得た教訓は、より広い目覚めの一部だとやはり思います、長年にわたる制度的人種差別の問題や様々な不正への認識にも見られる目覚めのね。ですから、やはり多くの人への警鐘になっていると思います。

今は、太陽光電気や風力電気、蓄電池技術、電気自動車のコストがかつてないほど低下していますし、他にもそれらほど知られていない多くの効率改善や、極めて効率的な選択肢なども現れて、まさに新たな手段の選択肢を生み出しているのです。昨年［2019年］は世界全体で、新たに設置されたすべての電力発電設備の80%が太陽光か風力によるものでした。現在、太陽光発電と蓄電池を組み合わせて新たに設置する費用は、新たにガス火力発電所を建設するよりかなり安くなっています。それはすでに化石燃料発電に（コスト面で）勝っているのです。

5年前、太陽光発電と風力発電が化石燃料発電より安かった地域は、世界の1%でした。それが今では世界の70%の地域で安くなっています。5年以内に、世界の100%の地域でそれらは（化石燃料発電より）安くなるでしょうね。

鍵となるのは、すでに地球の大気圏に蓄積したもの（温室効果ガス）です。それは平均で100年間ほど大気圏にとどまり、その蓄積したものはすでに、毎日ヒロシマ級の原爆60万個分が爆発して放出されるのと同等の余分な熱を閉じ込めているのです。

私たちは、この地球の薄い外殻である大気を下水溝のように使うのをやめなければなりません。それはつまり、化石燃料を一切燃やさない社会に、できるだけ早く移行するということです。

語句

release: ①～を発表する ②～を放出する／magnum opus:《ラテン語》最高傑作、代表作／*An Inconvenient Truth*:『不都合な真実』 ▶アル・ゴア氏が脚本・主演を担当した、地球温暖化を啓発するドキュメンタリー映画。／lay out: ～を明確に説明する／calamity: 大災害、大惨事／befall:〈良くないことが〉～に起こる／obvious: 明らかな／heed:（警告・忠告などを）心に留める／warning: 警告、注意／stress: ～を強調する／pandemic: 疫病の世界的流行、パンデミック／drought: 干ばつ／without thought to: ～について考えることなく／backlash: 反動、反発／wake-up call: 警鐘、注意喚起／leading: 一流の、優れた／virologist: ウイルス学者／epidemiologist: 疫学者、伝染病学者／warn of/about: ～を警告する／impending: 差し迫った／had best do: ～すべきである、～しないとまずいことになる／prepare: 備える／dire: 緊急の／terms: 言葉遣い／face: ～に直面する／consequences:（良くない）結果、影響／last:（ある期間）続く／get a handle on: ～を処理できるようになる、～に対処できるようになる／millennia: ▶ millennium（千年間）の複数形。／broad: 幅の広い／awakening: 目覚め、気づくこと／recognition: 認識／long-standing: 長年にわたる／institutional racism: 制度的人種差別／injustice: 不正／drop:（値段などの）低下、減少／solar electricity: 太陽光発電による電気／wind electricity: 風力発電による電気／battery: 蓄電池／electric vehicle: 電気自動車／well-known: よく知られている／efficiency improvement: 効率改善／hyper-: 超…／electricity generation: 発電／install: ～を設置する／storage: 貯蔵／significantly: かなり、著しく／gas plant: =gas power plant ガス火力発電所／beat: ～に勝る／coal-powered generation: 化石燃料発電／fossil electricity: 化石燃料による電気／accumulate:（徐々に）蓄積する、たまる／the earth's atmosphere: 地球の大気圏／roughly: 大体、おおよそ／accumulation: 蓄積物／trap: ～を閉じ込める／Hiroshima-class atomic bomb: 広島に落とされたのと同等の規模の原爆／explode: 爆発する／thin: 薄い／shell: 殻のような覆い／open sewer: 下水溝／elimination: 排除、廃止／burn: ～を燃やす／fossil fuel: 化石燃料

1. 正解 C

What is the main point made by Al Gore?

(A) Climate change is becoming a harder problem to solve.

(B) The pandemic has taken attention away from climate change.

(C) We are developing more ways to deal with the climate crisis.

設問訳 アル・ゴア氏の主な主張は何か。

(A) 気候変動は解決がより困難な問題になってきている。

(B) パンデミックは人々の注意を気候変動からそらしている。

(C) 私たちは気候危機に対処するためのより多くの方法を生み出している。

解説 pandemic はインタビュアーの話の中に出てくるが、ゴア氏の発言に「パンデミックは人々の注意を気候変動からそらしている」という内容は出てこない。よって、(B) は不適だと判断できる。We are seeing an historic drop in the cost of solar electricity, wind electricity, battery technology, electric vehicles, and a lot of other, less well-known efficiency improvements, hyper-efficiency options that are really creating new options.（今は、太陽光電気や風力電気、蓄電池技術、電気自動車のコストがかつてないほど低下していますし、他にもそれらほど知られていない多くの効率改善や、極めて効率的な選択肢なども現れて、まさに新たな手段の選択肢を生み出しているのです）から、(C) が正解だとわかる。さらに、And within five years, it will be cheaper in 100 percent of the world.（5年以内に、世界の100％の地域でそれら［太陽光発電と風力発電］は［化石燃料発電より］安くなるでしょうね）とも述べており、気候変動に対処するための環境が、技術面、コスト面で整いつつあると評価していることがうかがえるので、(A) も不適だと判断できる。

2. 正解 A

According to Al Gore, what lesson can the COVID-19 crisis teach us?

(A) It is important to listen to scientists' warnings.

(B) Virus outbreaks can become uncontrollable within months.

(C) Pandemics have a larger effect on racial minorities.

設問訳 アル・ゴア氏によれば、新型コロナウイルスの危機は、我々にどのような教訓を教えてくれる可能性があるか。

(A) 科学者の警告に耳を傾けることは大切である。

(B) ウイルスの大流行は、数カ月の間に手に負えなくなることもある。

(C) パンデミックは、人種的マイノリティーの人々に、より

解説 Well, it could be, because, first of all, it gives us obvious evidence that when the leading scientists—in this case, virologists and epidemiologists—start warning of an impending danger, we'd best listen to them and prepare.（ええ、そうでしょうね。まず、今回のコロナ禍は私たちに明白な証拠を示してくれましたから、優れた科学者たち——今回で言えばウイルス学者、疫学者ですが——彼らが迫り来る危険に警鐘を鳴らし始めたら、彼らの言うことに耳を傾け、それに備えるべきだという証拠をね）の部分に注目する。we'd best listen to them を言い換えた (A) が正解だとわかる。a danger whose consequences don't last months and years but centuries and, if we don't get a handle on it quickly, millennia（その危険の影響が残るのは数カ月や数年ではなく数世紀に及び、早急に対処しなければ数千年単位になる）という部分に months が出てくるが、ここは「気候変動」の話をしているので (B) は無関係。さらに、institutional-racism problems（制度的人種差別の問題）という表現は出てくるが、これはパンデミックとは関係ないので (C) も不適。

3. 正解 B

What does Al Gore say about alternative energy sources such as solar and wind?

(A) People mistakenly think they are unreliable.

(B) They are becoming cheaper to use.

(C) More efforts should be focused on battery storage.

設問訳 アル・ゴア氏は太陽光や風力などの代替エネルギー源について何と言っているか。

(A) 人々は、それらが信頼できないものだと誤解している。

(B) より安く使えるようになってきている。

(C) 蓄電池による電力貯蔵にもっと注力すべきである。

解説 Now, it's cheaper in 70 percent of the world. And within five years, it will be cheaper in 100 percent of the world.（それが今では世界の70％の地域で安くなっています。5年以内に、世界の100％の地域でそれらは［化石燃料発電より］安くなるでしょうね）より、(B) が正解。battery storage については、And we're seeing, now, the cost of new solar plus battery storage is significantly cheaper now than a new gas plant. It already beat coal-powered generation. (現在、太陽光発電と蓄電池を組み合わせて新たに設置する費用は、新たにガス火力発電所を建設するよりかなり安くなっています。それはすでに化石燃料発電に［コスト面で］勝っているのです) などと言されているが、特に「蓄電池による電力貯蔵に注力する」ことを訴えてはいないので (C) は不適。また、「人々の誤解」についても出てこないので (A) も選べない。

4. 正解 A

What point does Al Gore emphasize with regard to climate change?
(**A**) The atmosphere is already very polluted.
(**B**) Sewage systems contribute to the problem.
(**C**) Fossil fuels can be burned in different ways.

設問訳 気候変動に関して、アル・ゴア氏が強く主張していることは何か。
(**A**) 大気はすでにかなり汚染されている。
(**B**) 下水道システムが、その問題の一因である。
(**C**) 化石燃料は、様々な方法で燃やすことができる。

解説 The key fact is what is already accumulated in the earth's atmosphere. (鍵となるのは、すでに地球の大気圏に蓄積したものです) という発言は、「新エネルギーは安く使えるようになっているが、問題は、すでに地球の大気圏に蓄積したものだ」ということであり、(**A**) が正解である。We've got to stop using the thin shell of atmosphere around our planet as an open sewer. (私たちは、この地球の薄い外殻である大気を下水溝のように使うのをやめなければなりません) は、「たとえ」として「下水」の話を出しているだけなので、(**B**) は不適。また、「化石燃料を燃やすのをやめるべきだ」という主張はされているが、(**C**) のように「様々な方法で燃やすことができる」とは述べられていない。

問題文

The following is an interview with David Rubenstein, cofounder and co-executive chairman of the Carlyle Group.

Fareed Zakaria David Rubenstein is a leader. He is the cofounder and co-executive chairman of one of the world's largest investment firms, The Carlyle Group. He's been the chairman of the board of many of America's most important nonprofit institutions.

And now, he has edited a book about leadership called *How to Lead*. In it, he offers insight from many of the major leaders he's interviewed on his own eponymous TV show.

So, one of the things I've always wondered about leadership is, is it really possible to have a kind of theory of leadership? Because it does seem people have so many different traits that, you know, they're able to put to use.

Do you find there's any common trait that really spans all these different styles of leadership?

David Rubenstein Well, there's no one common trait, because if there were, everybody would pursue that trait. And I think many people have a view, as I do, that there are many different traits.

But they also include persistence, failing early in life and recognizing you need to be able to communicate with other people, learning how to communicate, learning how to empathize. And I think integrity is very important.

Now, there are many different leadership styles, and I tried to interview many people with different backgrounds and so forth. But there's no doubt that leadership is something you learn, in my view, and you learn it early in life, and then you work on the qualities, and you perfect them later on.

Zakaria You list a series of them, and the number-one quality, you say, is luck. Do you think most supersuccessful people recognize, as you clearly do, just what a large role luck plays?

Rubenstein Absolutely. Because suppose Bill Gates had not dropped out of Harvard; suppose Jeff Bezos had not read about the Internet; suppose many things had happened differently in people's lives.

I met many people that enabled me to do the things I've done. Had I not met those people, I might be doing something else, may not have been able to do what I...I'm proud that I've been able to do. So luck is everything, I think.

But you make your own luck. I think if you sit in your house and you don't do anything else, you're not likely to have luck. You have to go out, meet people, experiment and fail. Learning how to fail is very important, because if you don't fail, you're not likely to have the resilience you need to pick yourself up and achieve something.

Most of the people in the book are people that failed at some things in life. They picked themselves up, they got back on their feet, and they proved that what they wanted to do was actually something that could be done.

Zakaria You point out that a lot of people who are leaders, first of all, don't come from great backgrounds in terms of great wealth and privilege, and they often actually don't even do that well early on in life. Why do you think that is? Why do they then become successful?

Rubenstein Generally, the people who are the leaders in the world came from lower-income families or maybe middle-income families but not necessarily the wealthiest families.

So, take a look at the people running the world today. Generally, they were not student-body presidents, Rhodes Scholars and so forth. There are exceptions, but generally, they're people, maybe like me, who had some modest abilities early on. We just persevered like "The Tortoise and the Hare," and ultimately, we won out.

訳

カーライル・グループの共同創業者であり共同会長であるデービッド・ルーベンシュタイン氏へのインタビューです。

ファリード・ザカリア デービッド・ルーベンシュタイン氏はリーダーです。彼は、世界最大の投資会社の1つであるカーライル・グループの共同創業者であり共同会長です。アメリカ屈指の非営利機関の多くで理事会の理事長を務めてきました。

そして今度は、『How to Lead（いかに率いるか）』とい

うリーダーシップについての本を編集しました。その中で彼は、自身の名を冠したテレビ番組でインタビューしてきた一流のリーダーたちの多くから得られた見識を紹介しています。

リーダーシップについて私がずっと疑問に思っていたことの1つに、リーダーシップの理論といったものは実際のところあり得るのか、というのがあります。というのも、人が生かすことのできる資質は実に様々であるように思えるからです。

実際にその様々な型のリーダーシップに当てはまるような、共通した資質というのはあると思いますか。

デービッド・ルーベンシュタイン そうですね、これという共通した資質はありませんね、もしあるなら、みんなその資質を得ようとするでしょうから。そして多くの人は、私と同じように、（リーダーの）資質は多種多様であるという考えを持っていると思います。

しかしその資質には、粘り強さ、人生の早い段階での挫折、他者とコミュニケーションがとれる必要があると認識すること、コミュニケーションの方法を身につけること、他者に共感できるようになること、といったことも含まれます。誠実さも非常に重要だと思います。

リーダーシップには様々な型があり、私はバックグラウンドなどが異なる多くの人にインタビューを試みました。しかし私の考えでは、間違いないのは、リーダーシップとは学ぶものであり、そして人生の早い段階でそれを学んだ後、そのリーダーの資質を磨き、完成させていく、ということです。

ザカリア あなたはその資質をリストアップしていて、そのトップにくるのが運だと言っていますね。あなたは、ものすごい成功を収めている人たちの大半は、運がいかに大きな役割を果たしているか認識していると思いますか。あなたは明らかにそう認識されているわけですが。

ルーベンシュタイン もちろんです。仮にビル・ゲイツ氏がハーバードを中退していなかったら？ ジェフ・ベゾス氏がインターネットについて読んでいなかったら？（そういった成功した）人々の人生の中で多くのことが別の形で起こっていたらどうなっていたか。

私が成してきたことを可能にしてくれた人たちに、私はたくさん出会いました。その人たちに出会っていなかったら、私は何か別のことをしていたかもしれないし、私ができてよかったと誇りに思っていることもできていなかったかもしれません。だから運こそすべてだと私は思いますね。

でも運は自分でつくるものなんですよ。家の中で座っているだけでほかに何もしなければ、運はたぶん巡ってこないと思います。必要なのは、外に出て、人に会い、やってみて、失敗すること。失敗の仕方を学ぶのは非常に大切で、なぜなら失敗しなければ、そこから立ち直り、何かを成し遂げるのに必要な心の強さがなかなか得られないからです。

この本に出てくる人のほとんどは、人生で何かしらつまずいた人たちです。彼らは自らを奮い立たせ、立ち直り、自分が成し遂げたいと思っていたことが実際に成し遂げられるものであることを証明したのです。

ザカリア あなたは指摘していますね、リーダーの多くは、第一に、恵まれた出自ではないことを、富とか特権的な地位という意味で。実際、人生の早い段階ではあまりうまくいかないことすらよくあると。どうしてそうなのだと思いますか。なぜ彼らは後になって成功できるのでしょうか。

ルーベンシュタイン 一般的に、世界でリーダーの地位にある人たちは低所得の家庭の出で、もしかしたら中所得の家庭の出の人もいるかもしれませんが、必ずしも非常に裕福な家庭の出というわけではありません。

今日世界を動かしている人たちを見てみてください。概して、彼らは生徒会長やローズ奨学生などだったわけではありません。例外はありますが、一般的に彼らは、おそらく私と同様に、早い段階ではほどほどの能力の持ち主でした。私たちはただ「ウサギとカメ」（のカメ）のように耐え抜き、最終的に勝ち抜いたのです。

語句

cofounder: 共同創業者／co-executive chairman: 共同会長／investment firm: 投資会社／chairman of the board: 取締役会長、理事長／nonprofit institution: 非営利機関、非営利団体／edit: ～を編集する／insight: 見識／major: 一流の／eponymous: 作者や司会者の名前をタイトルにした／theory: 理論／trait: 特性、特徴／put...to use: …を活用する、生かす／common: 共通の／span:〈領域などが〉～にまたがる、及ぶ／pursue: ～を追求する、得ようとする／have a view that: ～という意見を持つ／persistence: 粘り強さ／fail: 失敗する／recognize（that）: ～ということを認識する／empathize: 共感する、感情移入する／integrity: 誠実さ、正直さ／background: 生い立ち、経歴／and so forth: …など／there's no doubt that: ～ということに

疑いの余地はない／work on: ～を鍛える、発達させようと努力する／quality: 特質、性質、特性／perfect: ～を完成させる、完全なものにする／later on: 後に、後で／list: ～をリストに挙げる、列挙する／a series of: 一連の、いくつもの／luck: 運／play a large role: 大きな役割を果たす／Absolutely.: まったくその通りだ／Suppose（that）...: 仮に…としたらどうだろうか／drop out of: ～を退学する、中退する／enable...to do: …が～できるようにする／be proud that: ～であることを誇りに思う／be not likely to do: ～しそうにない／experiment: 実験する、試みる／resilience:（逆境などから）立ち直る力／pick oneself up: 起き上がる、（失望・失敗などから）立ち直る／achieve: ～を成し遂げる／get back on one's feet: 立ち直る、回復する／prove that: ～ということを証明する／point out that: ～ということを指摘する／first of all: 何よりも、第一に／in terms of: ～に関しては、～について言えば／wealth: 富、財産／privilege:（富・家柄などによる）特権／early on: 早い段階で、初期に／generally: 一般的に、概して／lower-income: 低所得の／middle-income: 中所得の、平均的収入の／not necessarily: 必ずしも～ない／take a look at: ～を見てみる／run: ～を運営する、管理する／student-body president: 生徒会長／Rhodes Scholar: ローズ奨学生 ➤ Rhodes Scholarship（ローズ奨学金）はオックスフォード大学大学院で学ぶ者への奨学金。19世紀植民地時代の英国の政治家セシル・ローズの遺言により創設された。／exception: 例外／modest: ささやかな、そこそこの／persevere: 根気強くやり通す、へこたれないで続ける／"The Tortoise and the Hare":《イソップ物語》「ウサギとカメ」／ultimately: 最終的に／win out:（困難の末に）成功を収める、勝ち抜く

1. 正解 B

What are the speakers mainly discussing?

(A) Why some leaders are more effective than others

(B) Characteristics that are important for leadership

(C) The differences between leadership and success

設問訳 話者たちは主に何について話し合っているか。

(A) 一部のリーダーが、他のリーダーよりも有能である理由

（**B**）リーダーシップに重要な特性

（**C**）リーダーシップと成功の違い

解説 Do you find there's any common trait that really spans all these different styles of leadership?（実際にその様々な型のリーダーシップに当てはまるような、共通した資質というのはあると思いますか）というインタビューアーの質問と、その後のやりとりから、このインタビューの趣旨が（**B**）であることがわかる。「リーダーの能力の違い」や「リーダーシップと成功の違い」については触れられていないので、（**A**）および（**C**）は不適である。

2. 正解 A

What does David Rubenstein say about learning to lead?

（**A**）It happens early in life.

（**B**）It is not necessary for some leaders.

（**C**）It can have an unintended effect.

設問訳 デービッド・ルーベンシュタイン氏は、人を率いるのを覚えることについて、何と言っているか。

（**A**）若いころに起こることである。

（**B**）一部のリーダーにとって、それは必要ではない。

（**C**）予期せぬ効果が出ることもある。

解説 ルーベンシュタイン氏は、「様々な型のリーダーシップに共通した資質はあるか」と問われて答える中で、But there's no doubt that leadership is something you learn, in my view, and you learn it early in life, and then you work on the qualities, and you perfect them later on.（しかし私の考えでは、間違いないのは、リーダーシップとは学ぶものであり、そして人生の早い段階でそれを学んだ後、そのリーダーの資質を磨き、完成させていく、ということです）と述べていることから、（**A**）が正解と判断できる。（**B**）や（**C**）の内容について述べた箇所はない。

3. 正解 A

Why does Rubenstein mention Bill Gates?

（**A**）To support his point about the importance of luck

（**B**）To stress the importance of the Internet

（**C**）To explain how meeting certain people has helped him

設問訳 なぜ、ルーベンシュタイン氏はビル・ゲイツ氏について言及しているのか。

（**A**）運が重要だという自分の主張を裏づけるため

（**B**）インターネットの重要性を強調するため

（**C**）ある人々との出会いが彼を助けたことを説明するため

解説 ビル・ゲイツ氏について言及しているのは、「ものすごい成功を収めている人たちの大半は運がいかに大きな役割を果たしているか認識していると思うか」と聞かれ、Absolutely. Because suppose Bill Gates had not dropped out of Harvard（もちろんです。仮にビル・ゲイツ氏がハーバードを中退していなかったら？）と答えている箇所で、これは「運の重要性」を具体的に示している。よって、（**A**）が正解。（**B**）と（**C**）については触れられていない。

4. 正解 C

What does Rubenstein say about leaders?

（**A**）They tend to enjoy studying.

（**B**）Most begin to have success at a young age.

（**C**）Most are not raised in wealthy families.

設問訳 ルーベンシュタイン氏は、リーダーたちについて何と言っているか。

（**A**）リーダーたちは勉強を楽しむ傾向がある。

（**B**）たいていのリーダーたちは、若いころに成功をつかみ始める。

（**C**）たいていのリーダーたちは、裕福な家庭の出身ではない。

解説 Generally, the people who are the leaders in the world came from lower-income families or maybe middle-income families but not necessarily the wealthiest families.（一般的に、世界でリーダーの地位にある人たちは低所得の家庭の出で、もしかしたら中所得の家庭の出の人もいるかもしれませんが、必ずしも非常に裕福な家庭の出というわけではありません）という発言から、（**C**）が正解だと判断できる。You point out that a lot of people who are leaders...often actually don't even do that well early on in life.（あなたは指摘していますね、リーダーの多くは……実際、人生の早い段階ではあまりうまくいかないことすらよくあると）から（**B**）は除外できる。（**A**）の内容を述べた箇所はない。

Part 5　動画視聴問題

スマートフォンの場合はQRコードから、
パソコンの場合はURLから動画をご視聴ください。

No. 1

https://eqm.page.link/BZ95

オーストラリア英語

問題文

In Belgium, a record-breaking auction for a 2-year-old racing pigeon. Have a look at the bird. He's named New Kim [and] was sold for almost $2 million on Sunday, breaking last year's record by a significant margin. I think I saw one of those just outside in the car park. She was initially put up for auction at about $235, but bidding rose sharply. She ultimately sold to a buyer from China, where long-distance pigeon racing is becoming popular. One of the auctioneers says the new owner will likely want to breed her, because Belgium tends to produce elite birds and potential champions.

訳

ベルギーで、2歳のレース鳩をめぐる記録破りのオークションがありました。こちらがその鳥です。ニュー・キムという名前で、日曜日に200万ドル近い値で売れ、昨年打ち立てられた記録を大きく塗り替えました。こういう鳩なら私もさっきここの駐車場で1羽見たと思うんですけどね。その鳩は、最初は235ドルほどでオークションにかけられましたが、競りは高騰。最終的には中国の入札者に落札されました。中国では長距離鳩レースの人気が高まっています。競売人の1人が言うには、（落札者である）新たな所有者はおそらくその鳩を繁殖用に使いたがるだろう、というのも、ベルギーは優秀な、ひいては将来のチャンピオンとなりそうな鳩を生みだすことが多いからだ、ということです。

語句

record-breaking: 記録破りの ／ racing pigeon: レース鳩 ／ be named: 〜という名前である ➤ He's named... は She's named... の言い間違い。／ break a record: 記録を破る ／ by a significant margin: 〈競争の結果などが〉大差で ／ car park: 《英》駐車場 ／ initially: 初めは、当初は ／ put up...for auction: …をオークションにかける ／ bidding: 入札、競り ／ ultimately: 最終的に ／ long-distance: 長距離の ／ auctioneer: 競売人 ／ breed: 〜を繁殖させる ／ tend to do: 〜する傾向があ

る ／ elite: えり抜きの、精鋭の ／ potential: 〜になり得る

1.　正解 C

What is the main topic of this news report?

(**A**) A ban on the use of pigeons for racing

(**B**) A new way for racing pigeons to be sold internationally

(**C**) A racing pigeon that was sold for a record amount of money

---

設問訳 このニュースの主なトピックは何か。

(**A**) レースへの鳩の使用の禁止

(**B**) レース鳩を国際的に販売する新たな方法

(**C**) 記録的な高値で売られたレース鳩

解説 a record-breaking auction for a 2-year-old racing pigeon（2歳のレース鳩をめぐる記録破りのオークションがありました）から breaking last year's record by a significant margin（昨年打ち立てられた記録を大きく塗り替えました）までを聞いて、「レース鳩が高値で取引された」ことがわかれば、（**C**）にあたりをつけられる。ニュースでは高値が付いた経緯や落札者について述べられているが、（**A**）の「レースへの鳩の使用の禁止」や（**B**）の「販売方法」には触れられていない。正解は（**C**）。

2.　正解 A

According to the news report, what is happening in China?

(**A**) More people are becoming interested in pigeon racing.

(**B**) Pigeons are being raised for buyers in Belgium.

(**C**) Raising pigeons is becoming more difficult.

設問訳 このニュースによると、中国で何が起きているか。

(**A**) 鳩レースに興味を持つ人が増えている。

(**B**) ベルギーの購入者のために鳩が飼育されている。

(**C**) 鳩を飼育することがさらに難しくなってきている。

解説 She ultimately sold to a buyer from China（最終的には中国の入札者に落札されました）に続いて、where long-distance pigeon racing is becoming popular（中国では長距離鳩レースの人気が高まっています）と説明されていることから、中国で起きているのは

（**A**）だとわかる。Belgium tends to produce elite birds and potential champions（ベルギーは優秀な、ひいては将来のチャンピオンとなりそうな鳩を生みだすことが多い）と述べられているが、「中国でベルギー向けの鳩が飼育されている」わけではないから（**B**）はおかしい。「鳩の飼育の難しさ」の話も出ていないので、（**C**）も不適。

No.2

https://eqm.page.link/Ex7F

南アフリカ英語

問題文

So, researchers in the Netherlands have completed the first tests of a model airplane which could someday carry passengers in its wings. The Flying-V has the cabin, cargo hold and fuel tanks in the wings to make the plane more aerodynamic. Experts hope that design will cut fuel costs by 20 percent compared to today's airliners. The Delft University of Technology is working with Dutch k... airline KLM to make the idea a reality, with more tests planned.

訳

さて、オランダの研究者たちが、ある飛行機の試作機の初試験飛行を終えましたが、その飛行機はいつか乗客を翼の中に乗せて飛行するかもしれません。この「フライングV」は、客室、貨物室、燃料タンクを翼の中に配置して、機体をより空気抵抗を軽減する形状にしています。専門家らは、その設計によって今日の大型旅客機と比べて燃料費が20％削減されることを期待しています。デルフト工科大学がオランダの航空会社KLMと共同でこのアイデアを実現させようとしており、さらなる試験飛行が計画されています。

語句

the Netherlands: オランダ／complete: 〜を完了する、終える／model: ひな形の、試作品の／wing: 翼／
the Flying-V: フライングV　▶フライングVと言えば、ふつうはV字形のエレキギターのこと。新たに開発されているこの航空機もそれと同じV字形をしている。／
cabin: 客室／cargo hold: 貨物室／fuel tank: 燃料タンク／aerodynamic: 〈飛行機などが〉抗力を減らす形の／compared to: 〜と比較して／airliner:（大型の）定期旅客機／Dutch: オランダの／airline: 航空会社

1. 正解 B

What is this news report mainly about?

(**A**) The effects of airplane design on public safety

(**B**) An airplane with a new type of design

(**C**) An airline's effort to attract more customers

設問訳 このニュースは主に何に関することか。

(**A**) 飛行機の設計が公共の安全性に与える影響

(**B**) 新たなタイプの設計による飛行機

(**C**) 利用客を増やすための航空会社の取り組み

解説 ニュースは So, researchers in the Netherlands have completed the first tests of a model airplane ...（さて、オランダの研究者たちが、ある飛行機の初試験飛行を終えましたが……）で始まり、その後、その飛行機の特徴について述べている。よって、正解は（**B**）。（**A**）の「公共の安全性」や（**C**）の「利用客を増やすための航空会社の取り組み」の話は出てこない。

2. 正解 C

According to the news report, what do experts hope will happen?

(**A**) An airline will agree to collaborate with researchers.

(**B**) Airlines will design cabins with more space.

(**C**) Airplane fuel costs will become lower.

設問訳 このニュースによると、専門家が期待していることは何か。

(**A**) ある航空会社が研究者たちと協力することに同意する。

(**B**) 航空会社がより広い客室を設計する。

(**C**) 飛行機の燃料費が下がる。

解説 Experts hope that design will cut fuel costs by 20 percent compared to today's airliners.（専門家らは、その設計によって今日の大型旅客機と比べて燃料費が20％削減されることを期待しています）から、（**C**）が正解と判断できる。The Delft University of Technology is working with Dutch airline KLM to make the idea a reality から、すでにオランダのKLMがデルフト工科大学と共同でアイデアを実現させようとしていることがわかるので、（**A**）は不適。（**B**）の「客室を広くする」という話は出てこない。

Reading Section リーディングセクション

Part 1 語彙問題

No.1

問題文・解答

While Hollywood movies have stumbled in China lately, some films produced by Chinese studios and production companies have **flourished**.
(**A**) accomplished　(**B**) distinguished　(**C**) flourished

訳

ハリウッド映画が最近中国でつまずいている一方で、中国のスタジオや制作会社が作った映画のいくつかは成功している。

語句

stumble: つまずく／flourish: 繁盛する／accomplish: 〜を達成する／distinguish: 〜を見分ける

正解　C

No.2

問題文・解答

The concept of **immunity** passports remains deeply contentious, and anyone banking on it for a 2021 summer vacation could be disappointed.
(**A**) efficacy　(**B**) immunity　(**C**) vitality

訳

免疫パスポートという発想は依然として激しく議論を呼んでおり、2021年の夏季休暇に向けてそれをあてにしている人はがっかりする可能性がある。

語句

concept: 発想、概念／immunity: 免疫／contentious: 議論を呼ぶ／bank on: 〜をあてにする／be disappointed: がっかりする／efficacy: 効力、効きめ／vitality: 生命力、活力

正解　B

No.3

問題文・解答

Vincent van Gogh was **serially** undervalued throughout his career.
(**A**) progressively　(**B**) serially　(**C**) severally

訳

ビンセント・バン・ゴッホは彼の画家人生を通して何度も過小評価されていた。

語句

serially: 連続的に／undervalue: 〜を過小評価する／throughout: 〜の間ずっと／progressively: 徐々に、だんだん／severally: 別々に

正解　B

No.4

問題文・解答

US car sales have **picked up** again, and Americans are back to buying vehicles at their pre-pandemic pace.
(**A**) picked up　(**B**) pulled up　(**C**) rounded up

訳

アメリカの自動車の売り上げは再び好転し、アメリカ人はパンデミック前のペースでまた車を購入するようになっている。

語句

pick up: 上向く、好転する／vehicle: 乗り物／pull up: 〈車などが〉止まる、停車する／round up: 〜をかき集める、端数を切り上げる

正解　A

Part 2 短文読解問題

No.1

問題文

The pandemic has not only upended millions of lives around the world, it's now threatening the world's oceans. Discarded disposable masks, gloves and wipes are floating into waterways and oceans. The proof is in the waste that's already washed ashore on beaches.

As many as 62,210 PPE items, including single-use masks and gloves, were collected during the annual International Coastal Cleanup event in September 2020, according to preliminary data. It's the world's largest volunteer effort, held every September, involving participants from dozens of countries who remove and log a sample volume of plastics and marine waste from the ocean and waterways.

In 2020, 76 countries participated in the cleanup and collected at least 1.6 million pounds of trash, including tens of thousands of PPE products. It was the first time in the 35-year history of the event that PPE was added as a data category, along with cigarette butts, food wrappers, plastic straws and bottles, said Dr. George Leonard, chief scientist with Ocean Conservancy, a nonprofit working to protect oceans and advance marine conservation. "We absolutely believe that PPE waste is a significant threat to oceans and marine life," said Leonard.

訳

（新型コロナウイルスによる）パンデミックは世界中の非常に多くの人々の生活に大打撃を与えているだけでなく、今、それは世界の海洋をも脅かしています。廃棄された使い捨てのマスクや手袋、ウェットティッシュなどが河川や海に流れ込んでいるのです。それは、これまでに海辺に打ち上げられたごみを見れば明らかです。

2020年9月に実施された毎年恒例の「国際海岸クリーンアップ」イベントの間に、使い捨てのマスクや手袋など6万2210個ものPPE（個人用保護具）が回収されたことが、暫定的データで示されました。世界最大のボランティア活動であるこの催しは毎年9月に実施され、多数

の国の参加者が試料として使う分のプラスチック製品や海洋ごみを海や河川から除去し、記録します。

2020年には76カ国がこの清掃活動に参加し、少なくとも160万ポンド（約726トン）のごみを回収しました。その中には数万個のPPE製品も含まれていました。PPEが、たばこの吸い殻、食品パッケージ、プラスチック製ストロー、ペットボトルなどと並ぶデータ項目として加えられたのは、この催しの35年の歴史の中で今回が初めてであると、海を守り、海洋保全を推進する取り組みを行う非営利団体「オーシャン・コンサーバンシー」の主任研究員ジョージ・レナード博士は述べました。「われわれは、PPEのごみが海や海洋生物にとって深刻な脅威であることを確信しています」とレナード氏は語りました。

語句

pandemic: 疫病の世界的流行、パンデミック／upend: ～に大打撃を与える／threaten: ～を脅かす／discard: ～を捨てる、廃棄する／disposable: 使い捨ての／glove: 手袋／wipe:（手などをきれいにするための湿らせた）拭き取り用の布・紙・ペーパータオル、ウェットティッシュ／waterway: 河川、水路／proof: 証拠、証し／be washed ashore:〈漂流物などが〉海岸に打ち上げられる／as many as:《数詞を伴って》～もの数の／PPE: = personal protective equipment 個人用保護具／single-use: 使い捨ての／collect: ～を収集する、回収する／annual: 年1回の、例年の／International Coastal Cleanup: 国際海岸クリーンアップ ▶米NGO団体「オーシャン・コンサーバンシー」の呼びかけにより1986年に始まった、海岸ごみの調査活動。／cleanup: 清掃、掃除／preliminary: 暫定的な、仮の／volunteer effort: ボランティア活動／participant: 参加者／remove A from B: AをBから除去する／log: ～を（正式に）記録する／sample volume: 試料容量、サンプル量／marine: 海の、海洋の／pound: ポンド ▶1ポンドは約454グラム。／trash: ごみ／add A as B: AをBとして加える／cigarette butt: たばこの吸い殻／food wrapper: 食品パッケージ／plastic bottle: ペットボトル／chief scientist: 主任研究員／nonprofit: = nonprofit organization 非営利団体／advance: ～を推進する、促進させる／conservation:（自然環境などの）保護／significant: 深刻な、重大な／threat to: ～への脅威

1. 正解 A

What is the main point of the news report?

(A) Waste resulting from the pandemic is polluting the oceans.

(B) More equipment is needed to fight the pandemic.

(C) A new swimming event had to be canceled.

設問訳 このニュースの要点は何か。

(A) パンデミックによって生じたごみが海洋を汚染している。

(B) パンデミックと闘うために、もっと多くの用具が必要である。

(C) 新たに企画された水泳大会は中止されなければならなかった。

解説 第1段落には趣旨が述べられている可能性が最も高い。it's now threatening the world's oceans の it は直前の the pandemic を指すので、これは「パンデミックは世界の海洋をも脅かしている」という意味であるとわかる。続いて、「廃棄された使い捨てのマスクや手袋、ウェットティッシュなどが河川や海に流れ込んでいる」とあるので、正解は（A）。第2段落の1〜2行目に「6万2210個もの PPE（＝personal protective equipment 個人用保護具）のごみが回収された」という説明はあるが、「パンデミックと闘うためにもっと必要である」という話ではないので、（B）は不可。また、海で行われたイベントは水泳大会ではなく、International Coastal Cleanup event（「国際海岸クリーンアップ」イベント）である清掃活動なので、（C）も無関係とわかる。

2. 正解 C

What is reported about the September 2020 event?

(A) Some types of waste harmed volunteers.

(B) The volunteers used new methods to do their work.

(C) Volunteers from various countries participated.

設問訳 2020年9月に行われたイベントについて、何と報じられているか。

(A) ごみの種類によってはボランティアの人々に害を与えるものもあった。

(B) ボランティアの人々は新しい方法を用いて作業を行った。

(C) 様々な国のボランティアが参加した。

解説 設問のイベントとは International Coastal Cleanup event（「国際海岸クリーンアップ」イベント）のことで、第2段落で説明されている。participants を後ろから修飾している from dozens of countries に気がつけば、（C）の内容と一致することがわかる。さらに、第3段落の冒頭でも In 2020, 76 countries participated in the cleanup（2020年には76カ国がこの清掃活動に参加した）と具体的な数字を挙げて補足されているので、ヒントは多い。ニュースの最後で「PPE のごみ（PPE waste）が海や海洋生物にとって深刻な脅威（a significant threat to oceans and marine life）である」とは述べられているが、イベント参加者への害について触れられている箇所はない。よって、（A）は不適。（B）の「作業をするための新しい方法」の話も出てこない。

No.2

問題文

Two notebooks that once belonged to Charles Darwin, believed to be worth millions of pounds, have "likely been stolen" after being missing for two decades, Cambridge University Library said.

The notebooks—one of which contains Darwin's 1837 "Tree of Life" sketch—had been removed from the university's special collections strong rooms, where rare and valuable items are kept, to be photographed in September 2000, the library said in a statement.

The items were logged as photographed in November of the same year, but a routine check in January 2001 found that the small box containing the books had not been returned to its correct place.

Darwin sketched his ideas around an evolutionary tree in the summer of 1837 after returning from his round-the-world trip aboard HMS *Beagle*—decades before he published more developed ideas around the tree of life in *On the Origin of Species*.

For years, librarians at the university had assumed the books were simply lost in the vast library, which is home to more than 210 kilometers of shelving and some 10 million books, maps, and manuscripts.

"I am heartbroken that the location of these Darwin notebooks, including Darwin's iconic 'Tree of Life' drawing, is currently unknown, but we're determined to do everything possible to discover what happened," Jessica Gardner, university librarian and director of library services since 2017, said in a statement.

訳

かつてチャールズ・ダーウィンが所有し、その価値は数百万ポンドに上るとみられる2冊のノートが、20年前から紛失していることを受け、「盗まれた可能性が高い」とケンブリッジ大学図書館が発表しました。

これらのノート——そのうち1冊には、ダーウィンの1837年の「生命の樹」のスケッチが描かれています——は2000年9月、写真撮影のため、希少で価値あるものが保管されている同大学の特別コレクション金庫室から持ち出されたと、同図書館は声明で述べています。

これらのノートは同年11月に写真撮影されたと記録されていますが、2001年1月の定期点検の際に、ノートを保管した小さな箱が本来あるべき場所に戻されていなかったことが判明しました。

ダーウィンは、イギリス海軍帆船「ビーグル」での世界一周旅行から帰ってきた後、1837年の夏に、進化の系統樹に関するアイデアをスケッチしました。『種の起源』で「生命の樹」についてのさらに発展させたアイデアを発表する数十年前のことです。

何年もの間、ケンブリッジ大学の図書館員たちは、ノートは広大な図書館内で行方不明になっているだけだと考えていました。同図書館は、（全部で）210キロメートルを超える書架に約1000万の本、地図、原稿を所蔵する広さの施設です。

「悲嘆に暮れています。ダーウィンの象徴的な『生命の樹』のスケッチも描かれているこれらのノートが、今どこにあるのかわからないなんて。しかし私たちは、何が起きたのかを解明するためにできる限りのことをするつもりです」と、2017年から大学司書と図書館サービス長を務めるジェシカ・ガードナー氏は声明の中で述べました。

語句

be worth:（ある金額の）価値がある／pound:《英国の通貨単位》ポンド／likely: おそらく、たぶん／missing: 行方不明の／contain: 〜を含む、〜が入っている／sketch: ①描画、スケッチ ②〜をスケッチする／remove A from B: AをBから取り出す／strong room: 金庫室、貴重品室／valuable: 価値のある、貴重な／statement: 声明／log: 〜を（正式に）記録する／routine check: 定期点検／evolutionary tree: 進化の系統樹／round-the-world trip: 世界一周旅行／aboard:（乗り物に）乗って／HMS *Beagle:* イギリス海軍帆船「ビーグル」 ▶HMSはHer [His] Majesty's Shipの略。／publish: 〜を発表する、公表する／*On the Origin of Species*:『種の起源』 ▶ダーウィンの進化論についての著作。／librarian: 司書、図書館員／assume（that）: 当然〜であると思う、〜だと想定する／vast: 巨大な、非常に広い／be home to: 〜が存在する／shelving:《集合的》棚／manuscript: 原稿、草稿／be heartbroken: 悲嘆に暮れる／iconic: 象徴的な、伝説的な／drawing: スケッチ、線画／currently: 今のところ、当面／be determined to do: 〜しようと決心している／director: 館長、所長

---

1. 正解 C

What is the main point of the news report?
(A) An important library had to close down.
(B) A university lost much of its digital security.
(C) Valuable historical items have probably been stolen.

設問訳 このニュースの要点は何か。
(A) ある重要な図書館が閉鎖されなければならなかった。
(B) ある大学がデジタルセキュリティーの多くを失った。
(C) 貴重な歴史的アイテムがおそらく盗まれた。

解説 第1段落の内容を理解して、ニュースの要点を捉えよう。Two notebooks that once belonged to Charles Darwin, believed to be worth millions of pounds, have "likely been stolen"（かつてチャールズ・ダーウィンが所有し、その価値は数百万ポンドに上るとみられる2冊のノートが「盗まれた可能性が高い」）から、(C) の valuable historical items（貴重な歴史的アイテム）がダーウィンのノートを指していると考えれば、つじつまが合う。第5段落で the books were simply lost in the vast library（ノートは広大な図書館内で行方不明になっただけだ）という記述はあるが、「デジタルセキュリティーが失われた」という話は出てこないので、(B) は不適である。さらに、「図書館」に関するニュースではあるものの、「図書館の閉鎖」の話ではないため、(A) も不適。

2. 正解 B

When did Darwin do the drawing mentioned in this report?

(A) During his time aboard the *Beagle*

(B) A long time before *On the Origin of Species* was published

(C) Just before his round-the-world trip

設問訳 ダーウィンはこのニュースで述べられているスケッチをいつ描いたか。

(A) ビーグルに乗船中

(B) 『種の起源』が出版されるよりもずっと前

(C) 世界一周旅行の直前

解説 第4段落に Darwin sketched... とあり、その時期として、まず in the summer of 1837 after returning from his round-the-world trip aboard HMS *Beagle*（イギリス海軍帆船「ビーグル」での世界一周旅行から帰ってきた後、1837年の夏に）と説明されている。よって、(A) と (C) を除外できる。続く decades before he published more developed ideas around the tree of life in *On the Origin of Species*（『種の起源』で「生命の樹」についてのさらに発展させたアイデアを発表する数十年前）の decades before...（…する数十年前）を正しく理解できれば、これを A long time before... と言い換えた (B) を選べる。

No.3

問題文

Diamonds might be forever, but that doesn't mean they have to take eons to form. The gemstones are usually created after carbon is crushed and heated far beneath the Earth's surface over billions of years—which is what makes them so coveted.

Now, scientists in Australia say they have sped up the process into just a matter of minutes—and at room temperature. An international team of researchers led by the Australian National University（ANU）and RMIT University in Melbourne, Australia said they have created two types of diamonds at room temperature by using high pressure equivalent to 640 African elephants balancing on the tip of a ballet shoe.

The researchers said they were able to create two types of structurally distinct diamonds—one similar to those typically worn in jewelry, and another type called Lonsdaleite, which is found naturally at the sites of meteorite impacts and is harder than most diamonds.

Synthetic diamonds are not themselves new, and have already been created in labs since the 1940s in a bid to find cheaper, ethical and environmentally friendly stones. But researchers were excited to create such diamonds at room temperature, especially the harder Lonsdaleite diamond, which has the potential to be used to cut through "ultra-solid" materials on mining sites, they said.

訳

ダイヤモンドは永遠かもしれませんが、かと言ってダイヤモンドができるのに必ず何億年もかかるというわけではありません。ダイヤモンドの原石は通常、炭素が地表のずっと奥深くで数十億年にわたって押しつぶされ、熱せられることで生成されます——ダイヤモンドを誰もが欲するのはこのためです。

現在、オーストラリアの研究者たちは、ダイヤモンドを作る工程をわずか数分に加速させたと言っています——しかも室温でです。オーストラリア国立大学（ANU）とオーストラリアのメルボルンにあるRMIT大学（ロイヤルメルボルン工科大学）が率いる国際研究チームによると、アフリカゾウ640頭がバレエシューズのつま先に乗ってバランスを取っているのに等しい高圧を用いることで、室温で2種類のダイヤモンドを製造したということです。

研究者たちは、構造的に異なる2種類のダイヤモンドの製造に成功したと言います。1つは一般的に宝石として身に着けられているものに似たダイヤモンドで、もう1つは「ロンズデーライト」と呼ばれるタイプです。ロンズデーライトは、自然界では隕石が衝突した場所で見つかるもので、大半のダイヤモンドより硬いのが特徴です。

合成ダイヤモンド自体は目新しいものではなく、より安価で、エシカルで、環境にやさしい石を見つけるために、すでに1940年代から研究室で製造されてきました。しかし、研究者たちは、そのようなダイヤモンドを室温で製造したこと、特に、採掘現場で「超硬質」な物質を切断するのに活用できる可能性のある、より硬質なロンズデーライトダイヤモンドを製造したことに興奮している、と語りました。

語句

eons: 非常に長い年月［時間、期間］／form:〈ものが〉形を成す／gemstone: 宝石用原石／carbon: 炭素／crush:〜を押しつぶす、圧搾する／heat:〜を熱する／far beneath:〜のはるか下に／the Earth's surface: 地球の地表／coveted: 誰もが欲しがる、切望する／speed up:〜を加速させる／just a matter of minutes: わずか数分／room temperature: 室温、常温／RMIT University: = Royal Melbourne Institute of Technology ロイヤルメルボルン工科大学／high pressure: 高圧／equivalent to:〜と同等の、〜に相当する／tip:（とがった）先、先端／ballet shoe: バレエシューズ／structurally: 構造的に／distinct:（はっきり）異なる、別個の／typically: 主に、一般的に／jewelry: 宝石類、宝飾品／Lonsdaleite: ロンズデーライト ▶六方晶ダイヤモンド（hexagonal diamond）とも呼ばれる。／site: 場所、現場／meteorite impact: 隕石の衝突／synthetic: 人造の、合成の／lab: = laboratory 研究室、実験室／in a bid to do:〜することを目指して／ultra-: 極端な〜、超〜／solid: 硬い／material: 物質／mining site: 採掘現場

1. 正解 B

What is the main topic of the news report?

(**A**) The use of animals at a diamond-mining site
(**B**) A new method for making diamonds
(**C**) The discovery of a new type of diamond

設問訳 このニュースの主なトピックは何か。
(**A**) ダイヤモンドの採掘現場での動物の使用
(**B**) ダイヤモンドの新しい製造方法
(**C**) 新種のダイヤモンドの発見

解説 第2段落でNow, scientists in Australia say they have sped up the process into just a matter of minutes—and at room temperature.（現在、オーストラリアの研究者たちは、ダイヤモンドを作る工程をわずか数分に加速させたと言っています——しかも室温でです）と述べられ、synthetic diamonds（合成ダイヤモンド）の製造方法についての話が展開されている。よって、正解は(**B**)と判断できる。第3段落にtwo types of structurally distinct diamonds（構造的に異なる2種類のダイヤモンド）とあるが、「新種の発見」についての話ではないので、(**C**)は不適。第2段落のby using high pressure

equivalent to 640 African elephants balancing on the tip of a ballet shoe（アフリカゾウ640頭がバレエシューズのつま先に乗ってバランスを取っているのに等しい高圧を用いることで）という記述にゾウが登場するが、圧力の強さを表す例えで使われているだけなので、(**A**)も選べない。

2. 正解 A

What does the news report say about Lonsdaleite?

(**A**) It might be useful in mining.
(**B**) It was first discovered in the 1940s.
(**C**) It is not found in nature.

設問訳 このニュースはロンズデーライトについて何と述べているか。
(**A**) 採掘で役立つかもしれない。
(**B**) 1940年代に初めて発見された。
(**C**) 自然界では見つけられない。

解説 オーストラリアの研究者たちが製造したダイヤモンドは2種類あり、1つは「宝石として身に着けられているものに似たもの」、そしてもう1つが、Lonsdaleite（ロンズデーライト）である。最終段落の終わりにespecially the harder Lonsdaleite diamond, which has the potential to be used to cut through "ultra-solid" materials on mining sites（特に、採掘現場で「超硬質」な物質を切断するのに活用できる可能性のある、より硬質なロンズデーライトダイヤモンド）を製造したと述べられており、これと一致するのは(**A**)。「1940年代」に触れられているのは、同じく最終段落の「合成ダイヤモンド自体は、1940年代から研究室で製造されてきた」という文脈においてなので、(**B**)は不適。また、ロンズデーライトについて、第3段落でis found naturally at the sites of meteorite impacts（自然界では隕石が衝突した場所で見つかるもの）と説明されているので、(**C**)も除外できる。

Part 3　長文読解問題

No.1

問題文

As China grows richer, the waistlines of adults in the country are also expanding. More than half of Chinese adults are now considered overweight, a study conducted by the country's National Health Commission revealed on December 23, 2020. Obesity rates among Chinese adults have also more than doubled in less than two decades, from 7.1% in 2002 to 16.4% in 2020.

According to the report, 50.7% of Chinese adults are overweight, including those who are obese. In a country of 1.4 billion, that amounts to more than half a billion people—more than the entire US population.

That's a sharp increase over the past two decades. In 2002, 29.9% of Chinese adults were overweight, including obese. In 2012, that figure rose to 42%, according to previous reports released by Chinese health authorities.

"Our country's residents face a severe problem of overweight and obesity. The overweight and obesity rates among residents in both urban and rural areas and across all age groups are steadily rising," Li Bin, deputy director of the National Health Commission, said at a news conference.

It's partly due to huge changes in diet and eating habits brought on by the country's rapid economic growth. During the 1950s and 60s, famine saw an estimated 45 million Chinese people starve to death. And until 1993, people had to use government-distributed food vouchers to get staples such as rice, oil, eggs and meat.

The days of food shortages are long over. Now, Chinese people are free to eat largely as they choose, and the country's new wealth has brought ever more nutritious and calorie-rich food to the dining table.

The increase in spending power has also given rise to the problem of food waste, which Chinese President Xi Jinping has called "shocking and distressing." On December 22, 2020, a draft law on preventing food waste was submitted to the country's national legislature.

Rising overweight and obesity rates pose an additional burden to public health. Excessive weight increases the risk for serious disease and health conditions, including high blood pressure, diabetes, coronary heart disease and stroke, the US Centers for Disease Control and Prevention says.

"The overweight and obesity rates in China have been climbing fast, with a high prevalence and affecting all groups in the population. This brings enormous challenges," said Zhao Wenhua, chief nutritionist at the Chinese Center for Disease Control and Prevention.

According to the World Health Organization, at least 4 million people die each year as a result of being overweight or obese. Worldwide, obesity has been on the rise too, having nearly tripled since 1975, according to WHO. In 2016, 39% of adults globally—or more than 1.9 billion people—were overweight, including over 650 million who were obese.

In the United States, 71.6% of adults were classified as overweight, including obese, between 2015 and 2016, according to the CDC.

But China has a tougher measurement than global standards. WHO considers a body mass index(BMI)—a ratio of weight to height—over 25 to be overweight, and more than 30 obese. In China, a BMI greater than 24 is considered overweight, and over 28 is obese.

訳

中国が豊かになるにつれ、同国の成人のウエストラインも膨らみつつあります。現在、中国の成人の半数以上が過体重と見なされるということが、同国の国家衛生健康委員会によって実施された調査によって、2020年12月23日に明らかにされました。中国の成人の肥満率も20年に満たない期間で2倍以上になりました。2002年に7.1%だったのが、2020年に16.4%となったのです。

その報告書によれば、中国の成人の50.7%が、肥満である人を含め、過体重だということです。つまり人口14億人のこの国において、過体重の人の数は5億人以

上に達するということです——これは米国の全人口を上回る数です。

その数は過去20年の間に急増しました。2002年には、中国の成人の29.9%が、肥満である人を含め、過体重でした。2012年にその数は42%に増えたと、中国の保健当局が発表した過去の複数の報告書は述べています。

「わが国の国民は過体重と肥満という深刻な問題に直面しています。過体重と肥満の割合は、都市圏・地方を問わず、あらゆる年齢層で、着実に増加しつつあるのです」と、国家衛生健康委員会の副主任であるリー・ビン氏は記者会見で語りました。

この問題の一因として、同国の急速な経済成長によってもたらされた食生活と食習慣の大きな変化が挙げられます。1950年代と60年代には、飢餓によって推計4500万人の中国人が餓死しました。さらに1993年まで、中国の人々は米、油、卵、肉などの主たる食料を得るには、政府が配布する食料配給切符を使わなければなりませんでした。

食料不足の時代はとっくに終わっています。今、中国の人々はほぼ何でも好きなように食べられ、国の新たな富によってますます栄養豊かで高カロリーの食べ物が食卓にのぼるようになっています。

購買力の増進は食品廃棄問題も引き起こしており、中国の習近平国家主席はこれを「衝撃的で、悩ましい」と評しました。2020年12月22日に、食品廃棄を抑える法案が同国の国会（全国人民代表大会）に提出されています。

過体重と肥満の割合が増加すると、公衆衛生の負担がさらに増します。過体重は高血圧、糖尿病、冠動脈性心疾患、脳卒中など、深刻な病気や健康状態のリスクを増大させると、米疾病対策センターは述べています。

「中国における過体重と肥満の割合は急速に増加しており、発生率が高く、人口のあらゆる層に見られます。これは非常に大きな課題をもたらします」と、中国疾病予防管理センターの主任栄養士チョウ・ウェンホア氏は述べました。

世界保健機関（WHO）によれば、毎年少なくとも400万人が過体重や肥満が原因で亡くなっています。世界的に見ても肥満は増加傾向にあり、その数は1975年と比べて3倍近くになっていると、WHOは報告しています。2016年には世界の成人の39%——つまり19億人以上——が過体重で、そのうち肥満の人は6億5000万人を超えていました。

米国では2015年から2016年において、成人の71.6%が、肥満を含め、過体重に分類されました。これはCDCによる数字です。

しかし、中国は国際基準より厳しい測定基準を採用しています。WHOの基準では、体格指数（BMI）——身長に対する体重の比率——25以上を過体重、BMI30以上を肥満としています。中国では、BMI24以上の人が過体重、BMI28以上の人が肥満と見なされます。

語句

overweight: ①太り過ぎの、過体重の　②太り過ぎ、過体重／conduct: 〜を実施する／National Health Commission: （中国）国家衛生健康委員会／reveal（that）: 〜であることを明らかにする／obesity: 肥満／rate: 割合、比率／obese: （過度に）肥満の／amount to: 結果的に〜になる／figure: 数字／resident: 住民、在住者／face: （問題などに）直面する／severe: 厳しい、深刻な／steadily: 着実に／deputy director: 副長官、副所長／news conference: 記者会見／be due to: 〜が原因である、〜のせいである／partly: ある程度まで／diet: 日常の食事／bring on: 〜をもたらす、引き起こす／famine: 飢饉<ruby>飢饉<rt>ききん</rt></ruby>／see...do: …に〜させる、…が〜する原因となる／estimated: 推計の／starve to death: 餓死する／government-distributed: 政府が配布する／voucher: （食事などの）引換券、クーポン／staple: 必需食料品／be free to do: 好きなように〜できる／largely: ほとんど、大部分は／nutritious: 栄養のある、栄養価が高い／calorie-rich: 高カロリーの／spending power: 購買力／give rise to: 〜を生む、引き起こす／food waste: 食品廃棄物／distressing: 悩ましい、悲惨な／draft law: 法案／prevent: 〜を予防する／submit A to B: AをBに提出する／national legislature: 国民議会、国会／pose a burden to: 〜に負担を課す／public health: 公衆衛生／excessive weight: 過体重／high blood pressure: 高血圧／diabetes: 糖尿病／coronary heart disease: 冠動脈性心疾患／stroke: 脳卒中／the US Centers for Disease Control and Prevention: 米疾病対策センター／prevalence: 発生率／affect: 〈病気などが〉〜を冒す／enormous: 非常に大きな／challenge: 難題、課題／nutritionist: 栄養士、栄養学者／the Chinese Center for Disease Control and Prevention: 中国疾病予防管理センター／the World Health Organization: 世界保健機関、WHO／triple: 3倍になる／classify A as B: AをBとして分類する／tough: 厳しい、厳格な／measurement: 測定／body mass index: 体格指数、BMI　➤体重（kg）を身長（m）の2乗で割った値で肥満度を表す。／ratio of A to B: AとBの比率

1. 正解 C

What is the main topic of this news report?

(A) Changing attitudes about obesity among Chinese adults

(B) The failure of the Chinese government to reduce food waste

(C) Rising overweight and obesity rates in China

設問訳 このニュースの主なトピックは何か。

(A) 中国の成人の肥満に対する考え方の変化

(B) 中国政府の食品廃棄量削減の失敗

(C) 中国における過体重と肥満の割合の増加

解説 第1段落のMore than half of Chinese adults are now considered overweight（現在、中国の成人の半数以上が過体重と見なされる）や、第4段落のThe overweight and obesity rates among residents in both urban and rural areas and across all age groups are steadily rising（過体重と肥満の割合は、都市圏・地方を問わず、あらゆる年齢層で、着実に増加しつつあるのです）などの記述から、(C) が正解だとわかる。第7段落のThe increase in spending power has also given rise to the problem of food waste（購買力の増進は食品廃棄問題も引き起こしており）で食品廃棄問題について触れているが、「食品廃棄量削減の失敗」については出てこないので (B) は不適。「肥満に対する考え方の変化」についても言及されておらず、(A) も選べない。

2. 正解 A

What point is made by describing China in previous decades?

(A) The country's economic situation has improved.

(B) Food shortages today are dealt with more effectively.

(C) Some problems caused by poverty in the past still remain.

設問訳 過去の年代の中国について説明することで、何が主張されているか。

(A) 中国の経済状況が改善された。

(B) 今日の食料不足は、より効果的に対処されている。

(C) 過去に貧困によって引き起こされたいくつかの問題が、今も残っている。

解説 「過去の年代の中国」については、特に第5段落のDuring the 1950s and 60s,...以下で言及されている。ここで、中国ではかつて「餓死者が出て、米、油、卵、肉などの主たる食料を得るには、政府が配布する食料配給切符を使わなければならなかった」ことがわかる。そして第6段落でThe days of food shortages are long over. Now, Chinese people are free to eat largely as they choose...（食料不足の時代はとっくに終わっています。今、中国の人々はほぼ何でも好きなように食べられ……）と述べられているので、正解は (A) であり、同時に (C) は除外できる。また、「食品廃棄問題」が存在するほどの状況なのだから、(B) も不正解だとわかる。

3. 正解 C

What does the news report say about food waste in China?

(A) Its overall economic effects are not yet known.

(B) The availability of more-nutritious foods would help reduce it.

(C) The government is addressing the issue.

設問訳 このニュースでは、中国の食品廃棄物について何と言っているか。

(A) 食品廃棄物が経済全般に与える影響はまだわかっていない。

(B) より栄養価の高い食べ物が手に入るようになれば、食品廃棄物の減少に寄与するだろう。

(C) 政府はこの問題に取り組んでいる。

解説 第7段落でa draft law on preventing food waste was submitted to the country's national legislature（食品廃棄を抑える法案が同国の国会［全国人民代表大会］に提出されています）と述べられており、国がこの問題に取り組んでいることがわかるので、(C) が正解。第6段落にthe country's new wealth has brought ever more nutritious and calorie-rich food to the dining table（国の新たな富によってますます栄養豊かで高カロリーの食べ物が食卓にのぼるようになっています）とあるが、これが「食品廃棄物の減少につながっている」とは述べられていないので、(B) は不適。「食品廃棄物が経済に与える影響」については何も言われていないので、(A) も除外できる。

4. 正解 B

According to the WHO, what has happened since 1975?

(**A**) Deaths resulting from obesity have tripled in the United States.

(**B**) Obesity has become a bigger problem globally.

(**C**) Some obesity-related health problems have decreased.

設問訳 WHOによれば、1975年以来、何が起こっているか。

(**A**) アメリカでは、肥満に起因する死亡件数が3倍に増加した。

(**B**) 世界中で、肥満はより大きな問題となっている。

(**C**) 肥満に関連した健康問題の一部が減少した。

解説 第10段落の Worldwide, obesity has been on the rise too, having nearly tripled since 1975, according to WHO.（世界的に見ても肥満は増加傾向にあり、その数は1975年と比べて3倍近くになっていると、WHOは報告しています）という記述より、（**B**）が正解である。アメリカの肥満に起因する死亡件数についての記述はないので、（**A**）は不適。第8段落で Excessive weight increases the risk for serious disease and health conditions（過体重は深刻な病気や健康状態のリスクを増大させる）と述べられており、「問題が減少した」とは言われていないため（**C**）も不正解。

5. 正解 B

What is true about China's standards for determining obesity?

(**A**) They are often changed by the government.

(**B**) They are stricter than those used by the WHO.

(**C**) They have been criticized by the WHO.

設問訳 中国の肥満の判定基準に関して正しい記述はどれか。

(**A**) 基準は政府によってしばしば変更される。

(**B**) WHOの基準よりも厳しい。

(**C**) WHOによって批判されてきた。

解説 最終段落に But China has a tougher measurement than global standards.（しかし、中国は国際基準より厳しい測定基準を採用しています）という記述があ

る。そして、WHOの基準については「体格指数（BMI）25以上を過体重、BMI30以上を肥満」としていると説明されており、中国の基準では a BMI greater than 24 is considered overweight, and over 28 is obese（BMI24以上の人が過体重、BMI28以上の人が肥満と見なされます）とあるので、（**B**）が正解だと判断できる。「基準が変更されることがある」あるいは「WHOが中国の基準を批判している」という話は出てこないので、（**A**）と（**C**）は除外できる。

No.2

問題文

In an unusual collision, an airplane hit and killed a brown bear while landing at the Yakutat Airport in Alaska on November 14, 2020. Alaska Airlines Flight 66 was arriving from Cordova into Yakutat when the flight crew saw two bears crossing the runway, according to a statement by Alaska Airlines.

"The nose gear missed the bears, but the captain felt an impact on the left side after the bears passed under the plane," the airline's statement said. Pilots then spotted a bear lying several feet off the center of the runway while taxiing the Boeing 737-700 aircraft for parking.

The left engine cowl of the plane was damaged in the collision and maintenance technicians are currently working to repair the aircraft. Six passengers were on the flight at the time, but no injuries were reported.

After being informed of the incident, airport maintenance and operations crews removed the bear's carcass and brought it to a storage warehouse, according to Sam Dapcevich, a public information officer for the Alaska Department of Transportation and Public Facilities. The Alaska Department of Fish and Game was contacted to arrange for proper disposal of the bear.

"It's a rare occurrence for something like this to happen," Dapcevich told CNN. "I've been in Alaska my whole life and we've had aircraft strike birds and other animals—but this is the first instance of a bear that I've ever heard of."

The airport is partially fenced. The airport's operations crews are trained by the US Department of Agriculture to use pyrotechnics and vehicles to deter animals from coming near the runway and interfering with aircraft operations, Dapcevich said.

Crews had previously seen two bears in the area and believed them to be a female bear and a cub. On the day of the incident, crews had not seen any wildlife during snow removal operations, according to Dapcevich.

Local photographer and biologist Robert Johnson said he was surprised by the incident. He went out to capture the scene after speaking with his neighbors who were passengers on the flight. "It was an unusual occurrence, actually a first in Alaska at least," Johnson told CNN. "I've worked with bears most of my adult life up here."

In 1987, another unlikely collision occurred between wildlife and an Alaska Airlines airplane—but that aircraft hit a fish. An Alaska Airlines flight was departing from Juneau when a large fish hit the Boeing 737-200 aircraft just behind the cockpit window. An eagle that had crossed paths with the flight had been gripping the fish in its talons.

"In the process, the eagle either voluntarily released its meal or the rapid turn ripped it out of its claws," Anchorage-based Alaska Airlines pilot Captain Mac af Uhr wrote in a 2005 story about the incident, according to an Alaska Airlines blog post.

Dapcevich said it was too soon to say what steps would be taken to prevent a rare incident like the bear collision from happening in the future.

訳

珍しい衝突事故で、飛行機が1頭のヒグマに衝突し、命を奪いました。2020年11月14日、アラスカのヤクタット空港に着陸中の出来事でした。アラスカ航空のコードバ発66便がヤクタットに到着しようとするとき、2頭のクマが滑走路を横切るのを運航・客室乗務員が見たと、アラスカ航空は声明で述べました。

「前輪はクマとの衝突を回避したが、クマが機体の下に入った後に機長は機体の左側面に衝撃を感じた」と同航空会社の発表にはあります。その後、パイロットたちは、そのボーイング737-700機を駐機場へと走行させているときに、滑走路の中心から数フィート離れたところ

に1頭のクマが横たわっているのを見ました。

その衝突で機体左側のエンジンカウルが損傷を受け、現在、整備士が機体の修理を行っています。当時6人の乗客が乗っていましたが、けが人の報告はありませんでした。

事故の報告を受け、空港整備スタッフおよび空港運営スタッフがクマの死骸を撤去し倉庫に運んだと、アラスカ州運輸公共施設局の広報官であるサム・ダプチェビッチ氏は述べています。そのクマを適切に処理する手はずを整えてもらうために、アラスカ州漁業狩猟局が呼ばれました。

「めったにない事例ですね、こんなことが起こるなんて」とダプチェビッチ氏はCNNに語りました。「生まれてからずっとアラスカで暮らしていますが、そして飛行機が鳥やその他の動物と衝突することはありましたが、私の聞いた限り、クマ（との衝突）は今回が初めてです」

空港には一部フェンスが巡らされています。空港の運営スタッフは米農務省から、火工術や車両を使って、動物が滑走路に近づいて航空機運航の妨げにならないようにする訓練を受けている、とダプチェビッチ氏は言いました。

スタッフたちは以前この辺りで2頭のクマを見たことがあり、2頭はメスのクマと子グマだと考えていました。事故当日、スタッフたちは除雪作業中に野生生物を目撃しなかったと、ダプチェビッチ氏は言います。

地元の写真家で生物学者のロバート・ジョンソン氏は、今回の事故に驚いていると語りました。彼は、そのフライトの乗客だった隣人たちと話をした後、事故現場の写真を撮りに行きました。「珍しいことですね。実際、少なくともアラスカでは初めてです」とジョンソン氏はCNNに話しました。「私は大人になってからほぼずっとこの地域でクマにかかわる仕事をしてきたのですが」

1987年にも、野生生物とアラスカ航空機の意外な衝突が起きていますが、その航空機がぶつかったのは1匹の魚でした。アラスカ航空便がジュノーをたとうとした際、大きな魚がそのボーイング737-200機の操縦室の窓のすぐ後ろにぶつかったのです。その航空便と出くわしたワシがその魚をかぎ爪でつかんでいました。

アラスカ航空のブログ投稿によると、「その間に、ワシは獲物を自ら手放したか、急に向きを変えたせいで獲物がかぎ爪から落ちてしまった」と、アンカレッジを拠点とするアラスカ航空のパイロット、マック・アフ・ウア機長はその事故について2005年の報告書に記しているということです。

ダプチェビッチ氏によれば、今後クマとの衝突のよう

な珍しい事故の発生を防ぐために、いかなる措置が取られることになるかはまだわからないとのことです。

語句

collision: 衝突／brown bear: ヒグマ／land: 着陸する／Yakutat: ヤクタット ➤アラスカ州南東部の都市。／runway: 滑走路／statement: 発表、声明（書）／nose gear: （飛行機の）前輪／impact: 衝撃／spot...doing: …が〜しているのを見つける／taxi: （飛行機を）（滑走路から駐機場へ）滑走させる、タキシングさせる／parking: 駐機／engine cowl: エンジンカウル ➤飛行機のエンジンを覆うカバーのこと。／maintenance technician: 整備士／currently: 現在、目下／aircraft: 航空機、飛行機／inform A of B: AにBについて知らせる、報告する／remove: 〜を取り除く／carcass: 死骸／storage warehouse: 保管倉庫、貯蔵庫／public information officer: 広報官／the Alaska Department of Transportation and Public Facilities: アラスカ州運輸公共施設局／the Alaska Department of Fish and Game: アラスカ州漁業狩猟局／contact: 〜と連絡を取る／arrange for: 〜の手はずを整える／proper: 適切な／disposal of: 〜の処分、処理／strike: 〜にぶつかる、衝突する／instance: 例、実例／partially: 部分的に／fence: 〜に囲いをする、柵を巡らす／the US Department of Agriculture: 米農務省／pyrotechnics: 火工術／vehicle: 乗り物、車／deter...from doing: …に〜することを思いとどまらせる、やめさせる／interfere with: 〜を妨げる、阻む／cub: （クマなどの）子／wildlife: 野生生物、野生動物／snow removal operation: 除雪作業／biologist: 生物学者／capture: （カメラなどによって）〜を撮る、記録する／the scene: （事故などの）現場／neighbor: 近所の人、隣人／occurrence: 出来事、事件／unlikely: 起こりそうにない／depart from: 〜から出発する／Juneau: ジュノー ➤アラスカ州の州都。／cockpit: コックピット、操縦室／eagle: ワシ／cross paths with: 〜と出くわす／grip: 〜をつかむ、握る／talon: （猛禽類の）かぎ爪／voluntarily: 自発的に、自分の意思で／release: 〜を放す／meal: 食べ物、餌／turn: 方向転換、旋回／rip A out of B: AをBからはぎ取る／claw: （鳥獣の）かぎ爪／Anchorage: アンカレッジ ➤アラスカ州最大の都市。／-based: …を拠点とする／take steps to do: 〜するための措置を講じる／prevent...from doing: …が〜するのを防ぐ、防止する

---

1. 正解 C

What is the main topic of this news report?
(A) One airline's wildlife-conservation efforts
(B) The closure of an airport
(C) An accident at an airport

設問訳 このニュースの主なトピックは何か。
(A) ある航空会社による野生生物保護の取り組み
(B) ある空港の閉鎖
(C) ある空港で起きた事故

解説 ニュースのテーマは、冒頭のIn an unusual collision, an airplane hit and killed a brown bear（珍しい衝突事故で、飛行機が1頭のヒグマに衝突し、命を奪いました）という部分で提示されている。つまり、「ある事故が起きた」という話なので、(C)が正解である。第6段落で、野生生物が運航の妨げにならないようにする取り組みについては言及されているが、「野生生物保護」の話は出てこないので(A)は不適。また、空港の「閉鎖」の話も出てこないので、(B)も不適である。

---

2. 正解 B

Which of the following statements about the Flight 66 airplane is true?
(A) It was not carrying any passengers.
(B) It suffered some damage.
(C) Its design was criticized for being dangerous to animals.

設問訳 66便に関する以下の記述のうち、正しいものはどれか。
(A) 乗客は乗せていなかった。
(B) 多少の損傷を受けた。
(C) 動物にとって危険な設計であると批判された。

解説 66便に何が起こったかは、第3段落でThe left engine cowl of the plane was damaged in the collision（その衝突で機体左側のエンジンカウルが損傷を受けました）と説明されている。「機体が損傷した」ということなので、(B)が正解。同じく第3段落でSix passengers were on the flight at the time（当時6人の乗客が乗っていました）とあるため、(A)は不適。また、飛行機の設計についての話は一切出てこないので、(C)も不適である。

3. 正解 C

What does Sam Dapcevich say about what happened?

(A) The fence around the airport helped.

(B) The bear is lucky to have survived.

(C) Such an event is uncommon.

設問訳 サム・ダプチェビッチ氏は、起きたことについて何と言っているか。

(A) 空港を囲むフェンスが役に立った。

(B) そのクマが一命を取り留めたのは幸いだ。

(C) そのような出来事は珍しい。

解説 第5段落のIt's a rare occurrence for something like this to happen（めったにない事例ですね、こんなことが起こるなんて）という発言から、（**C**）が正解だとわかる。ニュースの冒頭でan airplane hit and killed a brown bearと述べられているので（**B**）は不適。また、第6段落にThe airport is partially fenced.（空港には一部フェンスが巡らされています）という記述はあるが、結局事故は起きてしまったのだから、（**A**）も選ぶことはできない。

4. 正解 B

What are the airport's operations crews trained to do?

(A) Contact the US Department of Agriculture if they see any bears

(B) Keep wildlife from getting in the way of airplanes

(C) Remove snow from the area without harming wildlife

設問訳 空港の運営スタッフは、どのような訓練を受けているか。

(A) クマを目撃した場合、米農務省に連絡する

(B) 野生生物が航空機の邪魔にならないようにする

(C) 野生生物を傷つけることなく、敷地内の除雪作業を行う

解説 第6段落にThe airport's operations crews are trained by the US Department of Agriculture to use pyrotechnics and vehicles to deter animals from coming near the runway and interfering with aircraft operations（空港の運営スタッフは米農務省から、火工術や車両を使って、動物が滑走路に近づいて航空機運航の妨げにならないようにする訓練を受けている）とある。このdeter animals from coming near the runway and interfering with aircraft operationsという部分を言い換えた（**B**）が正解。「クマを目撃した場合は米農務省に連絡する」という記述はないので（**A**）は不適。また、第7段落にOn the day of the incident, crews had not seen any wildlife during snow removal operations（事故当日、スタッフたちは除雪作業中に野生生物を目撃しなかった）という記述はあるが、「野生生物を傷つけることなく除雪する」とは書かれていないので、（**C**）も選べない。

5. 正解 A

What happened when an eagle flew near an Alaska Airlines plane in 1987?

(A) The bird dropped its meal on the plane.

(B) The bird suffered serious injuries.

(C) The plane had to land in the water.

設問訳 1987年に、ワシがアラスカ航空機のそばを飛んだ際、何が起こったか。

(A) ワシが獲物を飛行機の上に落とした。

(B) ワシは大けがを負った。

(C) その飛行機は水上着陸をしなければならなかった。

解説 第9段落にIn 1987, another unlikely collision occurred between wildlife and an Alaska Airlines airplane—but that aircraft hit a fish.（1987年にも、野生生物とアラスカ航空機の意外な衝突が起きていますが、その航空機がぶつかったのは1匹の魚でした）とあり、さらに第10段落で、the eagle either voluntarily released its meal or the rapid turn ripped it out of its claws（ワシは獲物を自ら手放したか、急に向きを変えたせいで獲物がかぎ爪から落ちてしまった）というコメントがある。この2つの記述から、「ワシが獲物を飛行機にぶつけてしまった」とわかるので、（**A**）が正解である。「ワシが飛行機にぶつかってけがをした」という記述はないので（**B**）は不適。また、「飛行機が水上に不時着した」という話も出てこないので、（**C**）も選べない。

General-Knowledge Section 国際教養セクション

Practice Test 1は2021年7月に公開されたもので、国際教養セクションの問題や解答・解説はその時点の事実・状況に即しています。一部変更を加えてあるものもあります。

No.1

正解 **A**

Which of the following statements about US President Biden is NOT true?

(A) He previously served as governor of Delaware.

(B) He was elected president on his third attempt.

(C) He is the oldest US president in history.

(D) He served two terms as vice president.

設問訳 米国のバイデン大統領に関する次の記述のうち、誤っているものはどれか。

(A) かつてデラウェア州知事を務めた。

(B) 3度目の大統領選挙挑戦で当選した。

(C) 米国史上最年長の大統領である。

(D) 副大統領を2期務めた。

解説 バイデン氏は1972年に29歳でデラウェア州選出上院議員に初当選した。2008年米国大統領選挙でバラク・オバマ氏が大統領に当選したのに伴い、副大統領に当選したため、2009年1月に上院議員を辞職した。デラウェア州知事を務めたことはない（**A**）。1988年、2008年の大統領選に挑んだがいずれも撤退、3度目の挑戦で当選した（**B**）。就任時の年齢は78歳で、トランプ前大統領の就任時年齢70歳を超え、米国史上最年長の大統領となった（**C**）。2009年から2017年までオバマ元大統領のもと、2期8年にわたり副大統領を務めた（**D**）。よって（**B**）（**C**）（**D**）は正しいが、（**A**）は誤り。

No.2

正解 **D**

Which of the following statements about US Vice President Harris is NOT true?

(A) She is the first female US vice president.

(B) Her father is from Jamaica and her mother was from India.

(C) She is qualified as a lawyer in the state of California.

(D) Before becoming vice president, she was a US House of Representatives member representing California.

設問訳 米国のハリス副大統領に関する次の記述のうち、誤っているものはどれか。

(A) 米国で初めての女性副大統領である。

(B) ジャマイカ出身の父とインド出身の母を持つ。

(C) カリフォルニア州の弁護士資格を持つ。

(D) 副大統領に就任する前は、カリフォルニア州選出の下院議員だった。

解説 これまでに女性では1984年に民主党フェラーロ元下院議員、2008年に共和党ペイリン元アラスカ州知事が副大統領候補となったが、どちらも副大統領にはなれなかった（**A**）。ジャマイカ出身の経済学者の父ドナルド・ハリス氏と、インド出身の乳がん研究者の母シャマラ・ゴパラン・ハリス氏の間に生まれた（**B**）。1989年に法務博士号を取得、1990年にカリフォルニア州の法曹資格を取得した（**C**）。2016年にカリフォルニア州の上院議員に選出され、以後副大統領に就任するまで務めた（**D**）。よって、（**A**）（**B**）（**C**）は正しいが、（**D**）は誤り。

No.3

正解 **B**

Which of the following statements about the United Nations Security Council (UNSC) is NOT true?

(A) The UNSC consists of a total of 15 permanent and nonpermanent members.

(B) The term for UNSC nonpermanent members is four years, and nonpermanent members can serve on the Council for consecutive terms.

(C) All United Nations members must comply with UNSC resolutions.

(D) If even one UNSC permanent member opposes a UNSC draft resolution, the resolution does not pass.

設問訳 国際連合安全保障理事会に関する次の記述のうち、誤っているものはどれか。

(A) 安保理は常任理事国、非常任理事国の合計15カ国からなる。

(B) 非常任理事国の任期は4年で、連続して任期を務めることができる。

(C) 安保理決議にはすべての国連加盟国が従わなければならない。

(D) 常任理事国のうち1カ国でも安保理決議案に反対すれば、その決議は否決される。

解説 国際連合安全保障理事会（安保理）の常任理事国は中国、フランス、ロシア、英国、米国の5カ国、非常任理事国は10カ国である。ちなみに常任理事国は国連憲章が改正されない限り恒久的にその地位にある（A）。非常任理事国は任期2年で、連続での再選は認められない（B）。国連憲章のもと、加盟国は安全保障理事会の決議を実施しなければならない（C）。理事国15カ国のうち、少なくとも9カ国が賛成すれば決議が認められるが、常任理事国5カ国のうち1カ国でも反対するとその決議は否決される。これを拒否権という（D）。よって、（A）（C）（D）は正しいが、（B）は誤り。

No.4

正解 C

Which of the following statements about the European Union（EU）is NOT true?

(A) The United Kingdom is the first state to have left the EU.

(B) Norway is not a member of the EU.

(C) All EU member states use the euro as their currency.

(D) Germany has the largest GDP of all EU member states.

設問訳 欧州連合（EU）に関する次の記述のうち、誤っているものはどれか。

(A) 英国は初のEU離脱国である。

(B) ノルウェーはEUに加盟していない。

(C) 加盟国はすべてユーロを通貨として使用する。

(D) 加盟国の中でGDPが最大の国はドイツである。

解説 1993年にEUが誕生して以来、英国は離脱した

最初の加盟国となった（A）。隣国のスウェーデンとフィンランドはEUに加盟しているが、ノルウェーは加盟していない（B）。EU加盟国の中で、2023年現在ユーロを通貨として使用しているのは加盟27カ国のうち20カ国であり、例えばスウェーデンは使用していない（C）。EU加盟国のGDP上位3国は順にドイツ、フランス、イタリアである（D）。よって、（A）（B）（D）は正しいが、（C）は誤り。

No.5

正解 C

Which of the following statements about Hong Kong is NOT true?

(A) It was a British colony for more than 150 years.

(B) In 2019, Hong Kong's average life expectancies for males and females were longer than Japan's, according to Japan's Ministry of Health, Labour and Welfare.

(C) The 2014 demonstrations against the Hong Kong government were called the Yellow Vests Movement.

(D) In June, 2020, the Chinese government passed a new security law to crack down on antigovernment activities in Hong Kong.

設問訳 香港に関する次の記述のうち、誤っているものはどれか。

(A) 150年以上にわたり、イギリスの植民地だった。

(B) 日本の厚生労働省によると、香港の2019年の平均寿命は男女共に日本を上回った。

(C) 2014年に起こった反香港政府デモは黄色いベスト運動と呼ばれた。

(D) 2020年6月、中国政府は、香港の反政府活動を取り締まるために新治安法を可決した。

解説 イギリスによる香港の植民地統治は1843年に始まり、1997年まで150年以上続いた（A）。2020年の厚生労働省の発表によると、国・地域別の平均寿命で、男女とも香港が1位で、いずれも日本人の平均寿命を上回った（B）。2014年の反香港政府デモは「雨傘革命」と呼ばれた。黄色いベスト運動は2018年から始まったフランス政府への抗議運動を指す（C）。香港での反政府活動を取り締まるため、国家分裂、政権転覆など4種類の活動を犯罪行為と定めた「香港国家安全維持法」を

可決した（**D**）。よって、（**A**）（**B**）（**D**）は正しいが、（**C**）は誤り。

No.6

正解 **B**

Which of the following statements about Jerusalem is NOT true?

(**A**) It is a sacred place in Judaism, Christianity and Islam.
(**B**) It has the second-largest population in Israel, after Tel Aviv.
(**C**) Israel has designated Jerusalem as its capital, but the United Nations does not recognize it as the capital.
(**D**) In 2017, President Trump officially recognized Jerusalem as the capital of Israel.

設問訳 エルサレムに関する次の記述のうち、誤っているものはどれか。
(**A**) ユダヤ教、キリスト教、イスラム教、それぞれの聖地である。
(**B**) エルサレムは人口では、テルアビブに次ぎイスラエル第2位である。
(**C**) イスラエルはエルサレムを首都と定めているが、国連は認めていない。
(**D**) 2017年に、トランプ大統領はエルサレムをイスラエルの首都として正式に認めた。

解説 ユダヤ教徒にとっては神殿のあった場所として、キリスト教徒にとってはキリストが処刑され、復活した場所として、イスラム教徒にとってはムハンマドが天へと昇った場所として、聖地とされている（**A**）。エルサレムの人口は約95万人（2020年）で、イスラエルの都市の中で最大である（**B**）。米国のトランプ前大統領は2017年12月にイスラエルの首都をエルサレムとして承認したが（**D**）、これに対し国連加盟国のうち128カ国（加盟国の約65％）が認定撤回を求める決議案に賛成した（**C**）。よって、（**A**）（**C**）（**D**）は正しいが、（**B**）は誤り。

No.7

正解 **B**

Which of the following statements about abbreviations used in the news is NOT true?

(**A**) The WHO is a specialized agency of the United Nations that was established to achieve health for people all over the world.
(**B**) The WTO is an international organization that sets various international rules regarding communications.
(**C**) ASEAN is a regional organization comprised of Southeast Asian countries for the purpose of co-operation in economic, political and other affairs.
(**D**) An ICBM is a ballistic missile with a very long effective range, able to fly from one continent to another.

設問訳 ニュースで使われる略語に関する次の記述のうち、誤っているものはどれか。
(**A**) WHOとは、世界中の人々の健康を実現するために設立された国連の専門機関である。
(**B**) WTOとは、通信に関する様々な国際ルールを定めている国際機関である。
(**C**) ASEANとは、東南アジア諸国から成る、経済・政治などで協力するための地域機構である。
(**D**) ICBMとは、有効射程が超長距離で大陸間を飛翔できる弾道ミサイルのことである。

解説 WHO は World Health Organization（世界保健機関）の頭文字（**A**）、ASEAN は Association of Southeast Asian Nations（東南アジア諸国連合）の頭文字（**C**）、ICBM は intercontinental ballistic missile（大陸間弾道ミサイル）の頭文字（**D**）であり、いずれも正しい。WTO は World Trade Organization（世界貿易機関）の頭文字で、国家間の貿易の規則を取り上げる国際機関のことである。よって、（**B**）は誤り。

No.8

正解 **C**

Which of the following statements about COVID-19 vaccines is NOT true?

(**A**) The first COVID-19 vaccine to be approved in the United States was of the new, mRNA type.
(**B**) No mRNA vaccines had been approved for use in humans until the COVID-19 vaccines were.

(**C**) The mRNA vaccines use inactivated pathogens.

(**D**) It is necessary to keep mRNA vaccines at extremely low temperatures to transport and store them.

設問訳 COVID-19用ワクチンに関する次の記述のうち、誤っているものはどれか。

(**A**) 米国で最も早く認可されたCOVID-19用ワクチンはmRNAワクチンという新しいタイプである。

(**B**) 今回のCOVID-19用ワクチン以前に、ヒトでの使用が認可されたmRNAワクチンはない。

(**C**) mRNAワクチンは、不活化した病原体を使っている。

(**D**) mRNAワクチンは超低温での輸送と保存が必要である。

解説 2020年12月に米国FDAが新型コロナウイルスワクチンとして最初に緊急使用を認可した米ファイザーと独ビオンテックの共同開発によるワクチンは、mRNAワクチンという新しいタイプである（**A**）。2020年12月以前は、人への使用が許可されたmRNAワクチンはなかった（**B**）。mRNAワクチンは、病原菌やウイルスを含まない（**C**）。このワクチンはメーカーによって異なるが、-90〜-60℃で輸送する必要があるなど、適切な温度管理が求められる（**D**）。よって、（**A**）（**B**）（**D**）は正しいが、（**C**）は誤り。

No.9

正解 A

Which of the following statements about the 5G mobile-communications system is NOT true?

(**A**) The "G" in "5G" stands for gigahertz.

(**B**) Mobile-communication systems have developed from 1G to 2G, 3G, 4G and 5G.

(**C**) The introduction of 5G will mean higher transmission speeds than with 4G.

(**D**) The introduction of 5G will enable more devices to be connected at the same time than with 4G.

設問訳 第5世代移動通信システム（5G mobile-communications system）に関する次の記述のうち、誤っているものはどれか。

(**A**) 5GのGは、"gigahertz"のことである。

(**B**) 移動通信システムは1Gから2G、3G、4G、5Gと進歩してきた。

(**C**) 5Gが導入されれば、通信速度は4Gより高速化するだろう。

(**D**) 5Gが導入されれば、4Gに比べてより多くの機器を同時に接続できるようになるだろう。

解説 第5世代移動通信システムは、英語ではFifth-generation mobile-communications systemと言う。5GのGはgenerationの頭文字である（**A**）。移動通信システムは、音声主体の1Gから、パケット通信に対応した2G、世界共通方式となった3G、LTE-Advancedなどの4G、次世代のネットワーク5Gへと進歩してきた（**B**）。5Gの通信速度は、4Gに比べ10倍以上になることが見込まれている（**C**）。同時接続台数も4Gに比べ10倍程度になることが見込まれている（**D**）。よって、（**B**）（**C**）（**D**）は正しいが、（**A**）は誤り。

No.10

正解 A

Which of the following is NOT mentioned in a 2020 World Bank report on global poverty?

(**A**) North Africa is the poorest region in the world.

(**B**) Half of the world's poorest people are children younger than age 15.

(**C**) Some 3.3 billion people live on less than $5.50 a day.

(**D**) It is estimated that climate change may drive 100 million people into poverty by 2030.

設問訳 次の記述のうち、世界の貧困に関する世界銀行の2020年の報告書で述べられていないものはどれか。

(**A**) 北アフリカは、世界で最も貧しい地域である。

(**B**) 世界の最貧困層の半数は、15歳未満の子どもである。

(**C**) 約33億人が1日5.50ドル未満で生活している。

(**D**) 気候変動によって2030年までに1億人が貧困に陥る可能性があると推定されている。

解説 世界銀行は隔年で発行している報告書「貧困と繁栄の共有2020」を2020年10月に発表した。この中で、

「世界で最も貧しい20カ国のうち、18カ国はサハラ砂漠以南のアフリカに属している」（**A**）、「2018年には貧困層の半数が15歳未満の子どもだった」（**B**）、「1日5.50ドル未満で暮らす人は世界人口の40%、約33億人を超える」（**C**）、「気候変動に対処しなければ、2030年までに1億人を超える人々が貧困に陥る可能性がある」（**D**）と記している。よって（**B**）（**C**）（**D**）は正しいが、（**A**）は誤り。

Practice Test 2
解答・解説

Practice Test 2 | 解答一覧

解答欄にご自身の解答を書き写しておくと、スコアを出しやすくなります。

Listening Section リスニングセクション

Part	No.	Question	解答欄	正解	測定する力
1	1	1		massive	書き取り
		2		evacuated	書き取り
	2	1		crisis	書き取り
		2		severe	書き取り
2	1	1		B	大意把握
		2		A	詳細理解
	2	1		C	大意把握
		2		A	詳細理解
	3	1		A	大意把握
		2		C	詳細理解
3	1	1		B	大意把握
		2		C	詳細理解
		3		B	詳細理解
		4		A	詳細理解
	2	1		A	大意把握
		2		B	詳細理解
		3		C	詳細理解
		4		A	詳細理解
4	1	1		A	大意把握
		2		C	詳細理解
		3		A	詳細理解
		4		B	詳細理解
	2	1		A	大意把握
		2		B	詳細理解
		3		A	詳細理解
		4		C	詳細理解
5	1	1		B	動画理解
		2		A	動画理解
	2	1		C	動画理解
		2		C	動画理解

Reading Section リーディングセクション

Part	No.	Question	解答欄	正解	測定する力
1	1	—		**B**	語彙
	2	—		**C**	語彙
	3	—		**C**	語彙
	4	—		**A**	語彙
2	1	1		**A**	大意把握
		2		**B**	詳細理解
	2	1		**B**	大意把握
		2		**C**	詳細理解
	3	1		**A**	大意把握
		2		**B**	詳細理解
3	1	1		**B**	大意把握
		2		**A**	詳細理解
		3		**B**	詳細理解
		4		**C**	詳細理解
		5		**A**	詳細理解
	2	1		**B**	大意把握
		2		**A**	詳細理解
		3		**C**	詳細理解
		4		**C**	詳細理解
		5		**B**	詳細理解

General-Knowledge Section 国際教養セクション

Question	解答欄	正解	Question	解答欄	正解
1		**D**	6		**B**
2		**A**	7		**C**
3		**A**	8		**D**
4		**B**	9		**D**
5		**C**	10		**B**

試験結果

Total Score	/120
L&R Score	/100

セクション	スコア
	あなたの得点／満点
Listening Section	/60
Reading Section	/40
General-Knowledge Section	/20

※ナレーター音声版の場合、実際のテストではCNN音声版に得点調整したスコアも算出されます。

pp.124-125の表から、リスニングセクションとリーディングセクションの「測定する力」の正解数を数え、下の欄に記入しましょう。あなたの強みと弱点がわかります。

リスニング	書き取り /4	大意把握 /7	詳細理解 /15	動画理解 /4
リーディング	語彙 /4	大意把握 /5	詳細理解 /11	

Practice Test 2 | 解答・解説

Listening Section リスニングセクション

Part 1 ディクテーション問題

No. 1　CNN音声版 ㊼↓　ナレーター音声版 ㊿↓
カナダ英語

問題文・解答

Living on the edge in central Mexico—the edge being a ①**massive** sinkhole which suddenly appeared in a family's backyard on Saturday. At first, it was 5 meters wide, but six days later, it's now at least 60 meters across and 20 meters deep. The family has been ②**evacuated**. Officials say farming and the extraction of groundwater may be to blame.

訳

メキシコ中央部で崖っぷちの暮らし——崖っぷちというのは、土曜日に、ある家族の家の裏庭に突如出現した巨大な陥没穴（の縁）のことです。当初、それは幅5メートルでしたが、6日後の今では少なくとも直径60メートル、深さ20メートルとなっています。家族は避難させられています。当局によれば、農作や地下水のくみ上げが原因かもしれないということです。

語句

live on the edge: 際どい生き方をする　▶ここでは文字通り「（穴の）edge（縁）で暮らしている」ということに掛けている。／ massive: 巨大な／ sinkhole: （路面などに）陥没で生じた穴／ appear: 現れる、出現する／ backyard: 裏庭／ be...wide: 幅…である／ be...across: 直径…である／ be...deep: 深さ…である／ evacuate: 〜を避難させる、立ち退かせる／ officials: 当局／ farming: 農作、農業／ extraction: 抜き取り、引き抜き／ groundwater: 地下水／ be to blame: 原因である

※リスニングセクションの各問題文の「アメリカ英語」などの記載は、CNN音声版の話者についてです。ナレーター音声版の話者の英語は、CNN音声版と異なる場合があります。
※ナレーター音声版の問題文は、スクリプトと多少異なる箇所があります。ご了承ください。

No. 2　CNN音声版 ㊽↓　ナレーター音声版 ㊿↓
オーストラリア英語

問題文・解答

Dire warnings about the hunger ①**crisis** in Ethiopia, and signs it's going to get worse: The United Nations and other aid groups have a new report saying more than 350,000 people in the country's Tigray Region are experiencing catastrophic levels of hunger, the most ②**severe** rating. The UN aid chief calls it a famine, and some compare the situation to Somalia's famine a decade ago.

訳

エチオピアの飢餓危機に対する緊急警告、そして事態がさらに悪化する兆しです。国連と他の支援団体は新たな報告書を出し、その中で同国ティグライ州の35万人以上が大惨事級——これは最も深刻な評価ランクですが——の飢餓を経験していると述べています。人道問題担当国連事務次長はこの事態を飢饉（ききん）と表現し、また、この状況を10年前のソマリアの飢饉になぞらえる向きもあります。

語句

dire: 〈警告や予測が〉恐ろしい、不吉な、先行きの暗い／ warning about: 〜に関する警告／ hunger: 飢餓／ crisis: 危機／ sign (that): 〜という兆候、兆し／ the United Nations: 国際連合、国連／ aid group: 支援団体／ Tigray Region: ティグライ州　▶エチオピア北部の州。2020年11月から国内紛争が続いていた。／ catastrophic: 壊滅的な、悲惨な／ severe: 深刻な、重大な／ rating: 評定、評価／ the UN aid chief: 人道問題担当国連事務次長　▶ここでは under-secretary-general for humanitarian affairs and emergency relief coordinator（人道問題担当国連事務次長兼緊急援助調整官）を指す。／ famine: 飢饉／ compare A to B: AをBに例える、AをBと同等と見なす／ decade: 10年

Part 2 ショートニュース問題

No.1
CNN音声版 問題文 50 設問 51
ナレーター音声版 問題文 70 設問 71
カナダ英語

問題文

A wild Asian elephant was found in the middle of the night rummaging through a woman's kitchen in Thailand. I still cannot believe this picture. Now, it stuck its head through a hole in the wall, which, stunningly, had already been made by another elephant that smashed through the wall last month. Wildlife experts believe the elephant was, of course, looking for food and say the house may have been targeted because it's near a national park. These types of encounters have been on the rise in Asia as wildlife habitats continue to shrink.

訳

1頭の野生のアジアゾウが、タイのある女性宅のキッチンを真夜中にごそごそ引っかき回しているところを発見されました。私はいまだにこの画像を信じられません。そのゾウは頭を壁の穴から突っ込んでいましたが、驚くべきことにその穴は、すでに先月、別のゾウが壁を突き破ってできたものでした。野生生物の専門家たちは、そのゾウは言うまでもなく食べ物を探していたと考えており、またその家が狙われたのは国立公園に近いためだろうと言っています。この種の遭遇は、野生生物の生息地が縮小し続ける中、アジアで増加しています。

語句

wild: 野生の／Asian elephant: アジアゾウ／in the middle of the night: 真夜中に／rummage through: （目的のものを探して場所を）引っかき回す／stick A through B: AをBから突き出す、突き通す／stunningly: 驚くべきことに／smash through: ～を破って突入する／wildlife: 野生生物／expert: 専門家／target: ～を標的にする、狙う／national park: 国立公園／encounter: 遭遇／be on the rise: 増加している／habitat: 生息地／shrink: 縮まる、小さくなる

1. 正解 B

What is the main point of this news report?

(A) An elephant injured a woman in a national park.

(B) An elephant attempted to get food from a person's kitchen.

(C) An elephant damaged a home as it fought with another animal.

設問訳 このニュースの要点は何か。

(A) あるゾウが国立公園内で女性にけがを負わせた。

(B) あるゾウが人の（家の）キッチンから食べ物を得ようとした。

(C) あるゾウが他の動物と戦った際に、家屋に損傷を与えた。

解説 冒頭の A wild Asian elephant was found in the middle of the night rummaging through a woman's kitchen in Thailand.（1頭の野生のアジアゾウが、タイのある女性宅のキッチンを真夜中にごそごそ引っかき回しているところを発見されました）と、途中の Wildlife experts believe the elephant was, of course, looking for food（野生生物の専門家たちは、そのゾウは言うまでもなく食べ物を探していたと考えている）の情報を合わせると、「ゾウが食べ物目当てに、夜中にある家のキッチンに侵入した」ことがわかるので、正解は (B)。(B) の attempt to do は「～しようとする」の意味。「女性の家のキッチンを荒らした」だけで「女性にけがを負わせた」わけではないから、(A) は不適。また、ゾウが他の動物と戦ったとは述べられていないので、(C) も選べない。

2. 正解 A

What does the news report say about Asia?

(A) Wild animals are losing their natural habitats.

(B) Funding for national parks has been decreasing.

(C) Illegal hunting of elephants is becoming a bigger problem.

設問訳 このニュースでアジアに関して述べられていることは何か。

(A) 野生動物がその生息地を失いつつある。

(B) 国立公園への財政支援が減少している。

(C) ゾウの密猟がより大きな問題となりつつある。

解説 ニュースの最後に、These types of encounters have been on the rise in Asia as wildlife habitats continue to shrink.（この種の遭遇は、野生生物の生息地が縮小し続ける中、アジアで増加しています）とあり、as（〜しているとき）以下で、この種の出来事の背景に言及している。「野生生物の生息地が縮小している」→「野生生物が生息地を失っている」ということなので、正解は（A）。（B）の「国立公園の財政支援」や（C）の「ゾウの密猟」には触れられていない。

No.2

CNN音声版	ナレーター音声版
問題文 52↓ 設問 53↓	問題文 72↓ 設問 73↓

オーストラリア英語

問題文

Well, hundreds of migrants tried their luck on land Wednesday to force their way from Morocco into the Spanish-controlled territory of Ceuta. Wednesday night, an even bigger group clashed with Moroccan riot police near the border. About 8,000 migrants have tried to swim from Morocco to Ceuta since Monday. This boy used plastic bottles to stay afloat but was arrested when he reached the shore. Spain says 5,600 migrants have now been sent back to Morocco.

訳

さて水曜日、何百人もの移民が陸路でモロッコからスペイン管轄領セウタへ無理やり入ろうと賭けに出ました。水曜日の夜、それ以上に大勢の集団がモロッコの機動隊と国境付近で衝突しました。月曜日以降、約8000人の移民がモロッコからセウタへと泳いで渡ろうとしました。こちらの少年は複数のペットボトルを使って浮かんでいましたが、岸辺に到達したときに逮捕されました。スペイン政府によれば、5600人の移民がすでにモロッコに送還されたということです。

語句

migrant: 移民／try one's luck: いちかばちかやってみる、運試しをする／force one's way from A into B: AからBへと無理やり進む、入る／...-controlled territory: …管轄の領土／Ceuta: セウタ ▶北アフリカ北西端に位置するスペイン領の港湾都市。モロッコとは国境を接する。／even:《比較級を強めて》さらに、一層／clash

with:〈軍隊などが〉〜と衝突する／Moroccan: モロッコ（人）の／riot police: 機動隊／border: 国境／plastic bottle: ペットボトル／stay afloat:（水面に）浮いたままでいる、沈まない／arrest: 〜を逮捕する／reach: 〜に到達する／shore: 岸、海岸／send A back to B: AをBに送り返す

1. 正解 C

What is this news report mainly about?

(A) A recent change in Spain's immigration policies
(B) The increasing danger faced by migrants who leave Morocco by sea
(C) Large numbers of migrants trying to enter a part of Spain from Morocco

設問訳 このニュースは主に何に関することか。
(A) スペインの移民政策における最近の変化
(B) 海路でモロッコから出た移民が直面する危険の高まり
(C) モロッコからスペインの領地に入ろうとする大勢の移民

解説 冒頭のhundreds of migrants tried their luck on land Wednesday to force their way from Morocco into the Spanish-controlled territory of Ceuta.（水曜日、何百人もの移民が陸路でモロッコからスペイン管轄領セウタへ無理やり入ろうと賭けに出ました）で、このニュースの要点が伝えられている。これを言い換えた（C）が正解。ニュースでは、移民と機動隊の衝突や、海から岸辺にたどりついた少年が逮捕されたことは述べられているが、海路の危険が増しているとは伝えていないので、（B）は不適。「スペインに入ろうとしている移民」についてのニュースであって、「スペインの移民政策」の話ではないので、（A）も無関係である。

2. 正解 A

What is true about the boy mentioned in the news report?

(A) He was caught by authorities.
(B) He is a legal resident of Spain.
(C) He helped other people survive in the water.

設問訳 このニュースで言及されている少年について正しいのはどれか。
(A) 当局に捕まった。

（**B**）スペインの合法居住者である。
（**C**）海上で人々を助けた。

解説 ニュースの後半で、ある少年について言及されている。This boy used plastic bottles to stay afloat but was arrested when he reached the shore.（こちらの少年は複数のペットボトルを使って浮かんでいましたが、岸辺に到達したときに逮捕されました）とあるので、was arrested を聞き取り、「逮捕された」とわかれば、正解を導き出せる。これを was caught（捕まえられた）と言い換えた（**A**）が正解となる。少年は、スペインの領土に違法に侵入しようと試みて逮捕されているので、（**B**）は誤り。（**C**）の「少年が人々を助けた」話は出てこない。

No.3　CNN音声版　問題文 54 設問 55　ナレーター音声版　問題文 74 設問 75　南アフリカ英語

問題文

The mystery of what causes one of the earth's greatest natural wonders has finally been solved after centuries of speculation. Scientists from the University of Iowa have confirmed a decades-old theory that the northern lights are produced by, quote, "powerful electromagnetic waves during geomagnetic storms." The extremely simple version of that is it's space weather. Scientists have been able to recreate the lights in a lab with plasma. They say the next step is predicting the strength of a geomagnetic storm.

訳

地球上で有数の自然の驚異の1つを何が引き起こしているかという謎が、何世紀にもわたる推論ののち、ついに解明されました。アイオワ大学の研究者たちは、数十年にわたって唱えられてきた説、すなわち北極光は、いわく「磁気嵐が生じている間の強力な電磁波」によって生じるという説を立証しました。それを極めて簡単に言えば、それは宇宙の天気だということです。研究者たちはプラズマによってラボ内でその光（北極光）を再現することに成功しました。次なるステップは磁気嵐の強さを予測することだ、と彼らは述べています。

語句

mystery: 謎／cause: 〜を引き起こす／natural wonder: 自然の驚異／solve: 〜を解く、解明する／speculation: 推論、臆測／confirm:（説などを）立証する／decades-old: 数十年前からの／theory: 理論、説／the northern lights: 北極光、北極のオーロラ／produce: 〜を生み出す／quote: 引用始め、以下引用／electromagnetic wave: 電磁波／geomagnetic storm: 磁気嵐／extremely: 極端に、極度に／version:（あるものに）対応するもの、版／space weather: 宇宙の天気／recreate: 〜を再現する／lab: ＝ laboratory 実験室、研究室／plasma: プラズマ／predict: 〜を予測する、予想する／strength: 力、強さ

---

1. 正解 **A**

What is this news report mainly about?
（**A**）The reason that the northern lights appear
（**B**）The decreasing strength of the northern lights
（**C**）The effect that the northern lights have on space weather

---

設問訳 このニュースは主に何に関することか。
（**A**）北極光が出現する理由
（**B**）北極光の強度が弱まっていること
（**C**）北極光が宇宙の天気に与える影響

解説 the northern lights とは「北極光」（北極のオーロラ）のこと。冒頭で The mystery of what causes one of the earth's greatest natural wonders has finally been solved after centuries of speculation.（地球上で有数の自然の驚異の1つを何が引き起こしているかという謎が、何世紀にもわたる推論ののち、ついに解明されました）と述べられ、続いて「アイオワ大学の研究者たちは、数十年にわたって唱えられてきた、北極光は、いわく『磁気嵐が生じている間の強力な電磁波』によって生じるという説を立証した」ことが述べられているので、what causes the northern lights（何が北極光を引き起こすのか）が主題である。よって、正解は（**A**）。（**B**）の北極光の強度や（**C**）の「北極光が宇宙の天気に与える影響」については言及されていない。

---

2. 正解 **C**

According to the news report, what have scientists been able to do in a lab?
（**A**）Use plasma to block electromagnetic waves
（**B**）Disprove a long-held theory about space

weather

(**C**) Reproduce the northern lights

設問訳 このニュースによると、研究者たちはラボ内で何を成し遂げたか。

(**A**) プラズマを利用して、電磁波を遮断する

(**B**) 宇宙の天気に関する長年の学説を反証する

(**C**) 北極光を再現する

解説 設問文と同様に、be able toを使って「科学者たち

が成し遂げたこと」を説明しているのが、Scientists have been able to recreate the lights in a lab with plasma.（研究者たちはプラズマによってラボ内でその光［北極光］を再現することに成功しました）である。recreate（～を再現する）は、reproduceと言い換えられるので、正解は（**C**）。同時に、（**A**）は「プラズマを使って北極光を再現した」という事実にそぐわないので不適。また、a long-held theory（長年の学説）は、「北極光が出現する理由についての学説」であり、反証したのではなく立証したので、（**B**）も選べない。

Part 3 ロングニュース問題

No.1　CNN音声版　問題文 57↓　設問 58↓　ナレーター音声版　問題文 77↓　設問 78↓　アメリカ英語

問題文

Taiwan's worst drought in more than half a century, making this island look more like a desert. Cracks snake across the bottom of Sun Moon Lake, Taiwan's largest body of water parched; reservoirs across the island evaporating. Recent rains put a small dent in a big problem, a problem scientists predict will only get worse.

Climate-change models paint a dire picture for Taiwan: stronger typhoons, more flooding, less-frequent rain, future droughts far more severe.

This mural gives you an idea of what Baoshan Reservoir usually looks like. This is what it looks like now. Water levels are right around 30 percent. They were less than 3 percent before monsoon season kicked off in mid-May.

Taiwan is experiencing its worst drought in decades. That's a big problem, because this reservoir is the primary water source for the Hsinchu Science Park, home to nearly 600 electronics companies, including the world's leading semiconductor manufacturer, TSMC.

"Why is this drought a problem for Taiwan's semiconductor industry?"（CNN）

"[For] every layer, we need a lot of chemical process[es]. And [for] every process, we need to clean the surface. We need to clean by [using] water—flowing, pure water."（Jefferey Chiu, electrical engineer, National Taiwan University）

Semiconductor manufacturers are searching for solutions: water recycling, purifying seawater—both years away from quenching the insatiable thirst of chip factories.

Making chips also requires huge amounts of energy. Taiwan, like the world, is trying to fight the climate crisis, cutting its carbon footprint while phasing out nuclear power. The island's semiconductor industry is investing big in green energy. Hundreds of giant wind turbines line the coast. Solar panels dot the landscape.

Just after we arrived, rolling blackouts hit the Taiwanese capital. Energy demand grows as temperatures rise. Taiwan's top energy consumer: semiconductors, vital to the global economy, powering everything from cars to computers. If Taiwan's power and water supply is in peril, the whole world could feel the pain.

訳

台湾で、ここ半世紀あまりの間で最悪の干ばつが発生しており、この島（台湾）はむしろ砂漠のように見えます。日月潭の底を蛇行するようにひび割れが生じています。台湾最大の水域（である同湖）がからからに乾いているのです。台湾全土の貯水池が蒸発しつつあります。最近降った雨が大きな問題——科学者たちが、この先悪くなる一方だと予測する問題です——を少しだけ緩和しました。

気候変動モデルは台湾にとって暗たんたる未来図を示しています。すなわち、台風はより勢力を増し、洪水は増え、雨の頻度は減り、そして今後の干ばつはこれまでよりはるかに深刻になるというのです。

　こちらの壁面は普段の宝山貯水池の様子を伝えています。こちらが現在の宝山貯水池の様子です。水量は（総貯水量の）ちょうど30％ほどです。5月半ばに雨期が始まる前は3％にも届いていませんでした。

　台湾は過去何十年かで最悪の干ばつに見舞われています。これは大問題です。なぜなら、この貯水池は新竹サイエンスパークの主要な水源であるからで、同パークは600社近くの電子機器会社の拠点となっており、世界最大手の半導体メーカー、TSMCもその1つです。

　「なぜ今回の干ばつが台湾の半導体業界にとって問題となっているのでしょうか」（CNN）

　「（半導体の）どの層でも多くの化学的処理が必要です。そしてどの工程でもその表面をきれいにする必要があります。水、流れる純水によってきれいにする必要があるのです」（ジェフリー・チュー　国立台湾大学の電気技師）

　半導体メーカー各社は解決策を模索しています。水のリサイクル、海水の浄化・淡水化——どちらも（半導体）チップ工場の尽きることのない水の需要を満たすにはまだ何年もかかります。

　チップ製造には膨大なエネルギーも必要です。台湾は、世界各国と同様、気候危機対策に取り組んでおり、原子力（発電）を段階的に廃止しながら自国のカーボンフットプリントを削減しています。台湾の半導体業界はグリーンエネルギーに多額の投資を行っています。沿岸には何百もの巨大な風力タービンが並んでいます。ソーラーパネルもそこかしこに点在しています。

　われわれ（取材班）が到着した直後、台湾の首都で輪番停電がありました。気温が上昇するにつれ、エネルギー需要は増します。台湾で最もエネルギーを消費するのは半導体（製造）です。それらは、世界経済に欠かせない存在であり、自動車からコンピューターまで、あらゆるものを動かしています。もし台湾の電力と水の供給が危機に陥れば、世界全体がその痛手を被りかねないのです。

語句

drought: 干ばつ、日照り／desert: 砂漠／crack: 裂け目、ひび、亀裂／snake across: ～を横切って蛇行する、くねくねと進む／the bottom of: ～の底／Sun Moon Lake: 日月潭　▶台湾中部にある湖。／body of water:

（湾・湖などの）水域／parched: 非常に乾いた、干からびた／reservoir: 貯水池／evaporate: 蒸発する／put a small dent in: ～を少し減少させる／predict: 予測する／climate-change model: 気候変動モデルやシミュレーション／paint a picture: 状態を表す、描く、示す／dire:〈警告や予測が〉恐ろしい、不吉な、先行きの暗い／typhoon: 台風／flooding: 洪水／less-frequent: 頻度がより少ない／far:《比較級の前に置いて》はるかに、ずっと／mural: 壁面／give A an idea of B: AにBがどのようなものかを示す／Baoshan Reservoir: 宝山貯水池／water level: 水位、水量／right around: ちょうど～くらい／monsoon season: 雨期、モンスーン期／kick off:《話》始まる／primary: 主な、主要な／water source: 水源／the Hsinchu Science Park: 新竹サイエンスパーク　▶新竹科学園区。科学技術産業を発展させることを目的として、1980年に創設された。／(be) home to: ～がある、～が拠点を置く／electronics company: 電子機器会社／leading: 先頭に立つ、最大手の／semiconductor manufacturer: 半導体メーカー／TSMC: = Taiwan Semiconductor Manufacturing Company　▶日本では「台湾積体電路製造」とも。／layer: 層、階層　▶ここでは、半導体基板の材料となるウェハー（wafer）という薄い板の層を指す。／chemical process: 化学工程／surface: 表面／flowing: 流れる／pure water: 純水／electrical engineer: 電気技師、電気技術者／National Taiwan University: 国立台湾大学／search for: ～を探し求める、模索する／solution: 解決策／purify: ～を浄化する／seawater: 海水／quench:（渇きを）癒やす、（欲求などを）満たす／insatiable thirst: 癒えることのない渇き、飽くなき欲求／chip: チップ　▶半導体の小片。／require: ～を必要とする／huge amounts of: 大量の、膨大な量の／climate crisis: 気候危機／cut: ～を削減する／carbon footprint: カーボンフットプリント、二酸化炭素排出量／phase out: ～を段階的に廃止する／nuclear power: 原子力／invest in: ～に投資する／big: 大規模に、大いに／green energy: グリーンエネルギー、環境にやさしいエネルギー／wind turbine: 風力タービン／line:（道などに）沿って並ぶ／coast: 沿岸、海岸／dot: ～に点在する／landscape: 景色、風景／rolling blackouts: 輪番停電／hit:〈災害などが〉（場所を）襲う、見舞う／the Taiwanese capital: 台湾の首都　▶台北のこと。／energy demand: エネルギー需要／(be) vital to: ～にとって不可欠である、極めて重要である／power: ～に動力を供給する、～を動かす／power supply: 電力供

給／water supply: 水の供給／be in peril: 危険にさらされている、危機的状況にある／feel pain:《比喩的に》痛手を被る、苦しむ

1. 正解 B

What is the main point of this news report?

(A) Businesses in Taiwan are being criticized for certain practices.

(B) A water shortage in Taiwan is affecting an important industry.

(C) Flooding in Taiwan is damaging facilities that produce electronics.

設問訳 このニュースの要点は何か。

(A) 台湾の企業が、ある慣習のために批判を受けている。

(B) 台湾の水不足が、ある重要な産業に影響を及ぼしている。

(C) 台湾の洪水が、電子機器を製造する施設に損害を与えている。

解説 冒頭で「台湾で、ここ半世紀あまりの間で最悪の干ばつが発生している」と述べられ、ニュース半ばあたりで、それが大問題である理由に言及されている。そしてリポーターが取材相手にWhy is this drought a problem for Taiwan's semiconductor industry?（なぜ今回の干ばつが台湾の半導体業界にとって問題となっているのでしょうか）と問いかけていることから、「台湾の半導体業界が、干ばつによって影響を受けている」ことがわかる。drought を water shortage、Taiwan's semiconductor industryを an important industry とそれぞれ言い換えた選択肢（B）が正解である。「台湾の企業の慣習」の話は出てこないし、「洪水が電子機器工場に損害を与えている」という説明もないので、（A）と（C）は選べない。

2. 正解 C

According to the news report, what is one thing that climate-change models show?

(A) Rain will occur more frequently throughout Taiwan.

(B) Rising sea levels will cause economic problems for Taiwan.

(C) Taiwan will experience stronger storms.

設問訳 このニュースによると、気候変動モデルによって示されることの1つは何か。

(A) 台湾全土でもっと頻繁に雨が降る。

(B) 海面の上昇により、台湾に経済的な問題が発生する。

(C) 台湾は、もっと強い嵐に見舞われる。

解説 気候変動モデルについては、Climate-change models paint a dire picture for Taiwan（気候変動モデルは台湾にとって暗たんたる未来図を示しています）で述べられている。a dire picture for Taiwan（台湾にとって暗たんたる未来図）の例として stronger typhoons が挙げられているので、正解は（C）。typhoons が storms に言い換えられている。stronger typhoons の後に less-frequent rain（雨の頻度は減り）と言っているので、（A）は矛盾する。（B）の「海面の上昇」についての言及はない。

3. 正解 B

What is one solution that semiconductor manufacturers are exploring?

(A) Changing the location of their factories

(B) Making seawater usable for chip production

(C) Producing new types of chips that require less energy

設問訳 半導体製造業者らが研究している1つの解決策は何か。

(A) 工場を移転すること

(B) チップの製造に海水を使えるようにすること

(C) これまでより少ないエネルギーで済む、新型チップを製造すること

解説 Semiconductor manufacturers are searching for solutions: water recycling, purifying seawater — both years away from quenching the insatiable thirst of chip factories.（半導体メーカー各社は解決策を模索しています。水のリサイクル、海水の浄化・淡水化——どちらも（半導体）チップ工場の尽きることのない水の需要を満たすにはまだ何年もかかります）とあり、「海水を浄化・淡水化して、チップの製造に用いること」を研究していることがわかるので、正解は（B）である。Making chips also requires huge amounts of energy.（チップ製造には膨大なエネルギーも必要です）とあるが、「製造に際して必要なエネルギーを減らす」研究については

言及されていないので（C）は選べない。また、「工場の移転」の話も出てこないので、（A）も不適である。

4. 正解 A

What does the news report suggest about Taiwan's semiconductor industry?

(A) Green energy is one of its priorities.

(B) It no longer requires large amounts of water.

(C) The Taiwanese people do not approve of its activities.

設問訳 このニュースが台湾の半導体産業について示唆していることは何か。

(A) グリーンエネルギーは、優先事項の1つである。

(B) 台湾の半導体産業はもはや大量の水を必要としていない。

(C) 台湾の人々は、半導体産業の活動を快く思っていない。

解説 半導体産業について「今は大量の水は必要ではない」とは言っていないので（B）は選べないし、「台湾の人々が半導体産業のことをどう思っているか」についても説明されていないので、（C）も不適。The island's semiconductor industry is investing big in green energy.（台湾の半導体業界はグリーンエネルギーに多額の投資を行っています）とあるので、正解は（A）。

問題文

A global minimum corporate-tax rate is closer to reality, with the Organization for Economic Cooperation and Development saying 130 nations, including China and India, have now endorsed the plan. CNN's Clare Sebastian explains what this could mean for some big multinational companies.

To have 130 countries agree to this is a massive step forward in a process that's taken the best part of a decade. Now, this deal aims to solve several problems.

One is that big international companies have been able to avoid taxes by shifting their headquarters or locations to lower-tax countries. This deal aims to solve that by allowing the profits of the biggest companies in the world to be taxed not only where they have a physical presence but [also] where they make their sales.

The other problem it aims to solve is that countries have been lowering their corporate-tax rates to attract these companies. The deal would avoid that by setting a global minimum corporate-tax rate of 15 percent.

Now, the deal targets primarily, though not exclusively, the big US tech giants: the likes of Facebook, Apple, Amazon, Microsoft and Google. And it was made possible by a compromise this year from the Biden administration, allowing the profits of these big companies to be taxed around the world in exchange for that global minimum tax, which is something the administration has been pushing for.

In a statement today, the US Treasury secretary, Janet Yellen, said "the race to the bottom is one step closer to coming to an end." Her French counterpart, Bruno Le Maire, called this the most important international tax agreement in a century.

訳

国際最低法人税率の実現がまた一歩近づきました。経済協力開発機構によれば、中国・インドを含む130カ国が現在その計画を支持しているのです。CNNのクレア・セバスティアン記者が、巨大多国籍企業にとってそれが何を意味しうるのかについて解説します。

130もの国にこの計画に同意してもらったというのは、ほぼ10年にわたって進められてきたプロセスにおける非常に大きな前進です。この合意はいくつかの問題を解決することを目指すものです。

（その問題の）1つは、今までは国際的な大企業が本社や拠点をより税率の低い国に移すことによって税金逃れをすることが可能であった、というものです。今回の合意は、世界各国の最大規模の企業の収益に対する課税を、その企業が物理的に拠点を置いている場所だけでなく、彼らが販売を行っている場所でも行えるようにすることで、その問題を解決しようというものです。

合意によって解決を目指すもう1つの問題は、複数の国がこうした企業を誘致するために法人税率を引き下げてきたということです。今回の合意が実現すれば、

15%の国際最低法人税率を定めることでそれが回避されます。

　合意が対象とするのは主に――とはいえ対象はこれらに限定されませんが――フェイスブック、アップル、アマゾン、マイクロソフト、グーグルといった米国のIT大手です。合意は今年、バイデン政権による譲歩により可能となりました。その譲歩とは、その国際最低税（率の導入）――これはバイデン政権が強く求めてきたものですが――と引き換えにこれらの大企業の収益に世界中で課税できるというものです。

　本日の声明で、米財務長官のジャネット・イエレン氏は、「底辺への競争は一歩終わりへと近づいた」と述べました。フランスのブリュノ・ルメール経済・財務相は、これをこの1世紀で最も重要な国際税協定だと言いました。

語句

global minimum corporate-tax rate: 国際最低法人税率／be close to reality: 実現間近である／
the Organization for Economic Cooperation and Development: 経済協力開発機構　▶略称OECD。／nation: 国家／endorse: 〜を支持する、是認する／mean: 〜を意味する、〜ということにつながる／multinational company: 多国籍企業／have...do: …に〜してもらう／agree to: （提案などに）合意する、同意する／massive: 〈程度・規模などが〉非常に大きな／step forward: 前進、進歩／process: 過程、プロセス／the best part of: 〜の大半、ほぼ〜／decade: 10年間／deal: 協定、合意／aim to do: 〜しようと意図する、〜することを目指す／avoid tax: （合法的に）税を逃れる、節税する／shift A to B: AをBに移す、移転する／headquarters: 本部、本社／location: （企業の支店・店舗などの）拠点、事業所／lower-tax: より税率の低い／profits: 利益、収益／tax: 〜に課税する／physical presence: 物理的な存在、現実の所在／make sales: 販売を行う／lower: 〜を下げる、引き下げる／attract: 〜を引き付ける、呼び寄せる、誘致する／set: 〜を設定する、設ける、定める／target: 〜を標的にする、対象とする／primarily: 主として／exclusively: まったく〜のみ／tech giant: IT大手企業／the likes of: 〜のようなもの、〜など／compromise from: 〜による譲歩／the...administration: …政権／in exchange for: 〜と引き換えに／push for: 〜を強く要求する／statement: 声明／the US Treasury secretary: 米財務長官／race to the bottom: 底辺への競争　▶企業の誘致などを目的に国家が法人税の引き下げや労働基準の緩和などを

競い、それにより国内の労働者の賃金や、環境、福祉が最低水準に下がっていくこと。／come to an end: 終わる、終了する／counterpart: 〈立場や地位などが〉対応関係にある人　▶Her（= Janet Yellen's）French counterpartとは、フランスにおける米国の財務長官に相当する人物、すなわちブリュノ・ルメール経済・財務相のこと。／international tax agreement: 国際的な税協定／century: 100年間

---

1. 正解 A

What is this news report mainly about?

(A) A new tax agreement that has received international support

(B) A trade agreement proposed by a number of multinational companies

(C) The global reaction to a proposed tax agreement between China and India

---

設問訳 このニュースは主に何に関することか。

(A) 国際的な支持を得ている、ある新しい税協定

(B) いくつかの多国籍企業によって提案された貿易協定

(C) 中国・インド間で提案された税協定に対する世界の反応

解説 冒頭のA global minimum corporate-tax rate is closer to reality, with the Organization for Economic Cooperation and Development saying 130 nations, including China and India, have now endorsed the plan.（国際最低法人税率の実現がまた一歩近づきました。経済協力開発機構によれば、中国・インドを含む130カ国が現在その計画を支持しているのです）から、「130カ国によって支持されている、国際最低法人税率の実現」がテーマであることがわかるので、正解は（A）。「中国・インドを含む……」とはあるが「中国とインドの間の税協定」の話ではないので（C）は除外できる。「企業によって提案された貿易協定」の話は出てこないので（B）も不適である。なお、このニュースは2021年7月に放映されたもので、同年12月時点では137の国と地域が合意した。

---

2. 正解 B

According to the news report, what is true of big international companies?

(A) They have been dishonest about their profits.

(B) They have been moving their headquarters

---

abroad.

(C) They have refused to sell products in certain countries.

設問訳 このニュースによれば、巨大国際企業について正しいのはどれか。

(A) 利益を虚偽申告している。

(B) 本社を国外に移転している。

(C) 一部の国で製品を販売することを拒否している。

解説 「巨大国際企業」については、One is that big international companies have been able to avoid taxes by shifting their headquarters or locations to lower-tax countries.（［その問題の］1つは、今までは国際的な大企業が本社や拠点をより税率の低い国に移すことによって税金逃れをすることが可能であった、というものです）と述べられている。ここで「本社を税率の低い国に移す」と説明されているので、正解は（B）である。（A）の「利益の虚偽申告」や（C）の「一部の国での販売拒否」についての話は出てこない。

3. 正解 C

What is one problem that the deal described in the news report addresses?

(A) The recent decrease in the profits of certain US companies

(B) The failure of the world's biggest companies to release their tax records

(C) The fact that countries have been reducing rates of tax on corporations

---

設問訳 ニュースの中で説明されている協定が対処する問題の1つは何か。

(A) ある複数の米国企業の収益が最近減少したこと

(B) 世界最大手の企業が、納税記録を発表しなかったこと

(C) 複数の国が法人税率を引き下げてきたこと

解説 One is that big international companies have been able to avoid taxes by shifting their headquarters or locations to lower-tax countries.（［その問題の］1つは、今までは国際的な大企業が本社や拠点をより税率の低い国に移すことによって税金逃れをすることが可能であった、というものです）という説明はあるが、大手企業の「納税記録」の話は出てこないので（B）は不適。

---

the profits of the biggest companies in the world（世界各国の最大規模の企業の収益）については言及されているが、「収益に対する課税」の話であり、「収益の減少」ではないので（A）も選べない。合意によって解決を目指しているのは、countries have been lowering their corporate-tax rates to attract these companies（複数の国がこうした企業を誘致するために法人税を引き下げてきたということです）と説明されており、これを言い換えた（C）が正解である。

4. 正解 A

What does the news report say about the Biden administration?

(A) A shift in its policy was a crucial step toward realizing the deal.

(B) Some of its recent decisions have been challenged by big tech companies.

(C) It has lowered its corporate-tax rate as part of a deal with certain companies.

設問訳 このニュースは、バイデン政権について何と言っているか。

(A) 政権の政策の変更が協定実現に向けて重要な一歩となった。

(B) 最近政権が決定したことの一部に対して、大手のIT企業から異論を唱えられている。

(C) 特定の企業数社との合意の一環として、法人税を下げた。

解説 it was made possible by a compromise this year from the Biden administration（合意は今年、バイデン政権による譲歩により可能となりました）という部分に注目。「譲歩」の具体的な内容は allowing the profits of these big companies to be taxed around the world（これらの大企業の収益に世界中で課税できるというもの）であり、この譲歩は政策の変更と言い換えることができるので、（A）が正解だとわかる。「IT企業からの異論」や「特定の企業との合意」の話は出てこないので、（B）と（C）は不適。

Part 4 インタビュー問題

No.1

CNN音声版	ナレーター音声版
問題文 62 設問 63	問題文 82 設問 83

アメリカ英語(Fareed Zakaria) / **アメリカ英語**(Eric Schmidt)

問題文

The following is an interview with former Google CEO, Eric Schmidt.

Fareed Zakaria Artificial intelligence first beat a human in a chess match 24 years ago. Since then, AI has grown exponentially. It is driving cars and diagnosing diseases. It can write news articles and create artistic masterpieces. It can fight the enemy on a battlefield. In coming years, it will do nothing short of reorganizing the world as we know it. But America is at great risk of falling behind China in the race to dominate this realm.

That last part is according to the National Security Commission on Artificial Intelligence. It is a blue-ribbon panel of top thinkers and executives who have just sent their final report to Congress and the president.

The chair of the commission, former Google head Eric Schmidt, joins me now.

Welcome, Eric. Let me ask you, first, are you confident in saying that, right now, your fear is that China is actually ahead?

Eric Schmidt We came to the conclusion that the United States is today ahead but may lose our lead fairly quickly. The reason is that China has decided to focus on leadership in AI by 2030 and is doing the necessary steps to provide that leadership.

They are a significant global competitor to the West and to America. They're organized in a central-planning way. And AI tends to benefit from having large sets of data and lots and lots of money. America is not organized that way.

Our recommendations include a top-level panel that would be convened under the vice president to focus on technology competitiveness and global competitiveness.

We estimate that winning the AI battle is a $50 trillion business over 20 years or so. So the amounts of money at stake here are huge, and we're not prepared. We need to double our R&D spending in our universities. We need to make sure we have a national research network for start-ups and small technical groups [and] university faculties to build the next generation of AI. The AI winner is not yet determined. It's the next great challenge.

Zakaria How much money in dollars do you think the United States should be investing in order to compete with China?

Schmidt In the report, we suggest a doubling of basic R&D every year, which I think is probably as fast as we can absorb it. And we estimate that that number should get to about $30 billion. Thirty billion seems like a lot of money, but when we're playing with trillions of dollars of industry profits, growth and value, you can see.

Imagine the worst case, which is we don't do this and the great next companies all come out of China and that the fantastic technology companies that have been built in the United States, which comprise 20 percent of our stock-market value, end up being in another country and not under our control.

I'm worried that because of the structure of China, they're going to move quicker than we are.

訳

Googleの元CEOであるエリック・シュミット氏へのインタビューです。

ファリード・ザカリア 人工知能が初めてチェスの試合で人間に勝ったのは24年前でした。以来、AIは飛躍的な進化を遂げています。車を運転すれば病気の診断も行い、ニュース記事を書くことも芸術的傑作を生み出すこともできます。戦場で敵と戦うことも可能です。AIは今後、われわれ人類が今知るこの世界をまさに再編成することでしょう。ところがこの領域の優位を巡る競争で、アメリカは中国に後れを取るリスクが非常に高くなっています。

この最後の部分は、人工知能国家安全保障委員会によるものです。これは一流の有識者や経営者など、えりすぐりのメンバーから成る委員会で、連邦議会と大統領に最終報告書を提出したばかりです。

この委員会の議長を務める、元グーグルのトップのエリック・シュミットさんにお話を伺います。

ようこそ、エリック。まず教えてください、確信をもって言えますか、あなたの懸念は中国が今現在、実際に先頭を行っていることだと。

エリック・シュミット われわれが達した結論は、今は米国が先頭に立っているが、かなり早い段階でそのリードを失うかもしれないというものです。なぜなら中国は2030年までにAI分野で主導権を手にすることに注力すると決断しており、その主導権を可能にするために必要な策を講じているからです。

彼らは西側諸国とアメリカにとってかなり手ごわい世界的競合相手です。彼らは中央計画的なやり方で組織化されています。そして、AIは、膨大な量のデータと巨額の金がある環境で恩恵を受ける傾向にあります。アメリカはそういう構造ではありません。

われわれが出した提案には、副大統領の下に招集される、技術的な競争力と世界で闘うための競争力に注力するトップレベルの委員会というものも含まれています。

われわれの概算では、このAI競争に勝つには、およそ20年で50兆ドルを要するでしょう。ですので、ここで必要となる金額は膨大なものであり、われわれにはその準備ができていません。大学における研究開発費を2倍にする必要があります。次世代のAIを構築するために、新興企業や小規模の技術者集団、大学の学部などのための全国的な研究ネットワークを確実に用意する必要があります。AI競争の勝者はまだ決まったわけではありません。これは次なる大きな難題なのです。

ザカリア 中国と張り合うためには、米国は具体的にどれだけの資金を投入すべきだと思いますか。

シュミット 報告書でわれわれが提案したのは、基本的な研究開発（費）を毎年2倍にすることです。これ（毎年2倍というペース）はおそらくわれわれが消化できる最大値だと思います。その金額は約300億ドルになると概算しています。300億というとものすごい金額のように思えますが、われわれが相手にしているのは数兆ドル規模の業界の利益、成長、価値であることを考えれば、お

わかりいただけるでしょう。

最悪のケースを想像してみてください。つまり、これをやらないケースです。その場合、次なる巨大企業はすべて中国から出てきて、米国で築かれてきた非常に優秀なIT企業——これらはわが国の株式時価総額の20%を占めているわけですが——がよその国に移転してしまい、われわれの手が及ばないものになってしまうのです。

中国という国の構造のために、彼らがわれわれより迅速に動いていくことを懸念しています。

語句

artificial intelligence: 人工知能、AI／beat: ～を打ち負かす／exponentially: 指数関数的に、爆発的に／diagnose: ～を診断する／disease: 疾患、病気／artistic: 芸術の、美術の／masterpiece: 傑作／battlefield: 戦場／in coming years: 今後、今後数年のうちに／nothing short of: まさに～にほかならない／reorganize: ～を再編成する、改造する／be at risk of: ～の危険にさらされている／fall behind: ～に後れを取る／dominate:（ある分野で）優位を占める／realm: 領域／the National Security Commission on Artificial Intelligence: 人工知能国家安全保障委員会／blue-ribbon: 最優秀の、精選された、卓越した（メンバーで構成される）／panel: 委員会、助言者の一団／thinker: 思索家、思想家／executive: 重役、幹部／final report: 最終報告書／Congress:（米国の）連邦議会／chair: 委員長／former: 前～、元～／head:（組織の）長／be confident in doing: 自信をもって～する／be ahead: 先を行っている、上回っている／come to the conclusion that: ～であるという結論に至る／lose one's lead: リードを失う／fairly: かなり／focus on: ～に重点的に取り組む／leadership: 指導力／step: 措置、対策／provide:（好ましい結果などを）もたらす／significant: 重要な、相当の／competitor: 競争相手／the West: 西側諸国、欧米諸国／organize: ～を組織化する／central-planning: 中央計画の／tend to do: ～する傾向にある、～しがちである／benefit from: ～から利益を得る、恩恵を受ける／that way: = in that way そのような形で、そのように／recommendation: 勧告、提案／include: ～を含む／convene:（会議などを）招集する／vice president: 副大統領／competitiveness: 競争力／estimate that: ～だと見積もる、概算する／trillion: 1兆／...or so: …かそれくらい、約…／(be) at stake: 問題となっている、賭けられている／huge: 巨大な、膨大な／be prepared: 準備ができている、用意がで

きている／double: 〜を倍にする、倍加する／R&D: ＝ research and development　研究開発／spending: 支出、出費／make sure（that）: 確実に〜であるようにする／start-up: 新興企業／technical group: 技術者集団／university faculty: 大学の学部／determined: 決定した、確定した／challenge: 難題、課題／invest:（金などを）投資する／compete with: 〜と競争する、張り合う／doubling: 倍加、倍増／basic: 基本的な、基礎の／absorb: 〜を吸収する／get to: 〜に達する／billion: 10億／profit: 収益、利益／growth:（経済的）成長、（資産価値の）増大／value: 価値／the worst case: 最悪のケース／comprise: 〜構成する、占める／stock-market value: 株式時価総額、市場価値／end up being: 結局〜になる／be under someone's control: 〜の支配下・制御下にある

1.　正解 A

What is the main issue that is discussed in this interview?

(A) China could soon get ahead of the United States in the field of AI.

(B) The US government believes China has used AI to damage US industries.

(C) US companies that develop AI are increasingly relying on Chinese technology.

設問訳 このインタビューで話されている主な問題は何か。

(A) AI分野において、中国がまもなく米国を追い抜く可能性がある。

(B) 米国政府は、中国がAIを使って米国の産業に打撃を与えていると考えている。

(C) AIを開発している米国の企業は、ますます中国の技術に依存している。

解説 インタビュアーのザカリア氏が、America is at great risk of falling behind China in the race to dominate this realm.（この領域の優位を巡る競争で、アメリカは中国に後れを取るリスクが非常に高くなっています）と人工知能国家安全保障委員会の見解を紹介している。さらに、同委員会の議長を務めるシュミット氏自身もWe came to the conclusion that the United States is today ahead but may lose our lead fairly quickly.（われわれが達した結論は、今は米国が先頭に立っているが、かなり早い段階でそのリードを失うかもしれないとい

うものです）と言い、その理由として「中国は2030年までにAI分野で主導権を手にすることに注力すると決断しており、その主導権を可能にするために必要な策を講じているからです」と述べている。これらの発言が、「AI分野で、中国が米国を追い抜く可能性がある」とする内容とマッチするので、正解は（A）。AI産業における競争の話ではあるが、（B）の「中国がAIを使って米国産業に打撃を与えている」と解釈できる箇所はない。また、仮定の話として、「次世代の巨大企業がみな中国で生まれ、米国のIT企業が外国に移転する」と述べているが、「AIを開発している米国の企業は中国の技術に頼っている」という話は出てこないので、（C）も選べない。

2.　正解 C

What does the interviewer say about the future of AI?

(A) The importance of AI will vary greatly depending on the industry.

(B) Use in military applications will remain the primary purpose of AI.

(C) The further development of AI will result in major changes in society.

設問訳 インタビュアーはAIの今後について何と言っているか。

(A) AIの重要性は、各産業で大きく異なるだろう。

(B) 軍事用途での利用は、AIの第一の目的であり続けるだろう。

(C) AIのさらなる発展は、社会に大きな変化をもたらすだろう。

解説 ザカリア氏のIn coming years, it will do nothing short of reorganizing the world as we know it. という発言に注目しよう。インタビューの冒頭からArtificial Intelligence＝AIの話をしているので、Since then, AI has grown exponentially.（以来、AIは飛躍的な進化を遂げています）以降の流れから、主語のit はAIを指していることがわかる。また、nothing short of... は「まさに…にほかならない」、reorganize は「〜を再編成する」、as we know it は名詞を後ろから修飾して「われわれが知っている」という意味を表すので、ここは「AIは今後、われわれ人類が今知るこの世界をまさに再編成することでしょう」と訳せる。これをresult in major changes in society（［結果として］社会に大きな変化をもたらす）を使って言い換えた（C）が正解。冒頭で様々な分野での

AIの活用方法に触れているが、(**A**)の「AIの重要性が産業により異なる」という話はしていない。military applications（軍事用途）も冒頭でAIができることの1つとして登場するだけなので、(**B**)も不適となる

---

3. 正解 **A**

What is one thing Eric Schmidt suggests about China?

(**A**) US tech companies might move there if US spending on AI is not increased.

(**B**) Some of its officials do not believe AI is worth investing more money in.

(**C**) Its central-planning structure has resulted in billions of dollars being wasted.

設問訳 エリック・シュミット氏が中国について示唆していることの1つは何か。

(**A**) 米国がAIへの投資を増やさなければ、米国のIT企業は中国へ移転してしまうかもしれない。

(**B**) 役人の一部は、AIにこれ以上の投資価値があるとは考えていない。

(**C**) 中央計画的な構造のせいで、数十億ドルを浪費した。

解説 シュミット氏は、中国がAI産業のトップに躍り出るかもしれない理由として、The reason is that China has decided to focus on leadership in AI by 2030 and is doing the necessary steps to provide that leadership.（中国は2030年までにAI分野で主導権を手にすることに注力すると決断しており、その主導権を可能にするために必要な策を講じているからです）と述べており、またAIの開発に巨額の資金が必要であるとも言っているので、(**B**) は除外できる。また、中国について、They're organized in a central-planning way.（彼らは中央計画的なやり方で組織化されています）と述べているが、これが「waste（無駄遣い）につながる」という話はしていない。よって、(**C**) も不適。シュミット氏はthe worst case（最悪のケース）として、AIへの投資を大幅に増加させるなどの必要な策を講じなかった場合に起こりうる事態を、the fantastic technology companies that have been built in the United States...end up being in another country（米国で築かれてきた非常に優秀なIT企業がよその国に移転してしまう）と述べている。このanother countryは文脈から中国を指すと判断できるので、正解は(**A**)。

4. 正解 **B**

What does Schmidt say the United States needs to do?

(**A**) Encourage foreign start-ups to move to the United States

(**B**) Significantly increase the amount of money it spends on AI development

(**C**) Open new universities where US and Chinese researchers can work together

---

設問訳 シュミット氏は、米国は何をする必要があると言っているか。

(**A**) 外国の新興企業に拠点を米国に移すように促す

(**B**) AI開発への投資を大幅に増やす

(**C**) 米国と中国の研究者が協力して働ける新しい大学を開校する

解説 university（大学）に言及しているのは、We need to double our R&D spending in our universities.（大学における研究開発費を2倍にする必要があります）だけで、米国と中国が協力する話も出てこないので、(**C**) はそぐわない。(**A**) のstart-ups（新興企業）の話は、We need to make sure we have a national research network for start-ups and small technical groups [and] university faculties to build the next generation of AI.の発言に出てくるが、「次世代のAIを構築するために、新興企業や小規模の技術者集団、大学の学部などのための全国的な研究ネットワークを確実に用意する必要があります」という内容なので、「拠点を米国に移す」という話は無関係。シュミット氏のwe suggest a doubling of basic R&D every year（私たちが提案したのは、基本的な研究開発［費］を毎年2倍にすること）やwe estimate that that number should get to about $30 billion（その金額は約300億ドルになると概算しています）といった発言から、正解は(**B**)。

問題文

The following is an interview with author Steven Johnson about his new book.

Fareed Zakaria My next guest says people live twice as long as they did 100 years ago. So, how on earth did it happen?

This fascinating story is the subject of Steven Johnson's new book, *Extra Life: A Short History of Living Longer*.

Steven Johnson, welcome. So, what you talk about as the big achievement between the two great pandemics—the Spanish influenza and this current one—is something, again, that we don't think a lot about, which is that the life span, the average life span of a human being, has doubled. How did that happen?

Steven Johnson Global life expectancy now is about 72, and a century ago it was half that. And that was partially because, up until that point, for really the whole history of civilization, even going back to hunter-gatherers, 40 percent of children died before adulthood. Two out of five of your kids would die. That was the average.

So, in about 100 years, depending on how you measure it, we've radically changed that experience. With this project, I was trying to go back and really look at what are the, kind of, big drivers of this momentous change.

One of the most important advances was the purification of the drinking-water systems. In the middle of the 19th century in cities around the world, it was extremely dangerous to drink water—and to drink milk too; that was another big factor in all of this.

And, you know, before we really had major medical breakthroughs, just being able to create a safe supply of drinking water—that was a major advance; and other basic forms of sanitation, like just washing your hands and things like that, that people didn't really understand until we understood the germ theory of disease.

So it's...you know, in some ways, it's basic infrastructure as much as it is, you know, medicine and, you know, taking a pill or going in to see the doctor that really makes a difference.

Zakaria Explain the milk one and pasteurization, 'cause that's another extraordinary thing. I didn't realize drinking milk used to be a very dangerous thing.

Johnson Milk in the middle of the 19th century was very dangerous. You could get tuberculosis from it. We didn't have refrigeration, and so milk would spoil, particularly in big cities, where you had to bring it in from outside the metropolitan area.

And in New York City in 1850, 60 percent of all deaths were children. And a lot of that had to do with them drinking contaminated milk.

Now, this is a classic story where we think, "Well, science solved this problem, because Louis Pasteur, in 1865, invented the technique of pasteurization.

But it took 50 years for pasteurized milk to become the standard in a grocery store in the United States.

And that's because the science on its own wasn't enough. It took activists to get pasteurized milk to become the standard. It involved persuading people to drink it. It involved persuading the milk industry to manufacture it. When we see big changes in human health, it's a combination of science and activism that really makes a difference.

訳

作家のスティーブン・ジョンソン氏への彼の新著に関するインタビューです。

ファリード・ザカリア 次にお迎えするゲストによれば、人間の寿命は100年前の2倍になっています。いったい何があったのでしょうか。

この興味を引かれる話はスティーブン・ジョンソン氏の新著『エクストラ・ライフ：より長く生きることについての短い歴史書』のテーマです。

スティーブン・ジョンソンさん、ようこそ。あなたが2つの大規模なパンデミック——スペイン風邪（のパンデミック）と現在のもの（新型コロナウイルスのパンデミック）——の間に起きた大きな成果として取り上げているものは、やはり私たちがあまり考えていないことで、それは寿命——人類の平均寿命——が2倍になったというものです。どうしてこのようなことが起きたのでしょうか。

スティーブン・ジョンソン 現在、世界の平均寿命は約72歳で、100年前はその半分でした。それは部分的には、その時点に至るまで、つまり、まさに人類の文明が始まって以来ずっと、狩猟採集の時代からでさえそうですが、子どもの40%が大人になる前に死んでいたためでした。あなたが子ども5人の親だとすれば、うち2人は死んでいたのです。それが平均でした。

約100年の間に、（年数は）計算次第で変わりますが、そうした事態を根本的に変えたと言えます。この（本の執筆や同テーマのテレビ番組の）プロジェクトで私は過去にさかのぼり、この極めて重要な転換をもたらした主要な要因はどのようなものであったのかについてしっかり調べようと思ったのです。

最も重要な進歩の1つに飲料水システムの浄化がありました。19世紀半ばは世界中どこの都市でも水を飲むのは極めて危険なことでした。牛乳を飲むことも同様で、この話全体の中で重要な要因でした。

真に大きな医学的躍進を迎える前は、飲料水の安全な供給を用意できるというだけで、それは大きな進歩だったのです。その他の基本的な衛生管理もそうです。例えば単純に手を洗うなどといったことですね。人々はこうしたことを、細菌が病気を引き起こすという理論を理解するまではちゃんとわかっていませんでしたから。

つまり、ある意味では、基本的なインフラは、医学や、薬を飲んだり医者にかかったりするのと同じくらいの改善をもたらすのです。

ザカリア ミルクとパスチャライゼーション（低温殺菌）の話をお聞かせください。ミルクのことも驚くべき話ですからね。牛乳を飲むことが非常に危険なことだったとは知りませんでした。

ジョンソン 19世紀半ばの牛乳は非常に危険でした。牛乳を飲んで結核になることがあったのです。冷蔵設備がなかったので牛乳は（すぐに）腐ってしまった、とりわけ大都市ではそうでした。都市部の外から運んでこなければなりませんでしたからね。

1850年当時のニューヨーク市では、総死者の60%が子どもでした。そしてその多くが、子どもたちが汚染された牛乳を飲んでいたことと関係していました。

こういう話になると、通常、皆こう考えるでしょう。「まあ、科学がこの問題を解決したのだ、ルイ・パスツールが1865年に低温殺菌法を発明したからだ」とね。

しかし、低温殺菌された牛乳が米国の食料品店に当たり前のように並ぶようになるには50年かかったのです。

それがなぜかと言えば、科学それ自体だけでは不十分だったからです。低温殺菌された牛乳がスタンダードになるには社会運動家たちが必要でした。そのためには人々にその牛乳を飲むように説得し、牛乳業界にそれを製造するよう説得することも重要でした。人類の健康において大きな変化があるとき、本当に違いをもたらすのは、科学と社会運動の両方なのです。

語句

on earth:《疑問詞を伴って》いったい／fascinating: 非常に興味深い、興味を引く／subject: 主題、テーマ／extra: 追加の、余分な／achievement: 功績、偉業／great: 大きな、大規模な／pandemic: 疫病の世界的流行、パンデミック／Spanish influenza: スペイン風邪／current: 現在の、今の／life span: 寿命／human being: 人間／double: 倍になる／life expectancy: 平均寿命、平均余命／partially: 部分的には、一部分は／up until: ～まで／civilization: 文明／hunter-gatherer: 狩猟採集民／adulthood: 成人期／depending on: ～次第で、～によって／measure: ～を測る、計算する、評価する／radically: 根本的に／driver: 推進力、原動力／momentous: 極めて重要な／advance: 進歩、前進／purification: 浄化／extremely: 極めて、極度に／factor: 要因／major: 大きな、主要な／medical: 医学の、医療の／breakthrough:（科学・技術などの）大躍進、大発見／sanitation: 衛生、公衆衛生／germ: 細菌／theory: 理論、学説／infrastructure: インフラ／medicine: 医学／take a pill: 錠剤をのむ／see a doctor: 医者に診てもらう／make a difference:（良い）変化をもたらす／pasteurization: 低温殺菌法、パスチャライゼーション　▶牛乳などを対象に、有害な細菌類を低温滅菌すること。低温のため、風味や成分の損失を抑えられる。名称は発明者のPasteur（パスツール）に由来。／extraordinary: 並外れた、驚くべき／tuberculosis: 結核／refrigeration: 冷却、冷蔵／spoil:〈飲食物が〉腐る、傷む／metropolitan area: 都市部、都市圏／death: 死亡事例、死亡者数／contaminated: 汚染された／classic: 典型的な、よくある／Louis Pasteur: ルイ・パスツール　▶フランスの細菌学者。本文中にもある牛乳等の殺菌法を考案したのみならず、狂犬病などのワクチンも開発した。／invent: ～を発明する／pasteurized: 低温殺菌された／become a standard: 標準となる、スタンダードになる／grocery store: 食料雑貨店／on one's own: 単独で／activist: 活動家、運動家／involve:（重要な要素として）

〜を伴う／persuade...to do: 説得して…に〜させる、…を促して〜させる／manufacture: 〜を製造する／combination of A and B: AとBの組み合わせ／activism:（政治的・社会的）運動、活動

1. 正解 A

What is the main topic of this interview?

(A) Factors behind the increase in people's life spans

(B) Mistaken ideas about modern diets and life-styles

(C) The effect of pandemics on scientists' view of human health

設問訳 このインタビューの主なトピックは何か。

(A) 人々の寿命が延びたことの要因

(B) 近代的な食事や生活に関する誤解

(C) パンデミックが人間の健康に対する科学者の見方に与えた影響

解説 the big achievement between the two great pandemics（2つの大規模なパンデミックの間に起きた大きな成果）という表現は登場するが、パンデミック自体が主な話題になっているわけではないので、(C) は不適。また、「食事や生活に関する誤解」の話題も出てこないので、(B) もおかしい。冒頭の My next guest says people live twice as long as they did 100 years ago. So, how on earth did it happen?（次にお迎えするゲストによれば、人間の寿命は100年前の2倍になっています。いったい何があったのでしょうか）で「人間の寿命が2倍になったこと」という主題が提示され、以下は「なぜ寿命が延びたのか」が話題の中心になっているので、正解は(A) だとわかる。

2. 正解 B

What is one thing Steven Johnson says about the middle of the 19th century?

(A) Water often had to be added to milk.

(B) The drinking water in cities was a danger to people's health.

(C) A significant number of people had no access to water.

設問訳 19世紀の半ばに関して、スティーブン・ジョンソン氏が述べていることの1つは何か。

(A) しばしば牛乳に水を足さなければならなかった。

(B) 都市の飲料水は人々の健康に危険であった。

(C) かなりの人々が、水を手に入れることができなかった。

解説 In the middle of the 19th century in cities around the world, it was extremely dangerous to drink water（19世紀半ばは世界中どこの都市でも水を飲むのは極めて危険なことでした）という記述を、be a danger to one's health（〜の健康に危険である）という表現を使って言い換えた(B) が正解。このあとに当時の「牛乳」の話は出てくるが、「加水する」という説明はないので (A) は不適。「水を飲むのが危険」という内容であって、「水が手に入りにくい」ということは述べられていないので、(C) も選べない。

3. 正解 A

What does Johnson say about New York City in 1850?

(A) More children than adults died.

(B) Lack of access to doctors contributed to poor human health.

(C) The work of transporting milk was done mostly by children.

設問訳 1850年のニューヨーク市に関して、ジョンソン氏は何と言っているか。

(A) 成人よりも子どものほうが多く亡くなった。

(B) 医者が身近にいないことは、人々の健康状態が悪かった理由の1つだった。

(C) 牛乳の輸送は、主に子どもたちによって行われていた。

解説 And in New York City in 1850, 60 percent of all deaths were children.（1850年当時のニューヨーク市では、総死者の60%が子どもでした）とあるので、(A) が正解である。続けて a lot of that had to do with them drinking contaminated milk.（その多くが、子どもたちが汚染された牛乳を飲んでいたことと関係していました）とあるが、「子どもが牛乳の輸送をしていた」とは述べられていないので、(C) は無関係。「医者が身近にいない」話は出てこないので、(B) は選べない。

4. 正解 C

What is one thing that is shown by the example of pasteurization?

(**A**) Scientists do not always think their studies can be put to practical use.

(**B**) Activists who support science sometimes do more harm than good.

(**C**) Scientific advances are not always quickly accepted in society.

設問訳 低温殺菌を例にとって示されていることの1つは何か。

(**A**) 科学者は、自身の研究が実用化できるとは必ずしも考えてはいない。

(**B**) 科学を支持する運動家たちは利益よりも損害を多くもたらすことがある。

(**C**) 科学の進歩が、すぐに社会に受け入れられるとは限らない。

解説 It took activists to get pasteurized milk to become the standard.（低温殺菌された牛乳がスタンダードになるには社会運動家たちが必要でした）という記述は、「運動家たちのおかげで、低温殺菌牛乳が広まった」ということを意味するので、（**B**）は誤りだと判断できる。また、「科学者が、自分の研究が実用化されると思っているかどうか」については触れられていないので、（**A**）も除外できる。正解は（**C**）で、it took 50 years for pasteurized milk to become the standard in a grocery store in the United States.（低温殺菌された牛乳が米国の食料品店に当たり前のように並ぶようになるには50年かかったのです）という部分の要約になっている。

Part 5　動画視聴問題

スマートフォンの場合はリスニング・トレーナー、またはQRコードから、パソコンの場合はURLから動画をご視聴ください。

No.1

https://eqm.page.link/E1UH

カナダ英語

問題文

Thousands of healthcare and essential workers [were] honored in the streets of New York on Wednesday. The city threw a ticker-tape parade for the hometown heroes who worked tirelessly throughout the pandemic. It was led by the nurse who became the first person in the US to receive a COVID vaccine. While New York City was one of the first COVID epicenters in the US, it now reports its lowest rate of infections since tracking began.

訳

水曜日、何千人もの医療関係者やエッセンシャルワーカーがニューヨーク市街でその栄誉をたたえられました。同市は、このコロナ禍を通じてたゆみなく働いた地元の英雄たちのために紙吹雪のパレードを行いました。パレードの先頭に立ったのは、米国で新型コロナウイルスのワクチンを受けた最初の人となった看護師でした。ニューヨーク市は、米国で最初期に最も感染が広まった都市の1つでしたが、今では（感染者の）追跡を開始して以来、最も低い感染率を報告するようになっています。

語句

healthcare worker: 医療従事者／essential worker: エッセンシャルワーカー　▶市民の日常生活を維持するのに不可欠な仕事に従事する人たち。／honor: ～をたたえる／throw: （催し物を）開く／ticker tape: （歓迎・祝福のために投げる）テープ、紙吹雪／hometown: 故郷の、地元の／tirelessly: 〈努力などが〉たゆまずに、疲れを知らずに／pandemic: 疫病の世界的流行、パンデミック／receive a vaccine: ワクチン接種を受ける／COVID: = coronavirus disease 2019（COVID-19）新型コロナウイルス感染症／epicenter: 中心地、発生地／report: ～を報告する／rate of infection: 感染率／tracking: 追跡

1.　正解　**B**

What was the main purpose of the event described in this news report?

(**A**) To raise money for pandemic relief efforts

(**B**) To recognize certain groups of workers for their contribution

(**C**) To celebrate the joining of two organizations in New York City

---

設問訳 このニュースで説明されているイベントの主な目的は何だったか。

(**A**) パンデミック救援活動のために資金を調達すること

(**B**) ある労働者グループの貢献をたたえること

(**C**) ニューヨーク市にある2団体の統合を祝うこと

解説 Thousands of healthcare and essential work-ers [were] honored in the streets of New York on Wednesday. (水曜日、何千人もの医療関係者やエッセンシャルワーカーがニューヨーク市街でその栄誉をたたえられました) と The city threw a ticker-tape parade for the hometown heroes who worked tirelessly throughout the pandemic. (同市は、このコロナ禍を通じてたゆみなく働いた地元の英雄たちのために紙吹雪のパレードを行いました) から、ニューヨーク市で「医療従事者」と「エッセンシャルワーカー」をたたえるパレードが行われたことがわかる。よって、「医療従事者」と「エッセンシャルワーカー」をcertain groups of workers (ある労働者グループ) と言い換えた (**B**) が正解となる。recognize A for B は「A (人) のB (功績など) をたたえる、表彰する」という意味。資金調達や、2つの団体が統合する話については触れられていないので、(**A**) や (**C**) は不適。

2. 正解 A

What is one thing that the news report suggests about New York City?

(**A**) Its situation with regard to COVID has improved greatly.

(**B**) It was the first US city to track its COVID infec-tion routes.

(**C**) Its COVID-infection rate is the lowest among all major US cities.

設問訳 ニューヨーク市について、このニュースが示唆していることの1つは何か。

(**A**) 新型コロナウイルスに関する状況は大きく改善している。

(**B**) その (地域の) 新型コロナウイルスの感染ルートを特定した米国で初めての都市だった。

(**C**) 米国の全主要都市の中で、新型コロナウイルスの感染率が最低である。

解説 While New York City was one of the first COVID epicenters in the US, it now reports its lowest rate of infections since tracking began. (ニューヨーク市は、米国で最初期に最も感染が広まった都市の1つでしたが、今では [感染者の] 追跡を開始して以来、最も低い感染率を報告するようになっています) という文から、ニューヨーク市が「米国で最初期に最も感染が広まった都市の1つ」であることがわかる。これは「その (地域の) 新型コロナウイルスの感染ルートを特定した米国で初めての都市」とは異なるので、(**B**) は選べない。また、ニューヨーク市における過去の感染率と比較して、「今が最も低い」と言っているので、「米国の全主要都市の中で」とする (**C**) は不適となる。感染率が低くなったことの言い換えとなる「新型コロナウイルスに関する状況は大きく改善している」という記述に誤りはないので、正解は (**A**)。

No.2
https://eqm.page.link/hzPF
オーストラリア英語

問題文

Airport authorities in the Galapagos Islands made a shocking discovery in a suitcase. They found nearly 200 newborn tortoises wrapped in plastic stuffed in it. Officials say the young tortoises were in poor condition and appear to be extremely underweight, and at least 15 of them have died. A police officer has been arrested in connection to the alleged smuggling. Ecuador's environment minister is furi-ous.

訳

ガラパゴス諸島の空港当局は、あるスーツケースの中にショッキングなものを発見しました。ビニールに包まれた200匹近いカメの赤ちゃんがスーツケースにぎっしり詰め込まれているのを見つけたのです。当局によれば、幼いカメたちの健康状態は悪かったそうです。また、体重も極度に少ないようで、少なくともそのうち15匹は死んだとのことです。警察官1人が密輸とされるこの事件に関連して逮捕されています。エクアドルの環境相は激怒しています。

語句

authorities: 当局 / the Galapagos Islands: ガラパゴス諸島 ▶東太平洋にあるエクアドル領の諸島。/ shocking: 衝撃的な / discovery: 発見 / newborn: 最近生まれた、生まれたばかりの / tortoise: カメ / (be) wrapped in: 〜にくるまれている、包まれている / plastic: プラスチック、ビニール / (be) stuffed in: 〜の

中に詰め込まれている／be in poor condition: 健康状態が優れない／extremely: 極度に／underweight: 標準の体重に達しない、低体重の／police officer: 警察官／arrest: 〜を逮捕する／in connection to: 〜に関連して／alleged: 〜と申し立てられた、疑われている／smuggling: 密輸／environment minister: 環境大臣／furious: 怒り狂った、激怒した

---

1. 正解 C

What is the main point of this news report?

(A) The Ecuadoran government will pass new laws to protect tortoises.

(B) Conservation practices in the Galapagos Islands have harmed tortoises.

(C) Someone in the Galapagos Islands cruelly tried to transport tortoises.

設問訳 このニュースの要点は何か。

(A) エクアドル政府は、カメを守る新法を可決する予定である。

(B) ガラパゴス諸島の保全活動はカメに害を与えている。

(C) ガラパゴス諸島にいた誰かが残酷な方法でカメを輸送しようとした。

解説 Airport authorities in the Galapagos Islands made a shocking discovery in a suitcase. They found nearly 200 newborn tortoises wrapped in plastic stuffed in it.（ガラパゴス諸島の空港当局は、あるスーツケースの中にショッキングなものを発見しました。ビニールに包まれた200匹近いカメの赤ちゃんがスーツケースにぎっしり詰め込まれているのを見つけたのです）から、誰かが残酷なやり方でカメを輸送しようとした事件だとわかる。よって、正解は（C）。ニュースの後半では、A police officer has been arrested in connection to the alleged smuggling.（警察官1人が密輸とされるこの事件に関連して逮捕されています）と補足されている。エクアドル政府に関連する話として、Ecuador's environment minister is furious.（エクアドルの環境相は激怒しています）とあるが、（A）の「新法」は出てこない。カメの密輸事件の話なので、（B）も的外れとなる。なお、イギリス英語ではturtleが主にウミガメを表し、tortoiseはリクガメを表す。

---

2. 正解 C

What does the news report say about the tortoises?

(A) Plastic was found inside their stomachs.

(B) Some of them have not yet been located.

(C) They were not in good physical condition.

設問訳 このニュースがカメについて述べていることは何か。

(A) 胃の内部にプラスチックが発見された。

(B) 一部のカメはまだ発見されていない。

(C) 健康状態がよくなかった。

解説 Officials say...（当局によれば……）に続いて、the young tortoises were in poor condition and appear to be extremely underweight, and at least 15 of them have died.（幼いカメたちの健康状態は悪かったそうです。また、体重も極度に少ないようで、少なくともそのうち15匹は死んだとのことです）と説明されている。be in poor condition（悪い状態である）ということは、be not in good (physical) condition（［体が］よくない状態である）ということなので、正解は（C）。（A）のplasticが出てくるのは、wrapped in plastic stuffed in it（ビニールに包まれ……スーツケースにぎっしり詰め込まれて）という文脈であり、Plastic was stuffed in their stomachs.（カメの胃にプラスチックが詰め込まれていた）という話ではないので不適。また、未発見のカメの話も出てこないので、（B）も選べない。

Reading Section リーディングセクション

Part 1 語彙問題

No.1

問題文・解答

Louisiana public schools are allowed to let parents choose whether they want to **quarantine** children after exposure to Covid-19.

(**A**) forbid (**B**) quarantine (**C**) disperse

訳

ルイジアナ州の公立学校は、子どもたちが新型コロナウイルスにさらされた場合、彼らを隔離するか否かを保護者に選択させることができます。

語句

public school: 公立学校／allow...to do: …に〜させる／quarantine: (伝染病予防のために) 〜を隔離する／exposure to: 〜にさらされること／Covid-19: = coronavirus disease 2019 新型コロナウイルス感染症 ➤COVID-19とも書く。ここでは、感染症というよりは、新型コロナウイルスの意味で使われている。／forbid: 〜を禁止する／disperse: 〜を分散させる、追い散らす

正解 B

No.2

問題文・解答

Tokyo is considered one of the world's top food cities, drawing travelers from around the world who spend their days sampling **renowned** Japanese dishes, from sushi to ramen.

(**A**) auspicious (**B**) reverent (**C**) renowned

訳

東京は世界でもトップクラスの食の都の1つとされており、世界中から旅行者が訪れ、すしからラーメンまで、名高い日本食を味わう日々を過ごします。

語句

consider A B: AをBとみなす／draw: 〜をひきつける、集める／sample: 〜を試食する／renowned: 有名な／dish: 料理／auspicious: 幸先の良い、吉兆の／reverent: うやうやしい

正解 C

No.3

問題文・解答

A growing power-supply **crunch** in China is triggering blackouts for households and forcing factories to cut production.

(**A**) crush (**B**) cramp (**C**) crunch

訳

中国における電力供給不足は悪化しており、家庭での停電を引き起こし、工場では減産を強いられています。

語句

power supply: 電力供給／crunch: 不足、逼迫 (ひっぱく)／trigger: 〜を引き起こす／blackout: 停電／household: 家庭／force...to do: …に〜するよう強いる／crush: 殺到、混雑／cramp: けいれん、引きつり

正解 C

No.4

問題文・解答

The Notre Dame cathedral is **on track to** reopen to the public in 2024.

(**A**) on track to (**B**) committed to (**C**) sitting tight to

訳

ノートルダム大聖堂は、2024年の一般への再公開に向けて予定通り進んでいます。

語句

The Notre Dame cathedral: ノートルダム大聖堂 ➤ フランス・パリにあるカトリック教会の大聖堂。2019年4月に大規模な火災が発生し、損傷した。正式名称はNotre-Dame de Paris。/ be on track to do: ～する予定通り進んでいる / the public: 公衆、一般の人々 / be

committed to doing: 断固たる決意で～し遂げようとしている、かならず～をやり遂げるつもりでいる / sit tight: （何かを待って焦らずに）じっとする、好機を待つ。

正解 **A**

Part 2 短文読解問題

No.1

問題文

As the climate crisis escalates, the world is banking on carbon-free energy to achieve a future with zero greenhouse gas emissions, or a net-zero future, where we remove just as much greenhouse gas from the atmosphere as we emit.

One potential form of clean energy is green hydrogen—which can be derived from sources like water, rather than fossil fuels, and is produced with renewable energy. It can be used to power heavy industry and fuel large vehicles, like planes and ships.

Facilities to produce this cleaner form of the gas have popped up across the globe — in the United States, Western Europe, China, Australia, Chile and South Africa, among other countries. The burgeoning global green hydrogen market is projected to be worth $11 trillion by 2050, by Goldman Sachs' estimates.

But critics of green hydrogen say using solar or wind energy to produce another fuel right now is a waste of precious renewables, as the world struggles to transition away from fossil fuels.

訳

気候危機が悪化するのに伴い、世界は非炭素エネルギーを利用することで、温室効果ガス排出量ゼロの未来、すなわち「実質ゼロ」の未来を実現しようとしています。排出したのとちょうど同じ量の温室効果ガスを、大気から除去するという未来です。

クリーンエネルギー候補の1つはグリーン水素です。これは、化石燃料ではなく水などから得ることができ、かつ再生可能エネルギーによって生み出されます。グリーン水素は重工業の電源として使用したり、航空機や船と

いった大型の輸送媒体の燃料として使用したりすることができます。

こうした、よりクリーンな形態の水素を生産する施設は世界各地に生まれています。米国をはじめ西ヨーロッパ、中国、オーストラリア、チリ、南アフリカなどの国々です。急成長を遂げるこのグリーン水素の世界市場は、ゴールドマン・サックスの推計によれば、2050年までに11兆ドル規模になると予想されています。

しかしグリーン水素を批判する向きもあり、彼らは、現状では別の燃料（水素）を生産するために太陽エネルギーや風力エネルギーを使用するのは、世界が化石燃料から脱却しようと苦心している現在にあっては貴重な再生可能エネルギーの無駄遣いだと言っています。

語句

climate crisis: 気候危機 / escalate: 〈量・程度などが〉次第に増大する / bank on: ～を当てにする、～に頼る / carbon-free: 炭素を含まない、炭素を排出しない / achieve: ～を実現する / greenhouse gas emissions: 温室効果ガス排出量 / net-zero: （温室効果ガスの排出量が）実質ゼロの / remove A from B: AをBから排除する、除去する / the atmosphere: （地球の）大気 / emit: ～を排出する / potential: ～となりうる / form: 形、形態 / clean energy: クリーンエネルギー、環境にやさしいエネルギー / green hydrogen: グリーン水素 ➤ 再生可能エネルギーで作られる水素。水を電気分解して得られるが、その電力は再生可能エネルギーで生み出すため、二酸化炭素を排出せずに製造できる。/ derive A from B: AをBから得る、引き出す、作る / source: 源 / rather than: ～ではなく / fossil fuel: 化石燃料 / renewable energy: 再生可能エネルギー / power: ～に電力を供給する / heavy industry: 重工業 / fuel: ①～を（燃料として）動かす、～の原動力となる ②燃料 / vehicle: 乗り物 / facility: 施設 / pop up: （急に）現れる、出現する / across the globe: 世界中で / burgeoning: 急速に成長している / be projected to do:

～すると予想されている／be worth: ～に値する、相当する／trillion: 1兆／Goldman Sachs: ゴールドマン・サックス ▶米金融大手。／estimate: 推定、推計／critic: 批判する者／solar energy: 太陽エネルギー／a waste of: ～の無駄／precious：貴重な／renewable: ＝renewable energy source 再生可能エネルギー源／struggle to do: ～するのに苦労する、なかなか～できない／transition away from: ～から移行する

---

1. 正解 A

What is the main topic of this news report?

(A) Key facts about one type of clean energy
(B) The high cost of producing clean energy
(C) A major shift to solar and wind energy

設問訳 このニュースの主なトピックは何か。

(A) あるクリーンエネルギーの主要な事実
(B) クリーンエネルギーの製造コストの高さ
(C) 太陽エネルギーや風力エネルギーへの大きな転換

解説 このニュースの主軸は、温室効果ガス排出量ゼロを実現するための、化石燃料に代わるエネルギーである「グリーン水素」である。One potential form of clean energy is green hydrogen...（クリーンエネルギー候補の1つはグリーン水素です）で始まる第2段落では、その原料や用途が、第3段落では、このグリーン水素の世界市場が急成長していることが、第4段落ではグリーン水素へ向けられる批判が説明されており、グリーン水素の概要がニュース全体で述べられているので、正解は(A)。クリーンエネルギーの製造コストの高さや、太陽・風力エネルギーへの大転換については触れられていないので、(B)と(C)は選べない。

2. 正解 B

What do critics of green hydrogen believe?

(A) It will not be widely used as a fuel.
(B) Making it with renewable energy is currently not a good idea.
(C) The facilities that produce it use a lot of fossil fuels.

設問訳 グリーン水素を批判する人たちは何を信じているか。

(A) 燃料としては広く使われないだろう。
(B) 再生可能エネルギーを使ってグリーン水素を生産す

るのは現段階では良いアイデアとは言えない。
(C) グリーン水素を生産する施設は、大量の化石燃料を使用している。

解説 最終段落の But critics of green hydrogen say using solar or wind energy to produce another fuel right now is a waste of precious renewables, as the world struggles to transition away from fossil fuels.（しかしグリーン水素を批判する向きもあり、彼らは、現状では別の燃料［水素］を生産するために太陽エネルギーや風力エネルギーを使用するのは、世界が化石燃料から脱却しようと尽力している現在にあっては貴重な再生可能エネルギーの無駄遣いだと言っています）を読み解こう。critics of green hydrogen say...（……とグリーン水素を批判する人たちは述べている）の後に、動名詞を使った長い主語（using...right now）とbe動詞のisの文が続く形。another fuel は「グリーン水素」を指している。ここでは「グリーン水素を生産するために、太陽エネルギーや風力エネルギーを消費するのは無駄遣いだ」と述べられており、これを言い換えた(B)が正解である。グリーン水素を批判する人たちの意見として、燃料として広く普及することはないとは書かれていないので、(A)は不適。第2段落に、グリーン水素は化石燃料ではなく水などから得られると書かれており、(C)も選べない。

No.2

問題文

Decades-long research into Leonardo da Vinci's purported remains has revealed how many people currently alive can claim to be descendants of the family of the Renaissance genius and *Mona Lisa* painter. It's 14.

The conclusion, published in the journal *Human Evolution*, comes from a new genealogical tree going through 21 generations and four branches. It's part of the Leonardo da Vinci DNA Project, which aims to confirm remains thought to be his and to "better understand his extraordinary talents and visual acuity through genetic associations."

The researchers wrote these results are "eagerly awaited from an historical viewpoint" as they will help researchers "scientifically explore the roots of his genius, to find information on his physical prowess and on his possibly precocious ageing, on his being left-handed and his health and possible hereditary sicknesses, and to explain certain peculiar sensory perceptions, like his extraordinary visual quality and synesthesia."

Researchers gathered data from historical documents in public and private archives and direct accounts by da Vinci descendants. The study did not provide much information on the living descendants, to protect their privacy.

訳

レオナルド・ダビンチのものとされる遺体に関する数十年の研究によって、ルネサンスの天才で「モナ・リザ」を描いた画家の一族の子孫と言える存命の人が何人いるのかが明らかになっています。14人です。

ヒューマン・エボリューション誌に発表されたこの結論は、21世代の4つに枝分かれした一族を網羅する新たな家系図から導き出されたものです。これは「レオナルド・ダビンチDNAプロジェクト」の一環です。このプロジェクトは、ダビンチのものと考えられている遺体が本当にそうなのかという実証と「遺伝的関連性を通じて彼の並外れた才能や鋭い視覚のより深い理解」を目的としています。

研究者たちは、これらの結果は「歴史的見地から待望されている」もので、というのもそれらは研究者たちが「彼の才能の源泉を科学的に探り、彼の秀でた身体性や、早期老化だった可能性、左利きだったことや健康状態、そして遺伝性疾患を患っていた可能性に関する情報を見つけ、また彼の類まれな視覚の特性や共感覚といった、ある特殊な知覚能力について説明する」のに役立つだろうから、と書いています。

研究者たちは、公文書や個人所蔵の史料と、ダビンチの子孫から直接聞き取った話からデータを集めました。この研究では、存命の子孫たちについては、プライバシー保護のためにあまり多くの情報を明らかにしていません。

語句

decades-long: 数十年続く、何十年にもわたる／ purported: 〜とされている、言われている／ remains: 遺体／ reveal: 〜を明らかにする／ currently: 今のところ、現在／ claim to be: 〜であると主張する／ descendant: 子孫、末裔／ Renaissance: ルネサンスの／ genius: ①（人を指して）天才、特殊な能力を持つ人

②天賦の才、ずば抜けた才能／ *Mona Lisa*:「モナ・リザ」／ painter: 画家／ conclusion: 結論／ publish: 〜を発表する／ journal: 雑誌、機関誌／
Human Evolution: ヒューマン・エボリューション ➤人間と人間以外の霊長類の物理的、社会的な進化を主に扱う雑誌。／ genealogical tree: 系図、家系を示す樹形図／ go through: 〜を貫く、網羅する／ generation: 世代／ branch: 分家／ be part of: 〜の一部である／ aim to do: 〜することを目指す、目標とする／ confirm: 〜を確認する、確証する／ better understand: 〜をよりよく理解する／ extraordinary: 類まれな、並外れた／ talent: 才能／ visual acuity: 鋭敏な視覚／ genetic association: 遺伝的関連／ result:（研究・調査などの）結果／ eagerly await: 〜を待ち遠しく思う／ from a...viewpoint: …な観点から／ an historical: ➤ historical の発音は子音で始まるので、a historical とする方が一般的。ただし、かつては h が発音されるいくつかの単語（hotel や historic など）に an が用いられることが今より多かったため、その名残で今でも人によっては特に historic や historical に an を用いることがある。／ scientifically: 科学的に／ explore: 〜を探究する／ roots: 根源、起源／ physical: 身体的な／ prowess: 並外れた腕前、すぐれた能力／ possibly: ひょっとして、ことによると／ precocious ageing: 早熟／ left-handed: 左利きの／ hereditary sickness: 遺伝疾患／ certain: ある〜、ある種の／ peculiar: 特殊の、特異な／ sensory perception: 知覚／ visual quality: 視覚の特性／ synesthesia: 共感覚 ➤ある音である色、ある色である匂いを感じる、といった特殊な感覚。／ gather: 〜を集める／ historical document: 歴史文書、史料／ archives: 記録文書集、古記録保管所／ account:（過去の出来事の）話、説明、記述／ protect someone's privacy: 〜のプライバシーを守る

---

1. 正解 B

What is the main topic of this news report?

(A) A disagreement among Leonardo da Vinci's descendants

(B) Effort to gain a better understanding of Leonardo da Vinci

(C) Mistakes in historical documents about Leonardo da Vinci

設問訳 このニュースの主なトピックは何か。

(A) レオナルド・ダビンチの子孫の間での意見の相違

（B）レオナルド・ダビンチをより深く理解するための取り組み

（C）レオナルド・ダビンチに関する史料の中にある誤り

解説 第1段落にレオナルド・ダビンチの子孫と考えられる人の人数が14人という研究結果が出たことが、第4段落にダビンチの子孫から話を聞いたこと、彼らの情報はあまり公開されていないことが記されているが、disagreement（争い）の話は出てこない。よって、（**A**）は不適。この14人という結論は、The conclusion...comes from a new genealogical tree going through 21 generations and four branches.（この結論は、21世代の4つに枝分かれした一族を網羅する新たな家系図から導き出されたものです）とあり、この研究の属するプロジェクトの意義や研究方法など、ダビンチについての研究の詳細がニュースの中で説明されているので正解は（**B**）。第4段落にResearchers gathered data from historical documents...（研究者たちは史料からデータを集めました）とあるように、史料は研究対象の1つではあるが、「誤り」の話は出てこないので（**C**）は不適である。

2. 正解 C

What does the news report say about the research?

（A）The researchers discovered new works by Leonardo da Vinci.

（B）The researchers were surprised by the findings of their study.

（C）Some of the data was provided by Leonardo da Vinci's relatives.

設問訳 このニュースは、研究について何と述べているか。

（A）研究者たちはレオナルド・ダビンチの新しい作品を発見した。

（B）研究者たちは自分たちの研究結果に驚いた。

（C）データの一部は、レオナルド・ダビンチの親族たちによって提供された。

解説 第4段落に、Researchers gathered data from historical documents in public and private archives and direct accounts by da Vinci descendants.（研究者たちは、公文書や個人所蔵の史料と、ダビンチの子孫から直接聞き取った話からデータを集めました）とある。direct accountsは、「（ダビンチの子孫たちから）直接話

を聞いた」という意味なので、「データの一部はダビンチの親族たちから提供された」とする（**C**）が正しい。（**A**）の「新しい作品」や（**B**）の「驚きの研究結果」に関する記述はない。

No.3

問題文

Hong Kong has reclaimed its status as the host of a marquee Asian tech conference it lost last year, as organizers cite the city's success in battling the coronavirus pandemic.

Rise, an annual tech conference whose recent speakers have included executives from Uber, Alibaba and Stripe, said that it would return to the city next year, with plans to stay for the next five years.

Organizers had announced in late 2020 that they would move the event to the Malaysian city of Kuala Lumpur, saying they wanted to seek opportunities in Southeast Asia's fast-growing tech scene.

At the time, the move raised questions about Hong Kong's ability to hold on to its image as Asia's premier global business hub as it was still grappling with the aftermath of mass protests in 2019.

Now, "Hong Kong has once again won as the host city of Rise for the coming five years," the event's organizers said in a joint statement with the Hong Kong Tourism Board.

The event in 2022 will be staged in-person. Hong Kong Secretary for Commerce and Economic Development Edward Yau touted this as "a testimony of Hong Kong's success in containing the pandemic and keeping the infection rate among the lowest in the world, thereby giving international event organizers confidence that they can stage their events here safely."

訳

香港が、昨年一度失った、アジア最高峰のITカンファレンスの開催地としての地位を取り戻しました。主催者はその理由として、香港がコロナ禍への対応に成功していることを挙げています。

「ライズ」は、最近ではウーバー、アリババ、ストライプなどの経営幹部が登壇した、年に1度のITカンファレン

スで、来年再び同地で開催され、さらに今後5年継続して開催される予定だと（関係者が）述べました。

　主催者側は2020年後半に、東南アジアで急成長を遂げているIT業界に機会を見いだしたいとして、同イベントの開催地をマレーシアの都市クアラルンプールに移すと発表しました。

　当時、その変更によって、アジアを代表するグローバルビジネスの中心地としてのイメージを香港が維持できるのかということが疑問視されました。香港はまだ2019年の大規模デモの余波に対処中でした。

　そして今、「香港は再び、今後5年ライズの開催都市となる地位を勝ち取った」とイベント主催者は香港政府観光局との共同声明の中で述べました。

　2022年に行われる同イベントは、（リモートなどではなく）対面で実施されます。香港のエドワード・ヤウ商務・経済発展局長は、これは「香港がコロナを封じ込め、感染率を世界でも最低レベルに抑えることに成功している証しであり、それが国際イベントの主催者たちに、ここなら安全にイベントを実施できると確信させたのだ」と誇らしげに宣伝しました。

語句

reclaim: 〜を取り戻す／status as: 〜としての地位／host: 開催地、開催国／marquee: 一流の、特にすぐれた／conference: 協議会、カンファレンス／organizer: 主催者／cite: （理由などとして）〜を挙げる、引き合いに出す／battle: 〜と戦う／pandemic: 疫病の世界的流行、パンデミック／annual: 年に1度の／executive: 幹部、役員／announce that: 〜だと発表する／seek an opportunity: チャンス・機会を求める／fast-growing: 急成長の／tech scene: 科学技術業界、IT業界／at the time: その頃、当時／raise questions about: 〜に関して疑問を呼び起こす／hold on to: 〜を手放さない、維持する／premier: 第一級の、一流の／business hub: ビジネス拠点／grapple with: （困難な問題などに）取り組む／aftermath: （大事件などの）余波、影響／mass: 大規模な／protest: 抗議、反対運動／joint statement: 共同声明／the Hong Kong Tourism Board: 香港政府観光局／stage: 〜を行う／in-person: 直接／secretary for commerce and economic development: 《香港》商務・経済発展局長／tout A as B: AをBだと誇らしげに宣伝する／testimony: 証拠、しるし、証し／contain: 〜を封じ込める、抑制する／keep A among B: AをBの間に保つ／infection rate: 感染率／thereby: それによって／give...confidence that: …に〜であると

いう確信を与える／safely: 安全に、無事に

---

1. 正解 A

What is the main point of this news report?

(A) Hong Kong will once again host a major event that it hosted in the past.

(B) Hong Kong companies will be celebrated at a global business conference.

(C) Hong Kong tech leaders will give aid to countries during the pandemic.

設問訳 このニュースの要点は何か。

(A) 香港が、かつて主催した大規模なイベントを再び主催する。

(B) 香港の企業が、あるグローバルビジネスカンファレンスで祝われる。

(C) 香港のテクノロジーリーダーたちが、パンデミック渦中の国々を援助する。

解説 冒頭のHong Kong has reclaimed its status as the host of a marquee Asian tech conference it lost last year（香港が、昨年一度失った、アジア最高峰のITカンファレンスの開催地としての地位を取り戻しました）および第2段落のit would return to the city next year, with plans to stay for the next five years（来年再び同地で開催され、さらに今後5年継続して開催される予定）などの文から、「もともと香港で行われていた、ある大規模なITカンファレンスが、他の国で開催されることになったが、再び香港で開催されることになった」という趣旨だとわかる。この内容と一致する選択肢は(A)である。第5段落のHong Kong has once again won as the host city of Rise...（香港は再びライズの開催都市となる地位を勝ち取った）などの表現から(B)のcelebrateを連想できるかもしれないが、香港の企業に関する記述はないので的外れである。(C)の「香港のテクノロジーリーダーたちが他国を支援する」話も出てこない。

---

2. 正解 B

What point does Edward Yau highlight with regard to Hong Kong?

(A) Its history as a center of global business

(B) Its ability to keep the pandemic under control

(C) The fact that its political situation has changed since the 2019 protests

---

設問訳 エドワード・ヤウ氏は香港に関してどんな点を強調したか。

(A) グローバルビジネスの中心地としての歴史

(B) パンデミックを抑え込めていること

(C) 2019年の抗議デモ以降、政治情勢が変化していること

解説 最終段落に書かれているエドワード・ヤウ氏の a testimony of Hong Kong's success in containing the pandemic and keeping the infection rate among the lowest in the world（香港がコロナを封じ込め、感染率を世界でも最低レベルに抑えることに成功している証し）というコメントから、「香港が新型コロナウイルスの感染拡大の抑え込みに成功したことを評価され、国際イベントを安全に開催できる都市と認められた」とヤウ氏が捉えていることがわかる。香港に以前から「グローバルビジネスの中心」としてのイメージがあったことも本文から読み取れるが、ヤウ氏が強調したポイントではないので(A)は不適。一度は開催地がクアラルンプールに変更されたことに関連して「2019年の大規模デモ」の話は出てくるが、それ以降の「政治情勢の変化」については触れられていないので、(C)もおかしい。正解は(B)。

Part 3　長文読解問題

No.1

問題文

The tiny goldfish you can pick up at pet stores for a few cents might not look like an environmental threat, but they can grow into a huge problem if set free in lakes or ponds—mainly because they can grow to be surprisingly huge.

Burnsville, Minnesota, which is south of Minneapolis, drew viral attention to the global issue when it posted pictures on social media of some of the whoppers that were caught during an ongoing survey of fish in Keller Lake. The city urged residents not to release their unwanted pet fish. They caught 10 goldfish last week and another 18 this week—each was more than a foot long, with the largest being 15 inches long and weighing about four pounds.

Burnsville natural resources specialist Caleb Ashling told CNN that the city partnered with neighboring Apple Valley and the company Carp Solutions to find out how many goldfish are in the lake. "We had some reports from residents of some increasingly large groups of goldfish out on the lake," Ashling said.

Goldfish root around on the bottom of lakes and ponds looking for food, which stirs up sediment and can uproot plants. This can impact water quality and the diversity of native species when the goldfish become established, said Carp Solutions owner Przemek Bajer, who is a research assistant professor at the University of Minnesota.

"Often, they don't eat aquatic plants, but the plants simply cannot establish roots in those lakes; they're just uprooted physically," Bajer said. "So if you have a lot of goldfish and carp in the lake, usually the first thing that happens is all the aquatic plants disappear." The fish also kick up nutrients that had settled on the bottom, and their waste, which can promote algae blooms that "turn clear lakes into green lakes."

Goldfish are native to China and eastern Asia and have traveled the world, thanks to their popularity as pets and ornamental fish. The US Geological Survey says that they've been established or reported in every US state, except Alaska, which eradicated a population of illegally introduced goldfish in 2019 from a pond in Anchorage. "All goldfish are invasive, basically worldwide," Bajer said. "In the whole of North America, Australia, parts of Europe, they are really, really widespread." They are closely related to the common carp, which are another invasive, non-native species, Bajer said.

"It's most likely that somebody just released them, but they can reproduce in the wild, too," Bajer said. "We don't know if these particular ones were released by somebody or they were spawned out in the lake from parents that maybe were introduced by somebody."

Ashling said they've worked hard to improve the water quality at Keller Lake and the communities want to protect their investment. He said the cities will decide what to do next once Carp Solutions finishes its assessment of how many goldfish are in the lake. "We know it's not good to have goldfish in the lake, but in some situations, goldfish can be in a lake and not be causing a lot of severe problems, but in the right lake in the right conditions they can cause a lot of problems," Ashling said. "So we're still in the process of trying to figure out what our situation is at Keller Lake."

訳

ペットショップで数セントで手に入るごく小さな金魚は、環境への脅威のようには見えないかもしれませんが、湖や池に放たれると大きな問題に発展しかねません——それは主に、金魚がびっくりするほど大きくなりうるということに起因します。

ミネソタ州のミネアポリスの南に位置するバーンズビル市が、ケラー湖で今も進行中の魚類の調査で捕獲されたとてつもないサイズの金魚の画像をいくつかSNSに投稿したところ、一気に拡散され、この世界規模の問題への注目を集めました。同市は住民に飼いたくなくなったペットの魚を（湖に）放さないよう要請しました。同市は先週10匹の金魚を捕獲し、今週さらに18匹を捕獲しました。そのどれもが1フィート（約30センチ）を超える体長で、いちばん大きいものは体長15インチ（約38センチ）、重さは約4ポンド（約1.8キロ）でした。

バーンズビル市の天然資源専門家であるケイレブ・アシュリング氏はCNNの取材に対し、同市はその湖に生息している金魚の数を把握するために、隣のアップルバレー市とカープ・ソリューションズ社と提携した、と述べました。「われわれは、個体数がどんどん増えている金魚の群れがいくつかその湖にいるという報告を複数の住民から受けました」とアシュリング氏は言いました。

金魚はえさを求めて湖や池の底を引っかき回し、それによって沈殿物が舞い上がり、（水生）植物を根から引き抜いてしまうこともあります。金魚が定着してしまうと、これが水質や在来種の多様性に影響を与えかねない、と話したのはカープ・ソリューションズ社のオーナーで、ミネソタ大学の研究助教授のプシェメック・バイエル氏です。

「多くの場合、金魚は水生植物を食べることはないのですが、植物は（金魚のいる）そうした湖ではとにかく根を張れないのです。物理的に根っこから引き抜かれてし

まうのです」とバイエル氏は言いました。「よって、金魚とコイが湖に大量にいる場合に往々にして最初に起こるのは、水生植物がすべて消えてしまうということです」。また、金魚は湖底に沈殿していた栄養分や自分たちの排せつ物を舞い上がらせ、それが藻の異常発生を促進することがあり、それによって「透き通った湖が緑色に濁った湖に変わってしまう」とのことです。

金魚は中国および東アジア原産の魚ですが、そのペットや観賞用の魚としての人気から世界中に広まっています。米国地質調査所によると、金魚は米国のすべての州で定着している、あるいは（いることが）報告されているとのことですが、唯一の例外がアラスカ州で、同州はアンカレッジの池に不法に持ち込まれた金魚の個体群を2019年に根絶しました。「金魚はすべて侵略種なのです、ほぼ全世界でね」とバイエル氏は言いました。「北米の全土やオーストラリア、そしてヨーロッパの一部の地域で、金魚は本当に、本当に広く生息しています」。金魚はコイに近い魚で、コイもまた侵略種であり、非在来種だ、とバイエル氏は述べました。

「おそらくは単に誰かが金魚を放したのでしょうが、金魚は野生でも繁殖できます」とバイエル氏は言いました。「現にここにいる金魚たちが何者かによって放たれたものなのか、それとも何者かによって導入されたかもしれない親たちからこの湖で生まれたものなのか、私たちには判別できません」

アシュリング氏によれば、彼らはケラー湖の水質改善に尽力しており、各コミュニティーはその労力が無駄にならないことを望んでいます。彼は、2つの市（バーンズビル市とアップルバレー市）は、カープ・ソリューションズ社がこの湖に生息する金魚の数を算出し終えた時点で次にどうするか決断するだろう、と話しました。「この湖に金魚が生息しているのはよくないということはわかっていますが、状況次第では、金魚が湖に生息していても大した問題はそれほど起こさないということもありえます。しかし、（問題が起こる）条件を満たした状況下の、条件を満たした湖では、金魚は多くの問題を引き起こしかねないのです」とアシュリング氏は言いました。「それで、私たちはまだ、ケラー湖がどのような状況に置かれているかを解明しようとしている最中なのです」

語句

tiny: とても小さな／goldfish: 金魚／pick up: 〜を手に入れる、買う／environmental threat: 環境への脅威／grow into: 成長して〜になる／huge: 巨大な／set... free: …を自由の身にする、解放する／pond: 池／

surprisingly: 驚くほど、意外に／draw attention to: 〜に（人の）注意を向ける、関心を集める／viral: （主にネット上で）急速に拡散した、バズった／post A on B: AをB（SNSなど）に投稿する／social media: ソーシャルメディア、SNS／whopper: 途方もないもの、巨大なもの／ongoing: 進行している、進行中の／survey: 調査／urge...to do: …に〜するよう強く求める／resident: 住民／release: 〜を解き放つ／unwanted: 望まれない、不要な／foot:《長さの単位》フィート ▶1フィート＝約30センチメートル。複数形はfeet。／inch: インチ ▶1インチ＝約2.5センチメートル。／weigh: 〜の重さがある、重さが〜である／pound:《重さの単位》ポンド ▶1ポンド＝約450グラム。／natural resources: 天然資源／specialist: 専門家／partner with: 〜と組む、提携する／neighboring: 隣接した、近隣の／find out: 〜を知る、解明する／increasingly: ますます／root around: （何かを探して）引っかき回す／stir up: （ほこり、沈殿物などを）舞い上がらせる／sediment: 沈殿物、たい積物／uproot: （植物を）根から引き抜く／impact: 〜に影響を与える／diversity: 多様性／native species: 在来種／become established: 〈生物が〉（新しい土地に）定着する／research assistant professor: 研究助教授／aquatic plant: 水生植物／establish roots in: 〜に根を張る／physically: 物理的に、力ずくで／carp: コイ／disappear: 消える、姿を消す／kick up: 〜を蹴り上げる、跳ね上げる／nutrient: 栄養素、栄養分／settle: 積もる、沈殿する／waste: 排せつ物／promote: 〜を促す、促進する／algae: 藻、藻類 ▶algaの複数形。／bloom: 異常発生、大発生／turn A into B: AをBへと変える／be native to: 〈動植物が〉〜の原産である、在来種である／travel: 〜を移動する／ornamental: 装飾用の、観賞用の／the US Geological Survey: 米国地質調査所 ▶自然災害や天然資源などについて科学的に研究する米国の調査機関。／report: 〜を報告する／eradicate: 〜を根絶する／population: （特定の地域に生息する動物の）個体群／illegally introduced: 不法に持ち込まれた／invasive: 侵略性の、侵略種の、外来種の／widespread: 広く行き渡った、はびこった／be closely related to: （生物学的に）〜と密接に関連している／common carp: コイ／non-native species: 非在来種の、外来種の／It is most likely that...: 恐らく…である、きっと…である／reproduce: 生殖する、繁殖する／in the wild: 野生で、大自然の中で／this particular: ほかならぬこの／spawn: 〈魚・カエルなどが〉（卵を）産む／work hard to do: 〜するために尽力する／

improve: 〜を改善する、向上させる／protect one's investment: 〜が時間や労力を投じたことを無駄にしない／once: いったん〜すると／assessment: 査定／situation: 状況／severe: 深刻な、重大な／right: （ある結果になるための）ちょうどいい、適切な／condition: 条件、状況／be in the process of doing: 〜している過程にある／figure out: （考えた末）〜を理解する、解明する

---

1. 正解 B

What is the main point of this news report?

(A) Fishing is having a negative effect on lake eco-systems.

(B) A population of invasive fish has been found in a lake.

(C) Poor water quality is harming a lake's goldfish population.

設問訳 このニュースの要点は何か。

(A) 釣りは湖の生態系に悪影響を及ぼしている。

(B) 侵略種の魚群が湖で見つかった。

(C) 水質の悪さが湖の金魚の個体群に害を及ぼしている。

解説 第1段落の、they [goldfish] can grow into a huge problem（金魚は大きな問題に発展しかねません）や、第2段落のBurnsville...drew viral attention to the global issue when it posted pictures on social media of some of the whoppers（バーンズビル市が……とてつもないサイズの金魚の画像をいくつかSNSに投稿したところ……この世界規模の問題への注目を集めました）などの記述から、ある湖で巨大な金魚が発見され、話題になったことがわかる。さらに、第4段落のThis can impact water quality and the diversity of native species when the goldfish become established（金魚が定着してしまうと、これが水質や在来種の多様性に影響を与えかねない）というプシェメック・バイエル氏の発言から、この金魚の個体群は「invasive（侵略的な、外来種の）」で、本来の生態系を乱しかねない存在であることもわかるので、正解は(B)。「金魚の群れが水質に影響を及ぼす可能性がある」という話なので、その逆の内容である(C)は選べないし、また、(A)の「釣り」の話も出てこない。

---

2. 正解 A

What is true with regard to the behavior of gold-fish in lakes and ponds?

(A) They make it difficult for plants to grow.

(B) They eat plants that native species need to survive.

(C) They destroy important fish that keep lakes and ponds clean.

設問訳 湖や池にいる金魚の習性に関して正しいのはどれか。

(A) 植物を育ちにくくする。

(B) 在来種が生存に必要な植物を食べてしまう。

(C) 池や湖をきれいに保つのに重要な魚を死滅させる。

解説 第5段落のバイエル氏の発言に、Often, they don't eat aquatic plants, but the plants simply cannot establish roots in those lakes; they're just uprooted physically（多くの場合、金魚は水生植物を食べることはないのですが、植物は［金魚のいる］そうした湖ではとにかく根を張れないのです。物理的に根っこから引き抜かれてしまうのです）とある。ここから、「多くの場合、金魚は水生植物を食べることはない」とわかるので、(B) は誤り。さらに、So if you have a lot of goldfish and carp in the lake, usually the first thing that happens is all the aquatic plants disappear.（よって、金魚とコイが湖に大量にいる場合に往々にして最初に起こるのは、水生植物がすべて消えてしまうということです）と続き、金魚によって水生植物が育ちにくい環境に変えられてしまう可能性が危惧されていることがわかるので、正解は(A) となる。金魚が他の種類の魚を食べたり攻撃したりするという記述はないので、(C) は不適。

3. 正解 B

What does the news report say about the popularity of goldfish?

(A) It has led to effects on common carp populations.

(B) It is the reason why goldfish are found in many places around the world.

(C) Goldfish are more popular in the United States than in other countries.

設問訳 このニュースは、金魚の人気について何と言っているか。

(A) コイの個体群に影響を及ぼしている。

(B) 世界各地で金魚が見られる理由である。

(C) 米国での金魚の人気ぶりは、他国のそれをしのいでいる。

解説「金魚の人気によって、どのような影響がもたらされたか」が問われている。第6段落の冒頭に、Goldfish are native to China and eastern Asia and have traveled the world, thanks to their popularity as pets and ornamental fish.（金魚は中国および東アジア原産の魚ですが、そのペットや観賞用の魚としての人気から世界中に広まっています）とあることに注目しよう。「人気があるので、世界中に広まった」ということであるから、これを端的に言い換えた (B) が正解である。「コイ」については、同じく第6段落で They are closely related to the common carp, which are another invasive, non-native species（金魚はコイに近い魚で、コイもまた侵略種であり、非在来種だ）という説明があるだけで、「金魚がコイになんらかの影響を与えている」とは言えないので、(A) は選べない。金魚の人気の国別比較の話も出てこないので、(C) も不適。

4. 正解 C

What is one thing Przemek Bajer says about the goldfish in Keller Lake?

(A) Their size will likely continue to increase.

(B) They probably cannot reproduce successfully in the lake.

(C) Whether they were put into the lake or born in it is unknown.

設問訳 プシェメック・バイエル氏がケラー湖の金魚について言っていることの1つは何か。

(A) 金魚のサイズはおそらく巨大化し続けるだろう。

(B) 金魚はおそらく湖でうまく繁殖することはできないだろう。

(C) 金魚が湖に入れられたのか、または湖で生まれたのかはわかっていない。

解説 第7段落のバイエル氏の発言を見ていこう。It's most likely that somebody just released them, but they can reproduce in the wild, too.（おそらくは単に誰かが金魚を放したのでしょうが、金魚は野生でも繁殖できます）とある。繁殖に関しては「できる」と言い切っているので、(B) は不可。続いてバイエル氏は、We don't know if these particular ones were released by somebody or they were spawned out in the lake from parents that maybe were introduced by somebody. (現にここにいる金魚たちが何者かによって放たれたものなのか、それとも何者かによって導入されたかもしれない親たちからこの湖で生まれたものなのか、私たちには判別できません) と言っており、これは (**C**) の内容と一致するので、(**C**) が正解となる。また、(**A**) に関しては、特に触れられていないので、不適。

5. 正解 A

What does Caleb Ashling suggest about the gold-fish?

(**A**) They may not have a significant negative effect on Keller Lake.

(**B**) There are a lot more of them than Carp Solutions says there are.

(**C**) They are hard to study, because conditions in Keller Lake change frequently.

設問訳 ケイレブ・アシュリング氏は金魚について何をほのめかしているか。

(**A**) 金魚は、ケラー湖に重大な悪影響を与えないかもしれない。

(**B**) カープ・ソリューションズ社が言うよりももっと多くの金魚がいる。

(**C**) ケラー湖の状態が頻繁に変化するので、金魚を研究するのが難しい。

解説 最終段落にあるアシュリング氏の We know it's not good to have goldfish in the lake, but in some situations, goldfish can be in a lake and not be causing a lot of severe problems (この湖に金魚が生息しているのはよくないということはわかっていますが、状況次第では、金魚が湖に生息していても大した問題はそれほど起こさないということもありえます) という発言から、「すべてのケースで、湖に放たれた金魚が大きな害を与えるわけではない」ことがわかる。また、ケラー湖について、どのような状況か解明しようとしている最中と最後に言っているので、ケラー湖の金魚が重大な悪影響を及ぼすか否かはまだ断定できる段階ではないことも示されている。したがって、正解は (**A**)。同じく最終段落で「カープ・ソリューションズ社がケラー湖に生息する金魚の数を算出し終えた時点で2つの市は次に何をするか決める」と書かれていることからカープ・ソリューションズ社はコイの数を算出中であることが読み取れ、(**B**) は選

べない。(**C**) の「ケラー湖の金魚は研究しにくい」といった話は出てこない。

No.2

問題文

Smartphone season is underway, and the headlines will almost certainly be the same as always: thinner, sleeker, faster models are coming to consumer pockets. But if a new push from the US government succeeds, future smartphones may also have to be designed for something extra—the ability to be repaired however a device owner chooses.

President Joe Biden last month urged the Federal Trade Commission to set rules preventing manufacturers from imposing restrictions on independent device repair shops and DIY repairs, a principle known as "right to repair." A week later, the FTC vowed to "root out" illegal repair restrictions on various products, including phones.

Companies such as Apple have been criticized for using tactics that make it harder for independent repair businesses to access devices, such as using non-removable memory or batteries, or sealing devices with special glue. (The companies argue that this is done to ensure the products are properly repaired.) New regulation would likely prohibit this practice and require smartphone manufacturers to make parts, tools, repair manuals, and diagnostics for out-of-warranty repairs more readily available to third-party businesses.

"In many cases, the price to fix a smartphone or computer is close to, if not more than, replacing it altogether—a strategy that encourages people to buy new devices rather than fixing them. This needs to change," Pedro Pacheco, a senior director at market research firm Gartner, told CNN Business. "Manufacturers will need to make design choices to keep the cost to repair devices down."

While smartphone makers aren't the only ones facing criticism for obstructing repairs, the order specifically calls them out for practices that make repairs "more costly and time-consuming." Regulatory pressure could change not only how consumers choose to fix their devices but how manufacturers build them in subtle ways.

"Current right-to-repair laws proposed in the US don't impact device design in any way, but a focus on repair opportunities could incentivize the manufacturers to swap screws for more standard ones or make the battery easier to remove," said Kyle Wiens, CEO and founder of iFixit, an online repair website for consumer electronics.

David McQueen, research director at market research firm ABI Research, agrees, noting even the smallest of changes could impact the construction of smartphones on some level. For example, adding new screws or more holes may impact a device's IP ratings—the degree of protection a device's components provide against dust and water. "Smartphone vendors have worked hard to get this to high levels, but if devices do have more screw holes and have to be easier to take apart, then would these ratings be compromised or have to be lowered?" said McQueen.

McQueen also pointed to a possible dilemma that some smartphone manufacturers might face in a right-to-repair world: "Would some companies still use high-end components across all their models if they know it will be easy to have them repaired or replaced?" On the one hand, companies may find more of their customers could replace these parts with cheaper components. On the other hand, he argues, "It could damage a vendor's brand value if they're selling products with noticeably inferior components to combat this possibility."

訳

スマートフォンの（最新機種が発表される）シーズンが到来しました。ヘッドラインはほぼ確実にいつもと同じになるでしょう。すなわち、より薄く、よりかっこよく、より高速なモデルが消費者たちのポケットへ——。しかし、米政府による新たな働きかけが成功すれば、未来のスマホはもう1つ新たな要素を加えるための設計が義務化されるかもしれません。それは、デバイス所有者の選択に応じて修理ができるようにすることです。

ジョー・バイデン大統領は先月、米連邦取引委員会（FTC）に対し、メーカーが独立系のデバイス修理店やDIY修理に制限をかけられなくする規制——「修理する

権利」として知られる原則——を設けるよう要請しました。その1週間後、FTCは、スマホを含むさまざまな製品に対する違法な修理制限を「根絶」していくと宣言しました。

アップル社など各社は、独立系修理業者がデバイス（内部）にアクセスしにくくなるような戦略、具体的には、取り外しできないメモリーやバッテリーを使用したり特殊な接着剤でデバイスを密封したりといった戦略を使っているとして非難を浴びてきました（これらの企業は、そうするのは製品の適切な修理を保証するためだと主張しています）。新たに設けられる規制はこの慣行を禁止し、スマホメーカー各社に対し、部品や工具、修理マニュアル、保証期間外修理の診断方法（の情報）が、第三者企業にとって利用しやすくなるよう要請するものになりそうです。

「多くの場合、スマホやパソコンの修理費は、丸ごと新品に取り換えるのとほぼ同等か、場合によってはそれ以上になります——これはデバイスを修理するのではなく新品を購入させるための戦略です。これは変わる必要があります」と、市場調査を手掛けるガートナー社のペドロ・パチェコ上級部長は「CNNビジネス」に話しました。「メーカー各社はデバイスの修理費を低く抑えるための設計を選ぶといったことも必要になってくるでしょう」

修理を妨げているとして非難を浴びているのはスマホメーカーだけではないものの、今回の命令は、修理を「より高額で、より時間のかかる」ものにしている慣行を理由に、スマホメーカー各社を特にやり玉に挙げています。規制圧力によって、消費者によるデバイス修理の選択の仕方だけでなく、メーカー側の製造面での細かいところでも変化がもたらされるかもしれません。

「現在米国で提案されている『修理する権利』の法律は、デバイスの設計に何ら影響を与えるものではありませんが、修理する機会（の増加）が注目を浴びることが、メーカーがねじをよりスタンダードなものに変更したり、バッテリーを取り外しやすくしたりするインセンティブになる可能性はあります」と、家電のオンライン修理サイトiFixit（アイフィックスイット）社のCEO兼創業者のカイル・ウィーンズ氏は語りました。

市場調査会社のABIリサーチ社の調査部長であるデービッド・マックイーン氏はこれに同意し、ごく小さな変化ですら、ある点でスマホの構造に影響を与えうると指摘します。例えば、新たなねじの追加や穴を増やすことでデバイスのIP評価に影響が出るかもしれません——IP評価とは、ほこりや水に対するデバイスの部品の保護等級のことです。「スマホの販売業者はこれを高めるべく努力してきましたが、実際にデバイスのねじ穴が増え、

分解しやすくならねばならないなら、この評価が犠牲になる、あるいは格下げする必要が出てくるのではないでしょうか」とマックイーン氏は言いました。

　マックイーン氏はまた、「修理する権利」が実現した際に一部のスマホメーカーが直面しうるジレンマの可能性についても指摘しました。「企業は、修理・交換が容易になるとわかっていてもなお自社の全製品に高品質の部品を使おうとするでしょうか」。一方では、企業各社は、今より多くの自分たちの顧客がこれらの部品をより安価なものと交換するということに直面するかもしれません。他方では——彼は主張します——「こうした可能性に対処するために各社が以前より著しく質の低い部品を使った製品を売るようになると、販売業者のブランド価値を傷つけることにもなりかねないのです」

語句

be underway: 進行中である／headline: ヘッドライン、大見出し／thin: 薄い／sleek:〈外観が〉スマートな、（流線形で）かっこいい／consumer: 消費者／push: 努力、ひと押し、推進／succeed: 成功する／be designed for: 〜のために設計されている／something extra: プラスアルファ、何か付け加わるもの／repair: ①〜を修理する ②修理／device:（電子）機器、デバイス／owner: 持ち主、所有者／urge...to do: 〜するよう…を促す／the Federal Trade Commission: 米連邦取引委員会 ▶略称FTC。／set a rule: 規則を定める／prevent...from doing: …が〜するのを防止する、…に〜させない／manufacturer: メーカー、製造会社（業者）／impose restrictions on: 〜に制限をかける／independent: 独立した／device repair shop: デバイス修理店／DIY repair: DIY修理 ▶DIYはdo-it-yourself（日曜大工）の頭字語。／principle: 主義、根本方針／vow to do: 〜することを誓う、確約する／root out: 〜を根絶する／illegal: 違法な／criticize...for doing: …を〜しているとして非難する、批判する／tactics: 戦術、戦略／make it hard for...to do: …が〜するのを難しくする／business: 企業／access:（コンピューター機器内部などに）アクセスする／non-removable: 取り外しができない、固定型の／memory: 記憶装置、メモリー／battery: 電池、バッテリー／seal A with B: AをBで封じる／glue: 接着剤／argue that: 〜だと主張する／ensure（that）: 確実に〜であるようにする／properly: 適切に、適正に／regulation: 規制／likely: 多分、恐らく／prohibit: 〜を禁止する／practice: 慣行、行為／require...to do: …に〜するよう義務付ける／part: パー

ツ、部品／tool: 道具、工具／repair manual: 修理マニュアル／diagnostics: 診断方法／out-of-warranty: 保証期間外の／（be）readily available to: 〜にとってすぐに利用できる、入手しやすい／third-party: 第三者の、サードパーティーの ▶IT用語としては、あるメーカーのコンピューターなどの機器の部品と互換できる部品などを作る他のメーカーを指す。／fix: 〜を修理する、直す／if not...: もしかすると…かもしれない、場合によっては…かもしれない／replace...altogether: …を丸ごと交換する、買い換える／strategy: 戦略／senior director: 上級部長／market research firm: 市場調査会社／Gartner: ガートナー社 ▶アメリカのハイテク関連市場を主に扱う調査会社。／keep...down: …を低く抑える／face:（問題や非難に）直面する／criticism: 非難、批判／obstruct: 〜を邪魔する、妨げる／order: 命令、指令／specifically: 特に／call A out for B:《話》Bのことで Aを非難する、AのB（不正行為など）を指摘する／costly: 高額な、費用のかさむ／time-consuming: 多くの時間を要する／regulatory pressure: 規制（当局）による圧力／in subtle ways: 微妙なことで、細かいところで／propose: 〜を提案する／not...in any way: 決して…ない／impact: 〜に影響を与える／focus on: 〜に対する注目／incentivize...to do: …に〜するインセンティブを与える、…に〜するよう促す／swap A for B: AをBと交換する／screw: ねじ／remove: 〜を取り外す、取り出す／consumer electronics: 家電製品／research director: 研究部長／note（that）: 〜ということを指摘する／construction: 構造／on some level: ある程度、ある点で／IP rating: =ingress protection rating IP評価 ▶デバイスの防水・防じんレベルの評価。／degree: 程度／protection against: 〜からの保護／component: 構成部品、パーツ／dust: ほこり／vendor: 販売会社・業者／screw hole: ねじ穴／take...apart: …を分解する／compromise: 〜を損なう／lower: 〜を下げる、低くする／point to: 〜を指摘する、挙げる／dilemma: ジレンマ、板挟み／high-end: 高級な、最上位の、高性能の／brand value: ブランド価値／noticeably: 著しく、目立って／inferior: 劣った、より低い品質の／combat: 〜と闘う、〜に立ち向かう

---

1. 正解 B

What is the main topic of this news report?

(A) A new feature of smartphones that would limit their life span

(B) Rules that would allow device users more freedom in repairing their devices

(C) An increase in illegal practices in the repair of devices like smartphones

---

設問訳 このニュースの主なトピックは何か。

(A) スマートフォンの寿命を制限する新機能

(B) ユーザーがもっと自由にデバイスを修理できるようにする規定

(C) スマートフォンなどのデバイス修理における違法行為の増加

解説 第1段落の But if a new push from the US government succeeds, future smartphones may also have to be designed for something extra — the ability to be repaired however a device owner chooses. (しかし、米政府による新たな働きかけが成功すれば、未来のスマホはもう1つ新たな要素を加えるための設計が義務化されるかもしれません。それは、デバイス所有者の選択に応じて修理ができるようにすることです) から、スマートフォンの修理に関する話題であることがわかる。さらに、第2段落の President Joe Biden last month urged the Federal Trade Commission to set rules preventing manufacturers from imposing restrictions on independent device repair shops and DIY repairs, a principle known as "right to repair." (ジョー・バイデン大統領は先月、米連邦取引委員会 (FTC) に対し、メーカーが独立系のデバイス修理店や DIY 修理に制限をかけられなくする規制——「修理する権利」として知られる原則——を設けるよう要請しました) という記述とあわせて、正解 (B) を導こう。「寿命を制限する機能」の話など出てこないので、(A) は完全に的外れ。第2段落の the FTC vowed to "root out" illegal repair restrictions on various products, including phones (FTC は、スマホを含むさまざまな製品に対する違法な修理制限を「根絶」していくと宣言しました) で illegal が出てくるが、「違法行為が増加している」という言及はないので、(C) も不適。

2. 正解 A

What is one thing that companies like Apple have faced criticism for?

(A) Making parts of their devices difficult to access

(B) Failing to use caution when repairing their devices

(C) Providing unclear information about the warranties they offer

---

設問訳 アップル社などの会社が直面してきた批判の1つは何か。

(A) デバイスの部品にアクセスしにくくしていること

(B) デバイスを修理するときに注意を欠いていること

(C) 保証に関して不明瞭な情報を提供していること

解説 第3段落の冒頭、Companies such as Apple have been criticized for using tactics that make it harder for independent repair businesses to access devices... によると、批判の矢は、アップル社をはじめとするメーカーが「修理しにくいスマートフォン」を製造していることへ向けられている。つまり、「デバイスの内部にアクセスしにくい (部品を取り出しにくい)」ということなので、(A) が正解となる。やはり第3段落の New regulation would likely prohibit this practice and require smartphone manufacturers to make...diagnostics for out-of-warranty repairs more readily available to third-party businesses. (新たに設けられる規制はこの慣行を禁止し、スマホメーカー各社に対し保証期間外修理の診断方法 [の情報] が、第三者企業にとって利用しやすくなるよう要請するものになりそうです) という部分で warranty (保証) について触れられてはいるが、「不明瞭な情報が提供されていた」という話は出てこないので、(C) は不適。(B) の「修理時の注意の欠如」も無関係。

3. 正解 C

What does Pedro Pacheco say about device manufacturers?

(A) The deals they make with other businesses are not good for consumers.

(B) The design choices they make lead to frequent problems with their devices.

(C) They make repairs costly to discourage users from having devices repaired.

設問訳 ペドロ・パチェコ氏は、デバイスメーカーについて何と言っているか。

(A) デバイスメーカーが他の企業と行う取り決めは、顧客にとって良いものではない。

(B) デバイスメーカーの設計選びが、デバイスに頻繁に問題をもたらしている。

(C) デバイスメーカーは、ユーザーがデバイスを修理してもらいたくなくなるように修理費用がかさむようにしている。

解説 パチェコ氏は「スマホやパソコンの修理費は、丸ごと交換するのとほとんど変わらない」と述べた上で、そのことがa strategy that encourages people to buy new devices rather than fixing them（デバイスを修理するのではなく新品を購入させるための戦略）と第4段落で説明している。これを言い換えた（**C**）が正解。「設計の不備によって、デバイスに問題が頻発している」とは述べられていないので、（**B**）は誤り。また、他の企業との取り決めの話題は出てこないので（**A**）も選べない。

---

4. 正解 **C**

According to David McQueen, what could result from changes in smartphone design?

(**A**) The devices could become more difficult to take apart.

(**B**) People might think the devices pose a danger to their safety.

(**C**) The devices could be more easily damaged by dust and water.

設問訳 デービッド・マックイーン氏によると、スマートフォンの設計の変更はどのような結果をもたらしうるか。

(**A**) デバイスを分解することがより難しくなるかもしれない。

(**B**) 人々は、デバイスが自分たちの安全を脅かすと考えるかもしれない。

(**C**) デバイスは、ほこりや水によってよりダメージを受けやすくなるかもしれない。

解説 マックイーン氏は第7段落で、even the smallest of changes could impact the construction of smartphones on some level（ごく小さな変化ですら、ある点でスマホの構造に影響を与えうる）と述べた上で、さらに、the degree of protection a device's components provide against dust and water（ほこりや水に対するデバイスの部品の保護等級）の指標であるIP ratings（IP評価）に言及している。「分解しやすいように（修理しやすいように）、デバイスのねじ穴を増やす」→「ほこりや水に対するデバイスの部品のIP評価が犠牲になる」という話の流れになっている。つまり、「設計変更によって、ほこりや水に弱くなる」ということであるから、正解は（**C**）。ここで話題になっているのは「分解しやすくする」という設計変更なので、（**A**）は正反対。また、「安全性」については触れられていないので（**B**）も不適。

---

5. 正解 **B**

What difficult choice does McQueen suggest smartphone manufacturers might have to make?

(**A**) Whether to stop selling cheaper models or try to improve their quality

(**B**) Whether to keep using high-end parts or switch to using cheaper parts

(**C**) Whether to change their marketing strategy or focus more on product quality

---

設問訳 マックイーン氏は、スマートフォンメーカーがどのような難しい選択をしなければならないかもしれないと示唆しているか。

(**A**) 安価なモデルの販売をやめるか、それともその品質改善を試みるか

(**B**) 高品質な部品を使い続けるか、それとも安価な部品に切り替えるか

(**C**) マーケティング戦略を変えるか、それとも製品の品質をより重視するか

解説 メーカーのdilemma（ジレンマ）について言及されている最終段落に注目しよう。設問のdifficult choiceはこのdilemmaを言い換えている。「高品質な部品（high-end components）を使用したところで、顧客が安価な部品に取り換えてしまう（＝以前ほどデバイスを買い換えなくなってしまう）かもしれない、かといって、安価な部品（cheaper components）を使用すると、販売業者のブランド価値を傷つけてしまうかもしれない」というジレンマなので、正解は（**B**）。（**A**）の「品質改善」や（**C**）の「マーケティング戦略」には触れられていない。

General-Knowledge Section 国際教養セクション

Practice Test 2は2021年11月に公開されたもので、国際教養セクションの問題や解答・解説はその時点の事実・状況に即しています。一部変更を加えてあるものもあります。

No.1

正解 **D**

Which of the following statements about NATO (the North Atlantic Treaty Organization) is NOT true?

(A) It was formed in 1949, after World War II.

(B) As of September 2023, the NATO alliance consisted of 31 European and North American countries.

(C) Turkey is a member of NATO.

(D) The NATO headquarters is located in Geneva, Switzerland.

設問訳 NATO（北大西洋条約機構）に関する次の記述のうち、誤っているものはどれか。

(A) 第2次世界大戦後の1949年に結成された。

(B) 2023年9月時点で、NATO同盟はヨーロッパと北アメリカの31カ国で構成されていた。

(C) トルコはNATOに加盟している。

(D) NATO本部はスイスのジュネーブに置かれている。

解説 NATOは第2次世界大戦終結後の1949年、英米が主体となって締結された北大西洋条約に基づいて設立された（**A**）。創設当初の加盟国は12カ国だったが、ソビエト連邦崩壊後の中欧・東欧諸国の加盟などによって、2023年9月現在、ヨーロッパと北アメリカの31カ国が加盟している（**B**）。ただし、2022年5月にスウェーデンがNATO加盟を申請しており、全加盟国が国内での批准手続きを終えればNATOは32カ国体制となる。トルコはNATOに1952年に加盟した（**C**）。よって、（**A**）（**B**）（**C**）は正しい。NATOの本部はベルギーのブリュッセルに置かれている。よって、（**D**）は誤り。

No.2

正解 **A**

Which of the following statements about China's political system is NOT true?

(A) The only officially recognized political party in China is the Communist Party of China.

(B) The Chinese Communist Party celebrated its 100th anniversary in 2021.

(C) The National People's Congress is a legislative body equivalent to Japan's Diet, and it convenes every March.

(D) There is currently no term limit for the office of president of the People's Republic of China.

設問訳 中国の政治体制に関する次の記述のうち、誤っているものはどれか。

(A) 中国で公式に認められている政党は、中国共産党だけである。

(B) 中国共産党は2021年に創立100周年を迎えた。

(C) 全国人民代表大会は、日本の国会に相当する立法機関であり、毎年3月に開催されている。

(D) 現在のところ、中華人民共和国の国家主席には任期の制限はない。

解説 中国では共産党以外に「民主党派」と称される8つの小政党が合法的に存在を認められている。よって、（**A**）は誤り。共産党は1921年7月、上海で秘密裏に第1回の党大会を開き、創立された（**B**）。全国人民代表大会は中国の立法府で、「全人代」と略される。年1回、3月に北京市で開かれる（**C**）。2018年の全人代で、これまで2期10年とされていた国家主席の任期に関する規定を撤廃した（**D**）。よって、（**B**）（**C**）（**D**）は正しい。

No.3

正解 **A**

Which of the following statements about Russia is NOT true?

(A) According to IMF statistics, Russia's nominal GDP in 2022 was the fifth largest in the world, after Germany.

(B) As of September 2023, the president of Russia was Vladimir Putin.

(C) Russia annexed the Crimean Peninsula in

Ukraine in 2014.

(**D**) As of September 2023, Russia was under economic sanctions from countries such as the United States and EU members.

設問訳 ロシアに関する次の記述のうち、誤っているものはどれか。

(**A**) IMF の統計によると、ロシアの2022年の名目GDPはドイツに次いで世界第5位である。

(**B**) 2023年9月の時点で、ロシアの大統領はウラジミール・プーチンだった。

(**C**) ロシアは、2014年にウクライナのクリミア半島を併合した。

(**D**) 2023年9月の時点で、ロシアは米国やEU加盟国などの国から経済制裁を受けていた。

解説 IMF の統計では、ロシアの2022年の名目GDPはフランスに次いで世界第8位である（**A**）。よって、（**A**）は誤り。プーチンは2018年5月より4期目の大統領を務めており、2023年9月の時点でもその職にあった（**B**）。2014年3月、ロシアはウクライナ南部のクリミア半島を併合した（**C**）。前述のロシアによるクリミア併合後、2023年9月の時点で欧米はロシアに対する経済制裁を継続していた（**D**）。よって、（**B**）（**C**）（**D**）は正しい。

No.4

正解 **B**

Which of the following statements about Myanmar is NOT true?

(**A**) According to the Myanmar Statistical Yearbook 2019, Buddhists make up nearly 90 percent of Myanmar's population.

(**B**) As of May 2023, most of the Rohingya refugees who had fled to Bangladesh have returned to Myanmar.

(**C**) In February 2021, the national armed forces of Myanmar staged a coup d'état and seized control of the government.

(**D**) As of September 2023, an armed resistance movement continued against the military forces that staged the coup.

設問訳 ミャンマーに関する次の記述のうち、誤っている

ものはどれか。

(**A**)「ミャンマー統計年鑑2019」によると、ミャンマーの人口の90%近くを仏教徒が占めている。

(**B**) 2023年5月の時点で、バングラデシュに逃れていたロヒンギャ難民のほとんどがミャンマーに戻った。

(**C**) 2021年2月、ミャンマーの国軍がクーデターを起こし、政府を掌握した。

(**D**) 2023年9月の時点で、クーデターを起こした軍に対して、武装化した抵抗運動が続いていた。

解説 ミャンマー中央統計局による「ミャンマー統計年鑑2019」によると、ミャンマーの人口の90%近くが仏教徒である（**A**）。2017年のミャンマー軍によるロヒンギャ武装集団の掃討作戦によってバングラデシュに逃げ込んだ民間人のうち、2023年5月の時点で約95万人が難民キャンプで暮らしていた（**B**）。よって、（**B**）は誤り。ミャンマー国軍は2021年2月1日にクーデターを敢行、アウン・サン・スー・チー国家顧問兼外相らを拘束して実権を掌握したが（**C**）、2023年9月の時点では、軍に対して武装化した抵抗運動が続いていた（**D**）。よって、（**A**）（**C**）（**D**）は正しい。

No.5

正解 **C**

Which of the following statements about abbreviations used in the news is NOT true?

(**A**) The IMF is a specialized agency of the United Nations whose purpose is to ensure the stability of the international financial system.

(**B**) The FDA is a government agency that sets rules for the safety of food, drugs and medical devices in the United States.

(**C**) OPEC is an organization that regulates oil production and oil prices on behalf of oil-importing countries.

(**D**) UNESCO is a specialized agency of the United Nations that aims to promote international cooperation in education, science and culture.

設問訳 ニュースで使われる次のアルファベットの略語に関する次の記述のうち、誤っているものはどれか。

(**A**) IMF は、国際金融システムの安定性を確保することを目的とした国連の専門機関である。

(**B**) FDA は、米国における食品、医薬品、医療機器の安全性に関する規則を定めている政府機関である。

(**C**) OPEC は、石油輸入国のために、石油の生産量と価格を調整する組織である。

(**D**) UNESCO は、教育、科学、文化における国際協力の推進を目的とした国連の専門機関である。

解説 IMF は International Monetary Fund（国際通貨基金）の頭文字（**A**）、FDA は Food and Drug Administration（米国食品医薬品局）の頭文字（**B**）、UNESCO は United Nations Educational, Scientific and Cultural Organization（国際連合教育科学文化機関）の頭文字（**D**）であり、いずれの記述も正しい。OPEC は Organization of the Petroleum Exporting Countries（石油輸出国機構）の頭文字で、石油産出国の利益を守るために設立された組織である。よって、（**C**）は誤り。

No.6

正解 **B**

According to the US Census Bureau's 2020 statistics, which of the following statements about population size and household income by race in the US is NOT true?

(**A**) The white population, not including Hispanics, makes up less than 60 percent of the overall US population.

(**B**) The black population in the US is larger than the Hispanic population.

(**C**) The estimated average household income of black people in the US is about 60 percent that of whites, not including Hispanics.

(**D**) The estimated average household income of Asians in the US is higher than that of whites, not including Hispanics.

設問訳 米国国勢調査局の2020年の統計によると、米国の人種別の人口および世帯収入に関する次の記述のうち、誤っているものはどれか。

(**A**) 米国のヒスパニック系を含まない白人の人口は、総人口の60％以下である。

(**B**) 米国の黒人の人口はヒスパニック系の人口よりも多い。

(**C**) 米国の黒人の推定平均世帯収入は、ヒスパニック系

を含まない白人のそれの約60％である。

(**D**) 米国のアジア系の推定平均世帯収入は、ヒスパニック系を含まない白人のそれよりも高い。

解説 米国国勢調査局2020年統計によると、米国全体の人口は約3億3140万人、そのうちヒスパニック系を含まない白人は約59％、ヒスパニック系は約19％、黒人は約14％を占めた（**A**）（**B**）。よって、（**B**）は誤り。また、同統計によると、米国の黒人の推定平均世帯収入（約4万8180ドル）は、ヒスパニック系を除いた白人の推定平均世帯収入（約7万8910ドル）の約60％である（**C**）。同様に、アジア系の推定平均世帯収入（約9万9620ドル）は、ヒスパニック系を除いた白人の推定平均世帯収入より高い（**D**）。よって、（**A**）（**C**）（**D**）は正しい。

No.7

正解 **C**

Which of the following statements about guns and gun control in the United States is NOT true?

(**A**) The Second Amendment to the US Constitution stipulates the "right of the people to keep and bear arms."

(**B**) According to the CDC, there were nearly 40,000 firearm-related deaths in the United States in 2019.

(**C**) The NRA is a pressure group that campaigns for gun abolition.

(**D**) Regulations regarding firearm ownership are not the same in every state in the US.

設問訳 米国における銃と銃規制に関する次の記述のうち、誤っているものはどれか。

(**A**) 米国憲法修正第2条は、"人民が武器を保持する権利"を明記している。

(**B**) CDC によると、2019年の米国での銃器関連の死亡者数は4万人近かった。

(**C**) NRA は、銃廃止のキャンペーンを行う圧力団体である。

(**D**) 銃器所有に関する規制は、米国のすべての州で同じではない。

解説 憲法修正第2条には、「規律ある民兵は自由な国

家の安全保障にとって必要であるから、国民が武器を保有し携帯する権利は侵してはならない」と記されている（**A**）。CDC（米疾病対策センター）によると、2019年の米国での銃が原因の死亡者数は3万9707人で、自動車事故の死者数並みだった（**B**）。NRA（全米ライフル協会）は米国市民が銃を所持する権利を保護することを目的とする圧力団体で、銃廃止のキャンペーンを行う圧力団体ではない（**C**）。よって、（**C**）は誤り。銃規制は州によって大きく異なる。カリフォルニアが最も厳しいが、フロリダ、バージニア、テキサスなどはより緩い（**D**）。よって、（**A**）（**B**）（**D**）は正しい。

No.8

正解 **D**

Which of the following statements about booster vaccinations for COVID-19 is NOT true?

(**A**) A COVID-19 booster vaccination is an additional vaccine dose given after the protection provided by the original shot(s) has begun to decrease.

(**B**) As of October 2021, the FDA had authorized booster doses of three COVID-19 vaccines already approved in the US.

(**C**) As of October 2021, some European countries had started providing booster vaccinations for COVID-19.

(**D**) According to the FDA, the COVID-19 vaccine used for a booster vaccination must be the same type as was used for the recipient's original vaccination.

設問訳 新型コロナウイルスワクチンのブースター接種に関する次の記述のうち、誤っているものはどれか。

(**A**) 新型コロナウイルスワクチンのブースター接種は、最初の接種で得られた予防効果が低下し始めた後に行われる追加のワクチン接種である。

(**B**) 2021年10月時点で、FDAは米国で既に承認されている3種類の新型コロナウイルスワクチンのブースター接種を許可した。

(**C**) 2021年10月時点で、ヨーロッパのいくつかの国では新型コロナウイルスワクチンのブースター接種が開始されていた。

(**D**) FDAによると、ブースター接種に使用される新型コロ

ナウイルスワクチンは、接種を受ける人に最初の接種で使用されたワクチンと同種類のものでなければならない。

解説 一般に新型コロナウイルスのワクチン接種で得られた免疫力は、時間が経過すると弱くなる。低下した免疫力を追加接種で強化することをブースター接種という（**A**）。米国FDAは、2021年10月時点でファイザー・ビオンテック、モデルナ、ジョンソン・エンド・ジョンソン製ワクチンのブースター接種を承認し（**B**）、さらにブースター接種ではそれら3種類のどのワクチンでも使うことができるとした（**D**）。2021年10月時点で、ドイツ、フランス、イタリアはすでにブースター接種を始めていた（**C**）。よって、（**A**）（**B**）（**C**）は正しいが、（**D**）は誤り。

No.9

正解 **D**

Which of the following statements about cyberattacks is NOT true?

(**A**) A ransomware attack is one that makes a computer inoperable until a fee is paid.

(**B**) IoT devices connected to the Internet may become targets of cyberattacks.

(**C**) Malware is any type of malicious software designed to interfere with, damage or destroy a programmable device, service, system or network.

(**D**) To prevent infection by malware, it is better not to update the OS.

設問訳 サイバー攻撃に関する次の記述のうち、誤っているものはどれか。

(**A**) ランサムウェア攻撃とは、料金を支払うまでコンピュータを操作できないようにするものである。

(**B**) インターネットに接続されているIoT機器は、サイバー攻撃の標的になる可能性がある。

(**C**) マルウェアとは、プログラム可能なデバイス、サービス、システム、ネットワークに対し、妨害したり、損害を与えたり、破壊したりすることを目的として設計された、あらゆる種類の害意のあるソフトウェアのことである。

(**D**) マルウェアへの感染を防ぐためには、OSのアップデートは行わない方が良い。

解説 ランサムウェア攻撃とは、PCやスマホ、タブレットなどさまざまな端末を使用不能の状態にし、元に戻すことと引き換えに身代金を要求するもの（**A**）。IoT機器は、ネットワークに接続して動作するため、マルウェア感染などのサイバー攻撃を受ける可能性がある（**B**）。コンピューターウイルスやスパイウェアなど、ユーザーのデバイスに不利益をもたらす悪意のあるプログラムやソフトウェアを総称してマルウェアと言う（**C**）。OSをアップデートすることで、マルウェアなどのサイバー攻撃の対象となりうるセキュリティー上の欠陥などが修正できる（**D**）。よって、（**A**）（**B**）（**C**）は正しく、（**D**）は誤り。

No.10

正解 **B**

Which of the following statements about space development is NOT true?

(**A**) According to China's state media, in 2019, a Chinese spacecraft became the first ever to land on the far side of the moon.

(**B**) The ISS is a space station operated exclusively by the United States and Russia.

(**C**) NASA has outsourced the development of manned spacecraft to the private sector since the Space Shuttle program ended in 2011.

(**D**) Three billionaires—Jeff Bezos, Elon Musk and Richard Branson—are competing in the space business.

設問訳 宇宙開発に関する次の記述のうち、誤っているものはどれか。

(**A**) 中国の国営メディアの発表によると、2019年に中国の宇宙船が史上初めて月の裏側に着陸した。

(**B**) ISSは、米国とロシアが独占的に運営する宇宙ステーションである。

(**C**) NASAは2011年にスペースシャトル計画が終了してからは、有人宇宙船の開発を民間企業に委託している。

(**D**) 3人の億万長者、ジェフ・ベゾス、イーロン・マスク、リチャード・ブランソンが宇宙ビジネスで競っている。

解説 中国国営中央テレビは2019年1月3日、中国の月無人探査機「嫦娥（じょうが）4号」が世界で初めて月の裏側への軟着陸に成功したと伝えた（**A**）。ISSは、アメリカ合衆国、ロシア、日本、カナダおよび欧州宇宙機関が協力して運用している宇宙ステーションである（**B**）。よって、（**B**）は誤り。NASAは民間企業として初の有人宇宙飛行を成功させたスペースXなどに有人宇宙船の開発を委託している（**C**）。ジェフ・ベゾスはブルーオリジン、イーロン・マスクはスペースX、リチャード・ブランソンはヴァージンギャラクティックをそれぞれ設立し、宇宙旅行を成功させている。よって、（**A**）（**C**）（**D**）は正しい。

MP3音声・電子書籍版（PDF）の入手方法

本書のご購入者は、下記URLまたはQRコードから申請していただければ、
本書の電子書籍版（PDF）を無料でダウンロードすることができるようになります。

申請サイトURL（ブラウザの検索窓ではなく「URL入力窓」に入力してください）

https://www.asahipress.com/eng/glentsguide/

※ PDFは本書の紙面を画像化したものです。
※ 本書初版第1刷の刊行日（2023年11月1日）より1年を経過した後は、告知なしに上記申請サイトを削除したり
　　電子書籍版（PDF）の配布をとりやめたりする場合があります。あらかじめご了承ください。

笹尾洋介 ささお ようすけ

京都大学 国際高等教育院附属国際学術言語教育センター 准教授。
京都大学総合人間学部卒業（2005年）、京都大学大学院人間・環境学研究科博士前期課程修了（2007年）。
ニュージーランド ヴィクトリア大学ウェリントン校（Victoria University of Wellington）より博士号を取得（2013年）。
応用言語学博士（Ph.D. in Applied Linguistics）。2012年より豊橋技術科学大学 総合教育院 講師を務め、
准教授を経て、2017年より現職。外国語としての英語教育を専門とする。とくに、言語テスト、
語彙習得、教育文法、教材開発、学術目的の英語などに関する研究論文を多数発表している。

オンラインテスト
CNN GLENTS 公式ガイド

2023年11月1日　初版第1刷発行

監修	笹尾洋介（京都大学 国際高等教育院附属国際学術言語教育センター 准教授）
発行人	小川洋一郎
発行所	株式会社 朝日出版社
	〒101-0065
	東京都千代田区西神田3-3-5
	TEL 03-3263-1230
	FAX 03-3239-7713
	https://www.asahipress.com/（HP）
	https://twitter.com/asahipress_com/（X）
	https://www.instagram.com/cnn.ee/（Instagram）
印刷・製本	図書印刷株式会社
表紙デザイン・DTP	大串幸子
表紙画像	Photo by Shutterstock
音声録音・編集	ELEC（一般財団法人 英語教育協議会）